ST. MICHAEL'S COLLEGE SERIES

— 7 —

COVER: St. Basil's Church in St. Michael's College, University of Toronto
(Photo © Francesco Guardiani)

ST. MICHAEL'S COLLEGE SERIES

Limina

Thresholds and Borders

Proceedings of
A St. Michael's College Symposium
(28 February – 1 March 2003)

Edited by

Joseph Goering, Francesco Guardiani, Giulio Silano

New York   Ottawa   Toronto

Library and Archives Canada Cataloguing in Publication

Limina: thresholds and borders: proceedings of a St. Michael's College symposium (28 February-1 March 2003)/edited by Joseph Goering, Francesco Guardiani, Giulio Silano.

(St. Michael's College series; 7)
Includes bibliographical references.
ISBN 1-894508-73-4

I. Guardiani, Francesco, 1949- II. Silano, Giulio, 1955-
III. Goering, Joseph, 1947- IV. Series.

AC5.L54 2005   081   C2005-900933-0

For further information and for orders:

http://www.legaspublishing.com

LEGAS

P. O. Box 040328	3 Wood Aster Bay	2908 Dufferin Street
Brooklyn, New York	Ottawa, Ontario	Toronto, Ontario
USA 11204	K2R 1B3	M6B 3S8

Printed and bound in Canada

CONTENTS

INTRODUCTION

In recent years, we have had frequent occasion to remember, perhaps with awed incredulity, that the community and the institution which is the University was born from the heart of the Church. Our own experience teaches us that, if it happens to be Catholic, a contemporary academic community is also sometimes, for better and for worse, on the margins of the modern University enterprise. This occasional sense of marginality is not entirely unfamiliar to the members of St. Michael's College in their relation to the behemoth which is the University of Toronto. Perhaps then it was inevitable that the St. Michael's College Symposium would sooner or later address the question of centers and margins.

Convinced, as we are, that both the center and the margins are important, we thought it might be good to explore their relations in more detail. Since the early twentieth century anthropologists have found particularly fruitful a consideration of boundaries and thresholds (*limina*) as makers and markers of significant human phenomena. Questions of inclusion and exclusion, of sacred and profane, of public and private have since become commonplace in the academy and beyond. We felt the time was ripe to put some of these issues into a conversation that would draw on the varied interests and expertise of the members of our College and their friends. And so for two days in the winter of 2003 we devoted the sixth in our series of annual Symposia to the topic: *Limina: Thresholds and Borders.*

The discussions were, as always, warm and wide-ranging. We were privileged once again to have Giuseppe Mazzotta join us; his usual erudition and his unusual insights set the tone for the Symposium. Other participants came from near and far, all revealing in their own ways the unexpected riches that can come from attending to thresholds and boundaries in our lives and cultures. The papers presented, and the discussions they engendered, will not necessarily serve to relieve the occasional feeling of marginality; they did and will show that such feelings can be fruitful. Besides, it turns out that tarrying in a liminal state brings with it its own portion of fun, and so we shall not rush toward a more peaceful postliminal condition.

We offer these essays now to the wider community, with the hope that they will continue to spark some of the same interest and pleasure that they generated among the participants. We are grateful to St.Michael's College for hosting the Symposium once again, and for making possible the publication of these proceedings.

THE EDITORS

GIUSEPPE MAZZOTTA

LIMINALITY AND UTOPIA OF LITERATURE: CAMPANELLA'S *CITY OF THE SUN*

ABSTRACT. The model of liminality/marginality has been theorized by anthropologists such as Victor Turner who patterned the notion of of liminality on the Mystical Body of the Church. This model, stripped of all theological implications, has been increasingly adopted by literary critics. The present talk will confront the limitation of the anthropological structure. By a series of references to "utopian" texts by authors such as Campanella, Shakespeare, and Cervantes, the paper will argue that literature provides an imaginary "space– in– between", an ambiguous middle area, wherein boundaries and barriers confront one another.

The term "liminality" – from the Latin *limen*, threshold, alludes also to *limes*, which means limit or border. Liminality, thus, contains ambiguous, self-contradictory senses. It designates margins, boundaries, frontiers, horizons, edges or thresholds in so far as they stand as intermediate spaces between two different worlds. Liminal is the ambiguous place both of separation and of a passageway from one area to another. Like a gate, it implies the existence of an "inside" and an "outside": it lets you in and out and it locates in between. The rhetorical term that defines it is *aporia*, from the Greek *aporos*, which lterally means "without passage." It conveys the insight that there is no easy way out of a logical confusion over the truth of a proposition or the bewilderment in the discovery that we stand at the border between two imaginary or real countries.

Cultural anthropology has recently given a new currency to the language of liminality or thresholds. Victor Turner, who takes it from *Rites de passage* by Arnold Van Gennep (1908), theorizes "liminality" as a metaphorical state of initiation ceremonies: liminal are the precincts where rituals occur; liminal are the privileged areas where the initiates withdraw from the "world," turn its values upside down, and begin their journey to their spiritual destination. In a text such as *From Ritual to*

Limina: Thresholds and Borders - A St. Michael's College Symposium
Joseph Goering, Francesco Guardiani, Giulio Silano eds. Ottawa: Legas, 2005

Theatre: The Human Seriousness of Play, Turner traces the map of a liminal or threshold experience, which ranges over numberless practices. Religious communities that remove themselves from public life; schools; universities; carnival rituals provisionally overhauling all conventions of order; esthetic interludes etc. crystallize the liminal condition. Such a condition is halfway between the rigor of the existing hierarchical structures of the world and the imaginary perfection of a future *communitas* or utopia. In its turn, the imaginary or dreamt *communitas* becomes the perspective disengaged from the reality of experience. Tied to the ludic or the imaginary status, the myth of *communitas* questions, counterfeits, and unveils the arbitrariness in all fictions of order.

In Turner's anthropology, liminality differs from marginality. Marginality marks a permanent condition at the edges of history. It names what can never be assimilated. It describes the eccentric or peripheral the "somewhere else" in relation to a center. It remains the irreducible residue of any experience. On the contrary, liminality designates the ambiguous movement of a break and a reconciliation. It is best figured as the situation of a man who is simultaneously on the road and at halt – "che va col cuore e col corpo dimora" (*Purg.* II, 12). As such, it shows that borders need not to be barriers and that apparent crossings may not be passable.

Anthropologists – from Van Gennep to Turner – have never explored the marginality or liminality of literature. In point of fact, they have marginalized literature. The question is crucial and from the very beginning of my career I have sought to confront the implications of these two categories. The second essay I ever published, "The *Decameron*: The Marginality of Literature" (*University of Toronto Quarterly* 42 (1972), 64-81), took the issue head on. Later, in a book that derived from it, *The World at Play in Boccaccio's Decameron* (Princeton, 1986), I argued that a narrative experience can be called liminal in the measure in which it marks the transition from one state of consciousness to another; and in the sense that it leads the reader past the threshold of what is known into new imaginative areas. At the same time, and ironically, however, that self-same narrative experience remains a discontinuous esthetic phenomenon forever shut within itself, outside any functional economy or social mechanism.

In effect, a narrative experience is characterized, as a thinker such as St. Bonaventure theorized in his *De reductione artium ad theologiam* (*The movement of the arts back to Theology*) by a double, aporetic trait. As in a ladder, where each step is independent and yet it leads to the one above or below, so does the literary experience stand at the edges of all concerns, and yet it involves within itself and leads to a whole universe of discourse. As such, a literary text subverts all binary oppositions anthropologists peddle: no easy distinction is possible between "in" and "out"; self and other; esthetics and politics etc. Paradoxically, then, in talking about literature one finds oneself deploying the lexicon of cultural anthropology while its meaning is altered. And the paradox has its own logic: anthropology stands as the discipline that focuses on man; literature, on the contrary, puts into question the sense of the human as well as the persistent myths about the centrality of man. From this point of view one can say that a literary text is not simply liminal or marginal. If we may coin a new term, it can best be defined as liminological in the sense that it stages a discourse of/about/at the limit.

No doubt, literary texts have a clear self-knowledge about their liminological status. Such a self-knowledge comes through as the awareness of man's finitude; it comes through as the realization that the literary discourse does not belong within the productive and rational perimeter of the city. Yet, these claims for the literary experience involve also philosophical discourse, whose place within the order of the city is never well-defined. Relegated nowadays to the schools, it does not belong to the public square, just as in the past it would on occasion leave behind the public forum, when it usually would parade or peddle its wares, and sought shelter under the porticos or the sacred gardens of the academy.

In Plato's *Phaedrus*, for instance, we read of Socrates, who never leaves the city till he meets Phaedrus. Together, they go outside the gates of the city, sit in the shade of a poplar tree, and there they engage in a dialogue about the manias of the soul, about love and, especially, about rhetoric. They converse about rhetoric's insidiousness to truth and about the links between rhetoric and the soul. In effect, Phaedrus and Socrates detach themselves from the city in order to re-think the discourses of the city. To do so, they need to retrieve a critical space or a perspective on the city from which they can reflect on the myths, on the lies and the fictions of all speech, and from which they can demolish the illusions and self-deceptions rampant in the city.

Socrates's self-reflexiveness lets philosophy overlap with rhetoric. This self-reflexiveness, however, sheds light on literary texts' own way of being. There is a historical difficulty scholars have traditionally encountered in locating where literature belongs within the organization of knowledge. We recall how Plato or Boethius banished it from the precincts of reliable knowledge, as a scandal to the rigor of reason. In Aristotle's *Poetics*, literature is a mimesis (i.e. imitation or simulation) and in this sense, it is unlike history or philosophy. The Renaissance commentaries on the *Poetics* by Castelvetro, Mazzoni, and Trissino (in much the way Philip Sidney's *Defense of Poetry* (1583) does) place literature in the intermediate space between philosophy and history.

Unlike analytical reason, which divides and separates, the poetic imagination is identified as a synthetic principle forging a similarity among disparate entities. I am paraphrasing Schiller's *Letters on the esthetic education of Man*, and such a conviction is available in Vico's *New Science* as well as Shelley's *A Defense of Poetry*.

There is no literary text that escapes the simultaneously marginal/liminal condition. Let us consider some texts that constitute the foundations of the Western canon. The *Odyssey* tells of the tortuous itinerary of the hero; the *Aeneid*, recounts the peripety of the hero to the new land and to a new history; the *Divine Comedy*, which places poetry within the horizon of exile and dramatizes the reality of the hero who comes face to face with death, questions the illusory barriers of life and death and summons us to consider that borders need not be thought of as barriers, but are passage ways to newer realities and wonders; the *Decameron*, finally, evokes the playful time of a *brigata* that, to flee the plague, withdraws to the hills of Fiesole in the enchanted playland of the imagination: here, in the intact frame of a garden, the young men and women reconstitute, however provisionally, a utopian community, yet they follow rigid rules and rituals. They turn the medieval *contemptus mundi* into *amor vitae*; they live paradoxically chaste even as they tell obscene stories; they take pleasure in recounting tales of deception and simulations and they enjoy recalling stories about the arbitrariness of all signs and sources. Within the horizon of their playful imagination, the storytellers even discover that though they are lords of all decisions, they themselves are under the lordship of death, from which providentially, they escape.

This paradigm of these literary experiences – forever poised at the threshold of the actual world from where they look critically at and re-invent the real world is far too common in literary history. One could fruitfully find it as the essential structure shaping the contents of works by Dante and Ariosto, Vergil, Leopardi, Shakespeare, Tasso, Montale etc. Yet one wonders what we gain by thinking about a literary text in these terms. In what way does such a way of thinking about literature open up a new critical perspective and lead us to a re-organization of knowledge? In effect, the most advanced and dominant theories of literature do not even raise this question. They focus on literature's ironic power to overhaul conventionally logical, rational ways of thinking and they stress metaphor's power to blur all binary oppositions and to denounce the illusoriness of all dualisms. But they keep away from raising the stakes.

I cannot answer all these questions in an abstract manner. I shall argue my case, instead, by looking in some detail at one utopian text, *La citta` del sole*, by Tommaso Campanella, written in 1602, while its author was in jail, and published in 1623.

As a utopia, *The City of the Sun* , as I will refer to this narrative, belongs to the rhetorical genre of Plato's *Republic*, and it recalls Thomas More's *Utopia*. Utopia, for More, contains ambiguous meanings: it resonates both with *ou-topia* and *eu-topia*: it leads us into the *nowhere* country and into a *good place,* as if the two implicated each other: the ambiguity suggests that the good place is to be found nowhere. There is another sense, however, to the ambiguity. A double meaning summons us to the need to think otherwise: it asks us to reflect on a plain sense from unknown and unpredictable perspectives. From this standpoint, both Plato and More had intuited the imaginative link binding utopia and otherness. They had grasped that utopia crystallizes the other discourse and it expresses itself fully through a dialogue or a double speech. In their wake, Campanella lucidly catches the link between dialogue and utopia.

The subtitle of *The City of the Sun* is "dialogo poetico"- poetic dialogue. What does it imply? First of all, the dialogical genre describes accurately the theatrical-dramatic figuration shaping the text that, as it unfolds, appears as an archive and a reorganization of knowledge. It evokes the traditions of Baroque encyclopedias as it lists the liberal and mechanical arts, politics, ethics, physics and, above all, astronomy as the tools by which the education of the Solarians is carried out. The narrative contains also references to the utility of the arts, such as painting, music, and singing. Poetry seems somehow to be bracketed, as the reader is made to face a rational utopia of science. Within this scientific framework all the various distinct forms of knowledge are subordinated to the sovereign eye of Metaphysics. Nonetheless, the educational program Campanella describes must be understood as a preamble to a political program, to the project of governing the "city of the Sun" in the best way possible. In point of fact, Campanella explores the boundaries among the various disciplines (pedagogy, ethics, science, geometry, and politics) and he seeks to reconstitute them into a unified order. Such an intention is signaled by his hybrid subtitle, "poetic dialogue."

In his *Poetica* (written in 1596), Campanella places the "poet" as the intermediary between nature and the work of art. "Poetic" for him connotes knowledge, a moral activity, akin and yet different from magic formulas, which produces freedom in the social world. On the other hand, "dialogue," a term designating a philosophical genre, points to the dramatic-philosophical structure of the text. Campanella's intent is clear: he moves in between the interstices that divide poetry and philosophy, and he wants to re-connect them. The two *dramatis personae* that figure in *The City of the Sun* , both anonymous and distinct from each other – the "Genovese" and the "Ospitalario" – embody the possibility of a dialogue between poetry and philosophy.

The "Genoese" belonged to Columbus's crew that reached America. He has experiences of real, scientific discoveries. The "Hospitaler" is a knight of the order of Hospitalers of St. John in Jerusalem. The Genoese comes forth as one who comes and goes. He is always on the way, with no time at hand and with other commitments to pursue. The Hospitaler, who, although circumscribed within traditional theological boundaries, has the curiosity to know about he new wonders of the world, questions the Genoese. His role is to inquire and to listen:

Hospitaler: Tell me, please, all that happened to you on this voyage.

Genoese: I have already told you how I sailed around the world and came to Taprobana, where I was forced to put ashore, how I hid in a forest to escape the fury of the natives, and how I came out onto a great plain just below the equator.

Hospitaler: What happened to you here (p.27).

The "here" is the City of the Sun, located under the equator, and it looks like a sacred precinct. Its circular temple, with a cupola on top, symbolically suggests that like the sun in the Copernican universe, the city stands at the center of the world. From these discretely mythical-religious references, one infers that this dialogue departs from the strictly philosophical ones. Most dialogues are to be understood within the tradition of dialectical disputations, such as those one finds in the Middle Ages, in the Renaissance dialogues or in the Platonic texts. They all share and are characterized by an ironic oppositional structure: they are debates aiming at bending the will of the interlocutor and at gaining control of the antagonist's mind.

Campanella stays within the Platonic context of the dialogue, but there is no trace in *The City of the Sun* of a philosophical refutation. Rather, the text is marked by a sense of adventure as well as of a scientific discovery. As such, it comes forth as the probing of the mysteries of knowledge, of the wondrous enigmas of reality. In so far as it is articulated as an adventurous quest, the Hopitaler questions the Genoese in order to find out how things are elsewhere. There is no effort to unify opposed view points or dissolve all contradictions. Quite to the contrary. At the end of the text, the "poetic dialogue" is interrupted and is left open-ended. When the Hospitaler asks how the Solarians interpret the religious wounds of modern Europe--the heresy of Luther, the role of the Jesuits, the religious colonization of Mexico by Ferdinando Cortes – the Genoese replies: "Non posso, non posso" (I cannot, I cannot).

The reply suspends as illusory the practice of "civil conversation." By being unable to reply, the Genoese seeks to avoid the authentic risk of responding to those who wish to know. On the one hand, the dialogue asks us to think otherwise and to open ourselves up to the adventure of discovery and thinking. On the other hand, the dialogue breaks down, bars the gate of knowledge, promises to pick up the conversation "un'altra volta,")(some other time). In the process, it discloses the gap existing between the solarity of transparent discourses and the enigmatic, murky fund of the unsaid and the unsayable. In this sense, "poetic dialogue" – a phrase that edges toward redundancy – reveals itself to be an oxymoron. It leads us to the boundaries of the sayable and the unsayable. It marks the utopian intersection of philosophy and poetry (a project Campanella relentlessly pursues in his *Poetics*).

The hoped for bond between philosophy and poetry, gains relief from another detail: the title itself, *Città del sole*. Its textual resonances are multiple. It alludes to the rhetoric of the new sciences and heliocentric theories, to ancient theologies, and to visionary, dantesque poetry. The antagonism between science and theology in Europe at the beginning of the seventeenth century hardly needs stressing. No doubt, Campanella aims at healing the political-moral rift between the two discourses. His title alludes to Ficino's *De sole et lumine* (1493). It echoes Dante's "Heaven of the Sun" (which houses "il calavrese abate Giovacchino" [*Par.* XII, 140]). Further, one catches the recall of Isaiah's prophecy (19:18) of the five cities in the land of Egypt. More poignantly, the Renaissance and baroque heliocentric theory of Copernican astronomy, which according to Bruno and Kepler ties together Pythagorean harmonies and modern scientific astronomy, is prominently staged.

Years later, Descartes criticized Galileo. He imputed to him the failure to articulate a metaphysics likely to give philosophical legitimacy to the new science. He blamed him because his scientific experiments have demolished the unity of the cosmos (Letter to Mersenne of Oct. 11, 1638). On his part, in his *Apologia pro Galileo*, Campanella had intuited, as Foscarini had done, the limits of the new scientific perspectives. The broad horizons of the new cosmology, of politics, ethics and theology (which Metaphysics gathers in an intelligible totality) remained unexplored. A new epistemology was needed. What was needed, more precisely, was an art that might reveal the esthetic unity of the ancient and new worlds. Traces of this quest for a new epistemology can be found in *The City of the Sun*.

Campanella's effort to join together knowledge and politics is rooted in Pythagorean philosophy, which in itself contains science, mathematical ideas of harmony, and theology. Plainly, the Pythagorean framework structures the imaginary world of the Solarians. The text tells that the utopian community of the Solarians had come into being as a philosophical community:

> Genoese: "This is a people that came from India, many of them being philosophers, who fled before the depredation of the Tartars and other plunderers and tyrants, and they resolved to live in a philosophic community... all things are held in common.... Not food alone, but arts, honors, and pleasure are also shared in common in such a way that no one can appropriate anything (pp. 37-39).

To the Machiavellian world of tyrants and predators Campanella juxtaposes the city of philosophy and its *libertas philosophandi*. More poignantly, the mathematical structure of the city is Pythagorean. Circular in shape, it is divided into 7 concentric circles bearing the names of the planets, with 4 gates disposed in the order of the 4 cardinal points. The center of the city features an altar, and above it, two spherical globes, a map of cosmic space and a map of the human world.

Ptolemaic cosmology is joined to the heliocentric hypothesis of Copernicus, as if no real rift exists between the two. On the other hand, this explicitly geometric-arithmetical symbolism is a throwback to Plato's *Republic* (VII, 525 b- 526c) and its proposition about mathematics as the discipline that crystallizes the purity of knowledge. Through this geometric-arithmetical description, Campanella, on his part, presents *The City of the Sun* as an architectural edifice – as la *città ideale*, in fact – and as an encyclopedia of the arts and sciences. As Vitruvius, who invented the phrase *artes liberales* knew, the two aspects – architecture and encyclopedism- are intimately connected. The city is built through and by education. Thus, all young people have to learn from one book, "ad usanza dei Pitagorici" (p.32). They all can be educated to and by the universalizing rationality of philosophy. This unity of knowledge both presupposes and is founded on the musical-religious principle of harmony of the world.

Their education, in short, merges together spiritual purification, moral discipline, and political organization. In point of fact, Campanella frames life within the rigidity of a system based on mathematical equalities.

The Solarians lead an ascetic life and own everything in common (as if excessive individuality caused moral evil). They address one another as "brother," with the intimation that the city has the spiritual structure of a monastic cloister. Equality, which is possible in the order of quantities and number, finds no room, plainly, in the order of quality. Consistently, Campanella draws the diffractions between the principle of quantity and that of quality. Thus political control of the city falls within the purview of scientific reason: a hierarchical and unequal organization of power shapes the order of the city. A Prince/Prelate (representing the conjunction of politics and religion), called Sun or the Metaphysician, makes all decisions. From this Sun radiates the political theology of the text.

He is the *pan-opticon* who exerts critical vigilance over the city and translates absolute knowledge into absolute power. In joining together as he does, politics and metaphysics, in casting the claim of absolute knowledge as the foundation of politics, Campanella captures and conveys the radical crisis of his times. More precisely, the mathematical intelligence of the astronomers has redefined the ancient scenarios of the encyclopedia. Campanella's Pythagorean cosmology re-proposes Plato's utopia or perfect city, ruled by a philosopher-king, whereby philosophy becomes the royal road to politics. With his version of Plato's *Republic*, Campanella responds to the political crisis of his time and confronts its fundamental problem: political machiavellism. In the *Atheismus triumphatus* he drafts the bonds of solidarity joining machiavellism and atheology, machavellism and the skepticism of the libertines. *The City of the Sun,* by contrast, claims, against Machiavelli, who abandons the utopian tradition of political philosophy, the value of utopias.

As we all recall, chapter XV of the *Prince* denies the logical validity of imaginary kingdoms. For Machiavelli, in fact, utopian schemes of happiness – such as those elaborated by Plato, More, and in the Renaissance myth of the "città felice" (Alberti, Leonardo, Filarete, Patrizi etc.) have no basis in fact. More than that, they interfere with "la verità delle cose."

In this sense, utopian writers are for Machiavelli counterfeiters of history. He liquidates them because they foment illusions about the perfectibility of mankind and because in their naivete or belief in an ethics of moderation they ignore the universe of infinite desires from which all human actions stem.

Modern science, whose symbol is Galileo's telescope, unveils the real structure of the world. Phenomena are illusory and deceptive, and the scientist's "spyglass" reveals the cosmos' false appearances and false immobility of the earth. Like Galileo's astronomy, Machiavelli's political science separates truth from falsehood and focuses on the systematic manipulation of illusory appearances, simulations and dissimulations. This knowledge of the truth is reserved only to scientists, who are in the know, and to the adepts of politics, who are aware of the secret essence of power. For Machiavelli, the paradigm for the cabal of power is made available by Pope Alexander VI (cf. *Il principe*, chapter XVII), while the myth encapsulating the surreptitious nature of political power is the Centaur Chiron, who covertly teaches Achilles the ciphers of power.

In point of fact, Machiavelli, who was the disciple of Marsilio Ficino, replaces the Neo-Platonic essences and metaphysical gradations articulated by his teacher, with the kingdom of simulacra and deceptive appearances. He stages the pragmatic artifices of a political theater. In the logic of his argument, the general criteria capable of distinguishing truth from falsehood are absent. We confront the gap between appearances and their substantial truth. As a consequence, in the Machiavellian world one can never believe (in) others. One can and should believe only in oneself.

If appearances delude and deceive, then Machiavelli ushers in Renaissance skepticism, which is to be understood as the limit of knowledge or as the triumph of a private form of knowledge. His idea of absolute power is rooted in skepticism and is expressed as the power to invest with sense events that are defined by a perpetual instability.

Many have objected to Machiavelli's political realism. Many – and especially the Christian thinkers, such as Scribani, Ribadeneira, and Botero – resented the overt rift between ethics and politics Machiavelli proposes or portrays. So did utopists, such as Campanella, Shakespeare, and Cervantes. Campanella is the first to have intuited the necessity of grounding politics on non-skeptical philosophical principles. His Pythagorean theory allows him the standpoint from which he can assimilate politics to a larger and harmonious circle of knowledge. As such, Pythagorean thought responds to the new realities of modern science and modern politics. But Campanella also intuited that Machiavelli's much vaunted political realism is naïve exactly in the measure in which it loses sight of the necessity of utopia. Why is utopia necessary? The answer lies in the weave of Plato/Pythagoras and Machiavelli available in *The City of the Sun*.

On the face of it, *The City of the Sun* is conceived as antithetical to the ethos of simulation described in *Il Principe*. Nonetheless, in spite of the divergences between the two texts, Campanella's utopian economy presents itself as the flip side of Machiavelli's practice of secrets. In the wake of Machiavelli, in *The City of the Sun* knowledge appears to be the arcane privilege of the philosophers and the Metaphysician. It is the absolute knowledge of the secrets of the city. Its circular topography, for instance, makes it a self-enclosed universe, one which is bent on excluding the outside world, keeping itself hidden, in order to safeguard its own existence. More than that, the city teems with invisible spies. Spies are sent abroad to steal other people's secrets.

In brief, Campanella retrieves the utopian tradition and casts it as the antidote to Machiavelli's skeptical political vision whereby politics come through as pure representation. In this context, utopia is understood as an alibi for power. Nonetheless, Campanella understands, as Plato did and Machiavelli did not, that the secret machinations of power are crucial to the up-keeping of the Platonic/Pythagorean ideals of the city. Campanella sees clearly that modernity's problems are simultaneously political *and* theological. It follows that the new modern science needs a new, unifying esthetics that would counter/contain the political / theological crisis. Let me briefly suggest how *The City of the Sun* provides this new esthetics.

In the final section of the text, the Genoese fears that his ship may sail away. Pressed by time he quickly recapitulates the synchretistic principles regulating the life of the Solarians. He recounts that they believe in the immortality of the soul; that the world – just as Bernardino Telesio had maintained – is animated; that they reject the notion of infinite worlds, which was held by Epicurus and Bruno; that they worship the Trinity and acknowledge Adam's sin. Theirs is a Christian ethics of nature.

Above all, the Solarians discern in modernity's scientific advances the prodigies and presages of the future. The art of flying; the invention of the telescope; and the imminent discovery of the "oricchiali" (by which one overhears the music of the spheres that have been silenced by the eclipse of the geocentric theories of the cosmos) – they are all signs of the new times and of the new esthetics. The new times, so we are told, are introduced by the women who at present rule all over Europe: Mary of Hungary, Elizabeth of England; Isabel of Spain; Mary of Scotland; Catherine of France; Bona of Poland etc. The new esthetics, on the other hand, is announced by the poetry of Ariosto, "poeta di questo secolo (che) incominciò dale donne dicendo: 'Le donne, I cavalieri, l'armi e l'amori."

Why does Campanella call Ariosto the poet of the modern age? To answer this question we have to keep in mind one detail: scientific optimism rules in utopia, and it expresses itself through the new instruments of the eye and the ear. Among the Solarians, Galileo's telescope dramatizes the triumph of the scientific perspective. The telescope, which is the mechanical prolongation of Alberti's perspective, reduces the perception of reality to the rigidity of a fixed viewpoint: in this perspective substances, just as happens in Machiavelli's universe, are transformed into pure phenomena. The "oricchiale", a phantasmatic hearing instrument, on the other hand, overhauls perspective's representation. As the musicologists of the Renaissance knew, the ear, unlike the eye, frees from the rigor of the fixed viewpoint and provides access to perceptions and invisible vibrations reaching us from all sides. In short, for Campanella ours can only be the time of music or Pythagorean harmony of the world.

The auricular esthetics of *The City of the Sun* projects its force through Ariosto's epic poetry. Ariosto's musical esthetics has been acknowledged throughout the Renaissance. Galileo prefers him to Tasso. In *La cena delle ceneri,* Florio and the Nolan, sailing at night along the river Thames and almost lost, sing some stanzas from the *Orlando Furioso* (Dialogue II). Bruno, in fact, stresses Ariosto's musicality, which had been vindicated by madrigalists, such as Giandomenico da Nola, Cipriano di Rore, Alessandro Striggio, and Francesco Rossello. Bruno grasps in Ariosto's song the harmony that Copernican science had stilled. In the wake of these debates Campanella sees the Pythagorean doctrine as the locus of reconciliation of music and philosophy as well as, in the wake of Ficino, the reconciliation between music and astronomy. Ariosto becomes for all of them the poet of Harmony or "concordia discors."

Like the *Orlando Furioso, The City of the Sun* gives itself as an epic adventure. If Ariosto highlights the tragic disintegration of reason, Campanella writes a text poised at the crossroads between philosophy and poetry. He gauges the distance separating them and, at the same time, unveils their hidden complicity, the complicity that joins any two interlocutors in dialogue, such as the Genoese and the Hospitaler. In this interlocution between philosophy and poetry, philosophy questions and asks if the poetic imagination can be constrained within the regime of philosophical reason. In a way, philosophy thinks against poetry: it wants to know and to define. Yet poetry always shows itself on the way to other destinations and experiences, as the Genoese does. It always pursues an elsewhere, displays its distance from abstract formulas, acknowledges its powerlessness, and, finally, evokes a utopian space where all oppositions endure and are not placated.

Finally, *The City of the Sun,* as I have argued here, shows the impossibility of a definitive discourse. It ends with the Genoese resisting his interlocutor's ongoing questions and saying: "Non posso, non posso." Their conversation breaks down. Its interruption signals the secret, paradoxical life of literature. It places us at the limit of any possible discourse, at the threshold of possible, alternate, and imaginary worlds. It can be said that Campanella has written an exemplary text of liminology: suspended between history and utopia, philosophy and poetry, sun and earth, madness and reason, Plato and Machiavelli, *The City of the Sun* traces the profile of different worlds in order to reconcile them and show their impossible distance. They are contradictory worlds that ceaselessly recall one another, implicate one another, and exclude one another. Campanella, a seventeenth century dominican friar, retrieves and deepens the theological, philosophical, and literary experiences he has inherited: he stands prodigiously balanced between equidistant worlds as if in the night of the equinoxes. Plunged into the depths of his Neapolitan jail he lives his solar, shadowy solitude and sketches the essential qualities of literature at the threshold.

JOSEPH GOERING

PENITENTIAL LIMINALITY
IN THE MIDDLE AGES

ABSTRACT. The rite of Penance in the early Church and the Middle Ages placed penitents in a liminal state – neither fully in communion with the Church, nor fully excluded.
During the thirteenth century penance and confession became one of the most popular
religious activities, and penitential liminality became a characteristic of the ordinary
Christian life. What might this mean?

Although Dante traverses three realms in his *Divine Comedy*, in only
two of them does he cross a threshold. The first, and most famous, he
reaches at nightfall on the evening of Good Friday in the year 1300.
Virgil has led him out of the Dark Wood where Dante found himself,
lost and afraid, on the morning of Maundy Thursday, to the gateway
into that eternal place where dwell "those who have lost the good of intellect," the place of the damned. Dante stops to read the ancient words
inscribed above the gateway:

> THROUGH ME THE WAY INTO THE SUFFERING CITY,
> THROUGH ME THE WAY TO THE ETERNAL PAIN,
> THROUGH ME THE WAY THAT RUNS AMONG THE LOST.
>
> JUSTICE URGED ON MY HIGH ARTIFICER;
> MY MAKER WAS DIVINE AUTHORITY,
> THE FULLEST WISDOM, AND THE PRIMAL LOVE.
>
> BEFORE ME NOTHING BUT ETERNAL THINGS
> WERE MADE, AND I ENDURE ETERNALLY.
> ABANDON ALL HOPE, YOU WHO ENTER HERE. (*INFERNO* 3, 1-9)

Virgil cheerfully leads Dante across this threshold, and into that tumul-
tuous and suffering world.

Three days later, on Easter Monday morning, Dante awakes to find
himself before another, and much more important, threshold. He had

Limina: Thresholds and Borders - A St. Michael's College Symposium
Joseph Goering, Francesco Guardiani, Giulio Silano eds. Ottawa: Legas, 2005

emerged from Hell and begun his slow and arduous climb up Purgatory Mountain early on the previous day, Easter Sunday. By nightfall on Sunday he and Virgil have reached a point perhaps one-third of the way up the mountain. While Dante sleeps, he is carried by St. Lucy, one of his patronesses, further up, to within sight of the walls of Purgatory itself. There, in the full light of morning, Dante sees the second, and final gateway through which he will pass – Peter's Gate – *la porta di San Pietro* (cf. *Inferno*, 1, 134).

Peter's Gate is not, as we have come to expect, one of the pearly gates of the Heavenly Jerusalem. It is found well below the ethereal realms, on the steep slopes of Mount Purgatory. Nor is this gate an imposing one, like the Gate of Hell. When Dante first sees it, he thinks that it is a mere breach or fissure in the wall of Purgatory. But as he and Virgil approach, he sees that it is a proper gate, guarded by a doorkeeper sitting on the threshold. The doorkeeper holds an unsheathed sword, "which so reflected rays toward us that I, time and again, tried to sustain that sight in vain" (*Purgatorio* 9, 83-85) He challenges Dante and Virgil, and Virgil replies that St. Lucy had shown them to the gate and bid them climb. With this, the doorkeeper invites them to mount the three steps that lead up to the gate. The first is of white marble, polished to a mirror-like clarity. The second step is darker than deep purple, rough-hewn and crumbling, with cracks running along both its length and breadth. The third, more massive, is made of porphyry, as flaming red as blood that spurts fresh from the veins.

On this top step the doorkeeper, an "Angel of God," traces seven "P"s on Dante's forehead with his sword-tip. He then withdraws from beneath his ash-colored robes two keys, one golden and the other silver, and with these he unlocks the massive metal doors. They swing open resoundingly, and Dante crosses the last threshold (*Purg.* 9, 73 - 10, 1).

These few lines in the ninth Canto of the *Purgatorio* constitute perhaps the single richest and most nuanced poetic description of the sacrament of penance that has ever been written. Dante is carried to Peter's gate by God's grace, not by his own efforts. Once there, he mounts the three steps that constitute the parts of the sacrament of penance. Since at least the twelfth century, penance had been described as entailing three distinct actions: contrition, confession, and satisfaction (cf. *Magistri Petri Lombardi* 4.16, vol. 2, pp. 336-342). The first step, of polished white marble, allows Dante to see himself reflected there and thus to recognize his sins and repent them. The second – dark purple, cracked and crumbling – represents the humbling of himself in confession, where he must admit to another the dark, cracked and crumbling state of his soul. The third step is blood-red; it represents not Dante's own satisfaction or penance for his sins – that will take place higher up in Purgatory – but rather the satisfaction for sins that makes all penance possible, namely, Christ's death on the cross. It is on this massive stone that Peter's gate rests, and from this foundation that Dante will embark on the second half of his journey. There is no further threshold to cross; the way to Paradise is henceforth open.

Dante's own penance or satisfaction is assigned by the gatekeeper. He traces with his sword point seven P's on Dante's forehead, each representing one of the seven deadly sins (*Peccata*), and it will be Dante's task to heal these seven wounds as he works his way through Purgatory. It is well to note that the marks or scars left by the sword are not, themselves, sins. The guilt (*culpa*) of Dante's sins is removed on the third step of the threshold, by Christ's sacrifice on the cross. Rather, the seven Ps represent the inclination to sin (called by medieval writers the *fomes peccati* – the kindling-wood of sin) that remain in the soul even after the sins themselves have been forgiven (cf. *Magistri Petri Lombardi* 2.30.8, vol. 1, pp. 499-500 et Thomas Aquinas 1-2, q. 91, a. 6).

Once the doorkeeper, the Angel of the Church, judges that Dante is truly sorry for his sins, has confessed them without reservation, and has undertaken to make amends for them in fitting ways, he opens Peter's gate to him. He opens the door with the keys that were entrusted to him by St. Peter. Peter himself had received them from Christ with the well-known words: "You are Peter, and upon this rock I will found my Church ... . And to you I will give the keys of the Kingdom of Heaven; whatsoever you bind on earth will be bound in heaven, and whatsoever you loose on earth will be loosed in heaven" (Mt. 16:18-19) From very early times it was considered that these were two keys, although occasionally Peter is shown with one or three.[4] That the one key was made of gold and the other of silver seems to be Dante's own invention – and it lives on today in the crossed keys, one golden and one silver, of the Holy See's Coat of Arms.

The gatekeeper tells Dante that the golden key is more precious, but that the silver one requires more skill in its use; both must work smoothly before the gate will open. The Angel turns first the silver key and then the golden one. Commentators have long agreed that the silver key is the one with which the Church unlocks the "entanglement of sin

---

[1]See the commentaries, from the fourteenth to the twentieth century, collected by The Dartmouth Dante Project. See also Ludwig Hödl.

in the human heart," and the golden one is the high authority given to the Church to open and to close the doorway of the Kingdom of Heaven (cf. Sayers 140, and the Dartmouth Project). Fortunately for Dante, and for us, the Angel of the Church has been instructed by Peter "rather to err in opening than in keeping this portal shut, whenever souls pray humbly"(*Purg.* 9, 128-129).

Peter's gate, this sacramental threshold between earth and heaven, represents a liminal passage that has been fundamental to the Christian Church from its beginnings. Both John the Baptist, the "precursor of the Lord," and Jesus himself, began their public ministries with calls to repentance (Matth. 3:2, 4:17). In the early Church a variety of practices grew up that gave physical shape to this penitential requirement. Most striking, perhaps, was the elaboration of baptismal rites that featured a period of teaching and penitential exercises culminating in the baptism itself, and the incorporation of the neophyte into the Christian community (Martimort, 3:13-83, 4:66-76). The creation of a sacred space in which this rite of passage took place was one of the earliest achievements of Christian art and architecture. Indeed, the earliest surviving Christian building, the house church of Dura Europos (ca. 250), already has a separate room set apart and decorated with appropriate images for the baptismal ceremony (Matheson).

By the early fourth century, and probably much earlier, the entire Christian community was sharing with the catechumens a period of penance and preparation leading up to the celebration of Baptism at Easter (Martimort, 4:66-72). This period, known as "Lent" in germanic-speaking countries (from a word designating the lengthening of days in the Spring), came to be one of the most popular observances in the Church. At Rome in the time of Pope Leo I (440-461) the period began on Quadragesima Sunday with a reading of the summons of St. Paul: "Now is the acceptable time" (2 Cor. 6:2). Pope Leo then reminded his Roman congregation that "all around the world thousands upon thousands of people are preparing for their rebirth in Christ." At the same time, Satan "sees those who had fallen washing themselves in the tears of repentance and being admitted to the healing of reconciliation as the Apostle's key opens the door of forgiveness to them" (Martimort, 4:67-68).

By the sixth century in Rome this liminal period began on the previous Wednesday with a penitential procession from the Church of St. Anastasia at the foot of the Palatine Hill to Santa Sabina where the first Mass of Lent was celebrated. During the procession, the people sang the antiphon *Immutemur habitu in cinere et cilicio* (Let us put on sackcloth and ashes). Perhaps first in the Rhineland, this "Ash Wednesday" came to be marked by the actual imposition of ashes, a practice that found its way back to Italy by the eleventh century. In Benevento in 1091 it was ordained that "on Ash Wednesday everyone, clergy and laity, men and women, will receive ashes" (Martimort, 4:68-69). On this day, too, those who were to undergo a public penance at the hands of the bishop were dismissed from the church, and would be received back again only at the end of the Lenten period (Martimort, 3:104-5; 110-112).

Ash Wednesday henceforth marked the beginning of a six-week liminal period of penitential observances that culminated during Holy Week. On Holy Thursday in Rome and Milan, and on Good Friday in Spain, public penitents who had been exiled from the community of the faithful were reconciled, and readmitted into full communion in the Church in an impressive ceremony presided over by the bishop (Martimort, 3:107). They were thus able to join the rest of the faithful in all the churches on the last stage or step of their penitential journey. As in Dante's *Commedia*, the last step on the threshold of Heaven is Christ's death on the cross on Good Friday. It is this sacrificial death that makes possible the crossing of the threshold to Easter and to Heaven.

Some form of this ritual passage from death to life was reenacted annually in all the churches of Christendom, but it never exhausted the possibilities and the imaginations of those wishing to make the penitential journey. Leaving aside, for lack of good scholarship, what must have been one of the most important *loci poenitentiae*, penance in the hour of one's death, other practices also developed to give shape and form to the crossing of the penitential threshold. The most influential, in the long run, was the emergence of a system wherein a penitent could seek out a skilled confessor – a soul friend or what we today might call a "personal trainer" – who would direct his or her penitential journey. This practice grew up first, it seems, in Celtic Ireland, and by the eighth century it was known throughout Europe.[8] It opened up many new possibilities. One could enter the penitential state at any time, not just during prescribed seasons. And one could confess all one's sins, not just the great ones, and receive expert direction from a skilled physician and judge of souls.

The first kind of penance, that which begins on Ash Wednesday and ends with the Easter triduum, emphasizes the power and effectiveness of Dante's golden key, namely, the authority given by Christ to Peter

---

[7]The literature on the origins of private or personal confession and penance is enormous. For a general orientation, see Poschmann, and Martimort 3:101.

and his successors to open and close heaven's door. The second kind emphasizes the skill of the individual penitent and confessor in using the silver key to untangle the knots of sin in the soul. Both keys are necessary, as Dante's Angel explains, and it was especially in the twelfth century that concerted efforts were made to bring together the operation of both in the sacrament of penance (cf. Anciaux and Hödl).

The result was a bold and seemingly foolhardy gesture by Pope Innocent III in the Fourth Lateran Council of 1215. In the decree *Omnis utriusque sexus*, the Council required that every adult Christian, both male and female, both cleric and lay, must confess all of their sins at least once a year to their proper priest or to a licenced substitute, strive to fulfill the penance enjoined, and receive the Eucharist at Easter (*Decrees* 1:245). This decree neatly wove together the older penitential regimes. Without taking anything away from the traditional Lenten rite and its authority, the decree made possible, indeed it required, that this rite be accomplished by means of a personal and individual confession to one's proper priest and an attempt to fulfill an individualized penance.

A bold and seemingly foolhardy gesture this surely was. There can have been no framework at the time, whether social or liturgical, for putting such a decree into practice. Some priests, no doubt, were skilled confessors, and some penitents were accustomed to searching their consciences, confessing their particular sins, and seeking an appropriate penance. But that every parish priest, and every parishioner of all estates and walks of life should develop the skills necessary for fulfilling this decree was surely a far-fetched idea.

It is only with historical hindsight that we can see how fruitful Pope Innocent's initiative was. Whether it took a few decades or a few centuries we cannot say with confidence, but henceforth, and for at least the next 750 years, it would be in this personal encounter between priest and penitent in confession that most Christians would cross the *limen* of penance. During the thirteenth century alone, literally thousands of treatises were written to help prepare priests and penitents for this encounter (cf. Goering). From vast *summae de penitentia* to little handbooks and didactic poems, the literature of penance and confession that sprang up in this period gives eloquent testimony to widespread eagerness, among clerics and lay people alike, to learn about and to master this new penitential regime.

Dante's *Divine Comedy* is only one, if surely the most sublime, evocation of the power of penitential liminality at the beginning of the fourteenth century. By the end of the century, another layman, Geoffrey

Chaucer, will cap his own literary career by elaborating for his English-speaking audience a full-scale exposition of the penitential way. Chaucer knew Dante's *Commedia* well; even his Wife of Bath can quote Dante as an authority! ("The Wife of Bath's Tale" lines 1126-1133, from Dante's *Purgatory* 7, 121-123). And when Chaucer had finished writing his delightful *Canterbury Tales*, sometimes bawdy, and sometimes, as he says, "tending toward sin," he penned his "Parson's Tale." This Tale summarizes, as well as anything in print, the common, and detailed, understanding of penance that had developed during the two preceding centuries. It can be read almost as a gloss on Dante's concise evocation of the penitential way.

The Parson begins:

> Our sweet Lord God of Heaven, Who wishes to destroy no man, but would have all come into the knowledge of Him and to the blessed life that is everlasting, admonishes us by the Prophet Jeremiah, who says thus: "Stand ye in the ways, and see, and ask for the old paths (that is to say, the old wisdom) where is the good way, and walk therein, and ye shall find rest for your souls." Many are the spiritual ways that lead folk unto Our Lord Jesus Christ and to the Kingdom of Glory. Of which ways there is a right noble way and a proper one, which will not fail either man or woman who through sin has gone astray from the right way to the Heavenly Jerusalem; and this way is called penitence. ("The Parson's Tale," 288)

Many pages later, after guiding the Canterbury pilgrims up the three steps of contrition, confession, and satisfaction, he concludes, like Dante, by describing the end of this penitential journey:

> Then shall men understand what is the fruit of penance ... it is the endless bliss of heaven. ... This blessed kingdom may man acquire by poverty of spirit, and the glory by humbleness, and the plenitude of joy by hunger and thirst, and the ease and rest by labour, and life by death and mortification of sin. ("The Parson's Tale," 327)

As unlikely as it may seem, penance has become one of the most popular religious activities of the Christian life, and penitential liminality one of its most common states.

WORKS CITED

Alighieri, Dante. *The Divine Comedy*, transl. Allen Mandelbaum. Knopf: New York, 1995.

Anciaux, Paul. *La théologie du sacrement de la pénitence au XIIe siècle*. Louvain: Nauwelaerts, 1949.

Chaucer, Geoffrey. *The Riverside Chaucer*. Larry D. Benson, ed. Boston: Houghton Mifflin, 1987.

Dartmouth Dante Project. *www.dartmouth.edu/~library/explain/Dartmouth %20Dante%20Project/#General*.

Decrees of the Ecumenical Councils. Norman P. Tanner, ed. and transl. 2 vols. London, 1990.

Goering, Joseph. "The Internal Forum and the Literature of Penance and Confession." *Traditio* (forthcoming).

Hödl, Ludwig. *Die Geschichte der scholastischen Literatur und der Theologie der Schlüsselgewalt* (Münster: Aschendorff, 1960).

Magistri Petri Lombardi Sententiae in iv libris distinctae. 2 vols. Grottaferrata: Collegii S. Bonaventurae, 1971-1981.

Matheson, Susan B. *Dura-Europos, the ancient city and the Yale collection*. New Haven: Yale University Art Gallery, 1982.

Martimort, Aimé G. *The Church at Prayer: An Introduction to the Liturgy*. Collegeville: The Liturgical Press, 1992.

Poschmann, B. *Penance and Anointing of the Sick*. Freiburg: Herder, 1964.

Sayers, Dorothy (transl. and comment.). *Dante: The Divine Comedy, 2, Purgatory*. Penguin: Harmondsworth, 1955.

Thomas Aquinas. *Summa theologiae*.

ANTONIO CALCAGNO

DERRIDA, TIME AND POLITICS: A PRAGMATIC AND UNDECIDABLE RELATION?

ABSTRACT. Derrida's democracy to come is sometimes seen as excluding the possibility of any sort of decisive political action or intervention. This paper will argue that the democracy to come makes clearer the responsibly defining limits of political decisions through the very impossibility contained in such decisions.

It would be an understatement to say that contemporary French thinkers, including Jacques Derrida[1], Alain Badiou,[2] Alain Finkielkraut[3] and Sylvain Lazarus,[4] are dissatisfied with the present-day status of political thinking and politics in general. Each of these thinkers has his own approach to the present-day political dissatisfaction and it would be gross presumption to try and reduce all of these thinkers to one over-arching political framework. This paper will have as its focus the response of Jacques Derrida to the above-mentioned dissatisfaction. Derrida's recent philosophy has been devoted to questions of ethics, religion and politics. In part, this is an attempt to answer critics who have often charged Derrida's deconstructive project with being confined to textual analysis, thereby having more to do with reading than with concrete practical matters. Richard Rorty complains,

> I see romantic and utopian hopes of the sort developed in the 'The Politics of Friendship' as a contribution to Derrida's private fashioning...[b]ut I do not see texts such as the 'The Politics of Friendship' as contributions to po-

---

[1] Jacques Derrida, *Spectres de Marx* (Paris: Galilée, 1993); *Politiques de l'amitié* (Paris: Galilée, 1994); *L'autre cap suivi par La démocratie ajournée* (Paris: Minuit, 1990); *Voyous* (Paris: Galilée, 2003).

[2] Alain Badiou, *Manifeste pour la philosophie* (Paris: Seuil, 1988); *Peut-on penser la politique?* (Paris: Seuil, 1985); *Abrégé de métapolitique* (Paris: Seuil, 1998).

[3] Alain Finkielkraut, *La défaite de la pensée* (Paris: Gallimard, 1987); *L'imparfait du présent* (Paris: Gallimard, 2002).

[4] Sylvain Lazarus, *L'anthropologie du nom* (Paris: Seuil, 1993).

Limina: Thresholds and Borders - A St. Michael's College Symposium
Joseph Goering, Francesco Guardiani, Giulio Silano eds. Ottawa: Legas, 2005

litical thought. Politics...is a matter of pragmatic short-term reforms and compromises...Political thought centres on the attempt to formulate some hypotheses about how, and under what conditions, such reforms might be effected.[5]

In sum, though Derrida may provide an interesting approach to textual criticism, Derrida's claim that his deconstructive project, especially as articulated in his "concept" of différance, extends to cover and archstructure all of human experience,[6] including political experience, is taken cum grano salis.[7] Very few, if any, pragmatic political applications can be seen to be drawn from his recent meditations on politics.[8] But Derrida's recent philosophy is not to be understood as merely textual, for he also recognises that if he is to be consistent to the claims of deconstruction, he must also show how indeed all is to be read as text,[9] that is, how deconstruction can be extended to political philosophy and politics in general.

It is the contention of this paper that Derrida articulates for his readers the possibility, though, as we shall see later, this possibility is laced with impossibility as well, of a deconstructivist politics. Derridean politics is to be understood under the arch-structure of what Derrida calls the democracy to come, *la démocratie à venir*. Certainly, what Derrida means by the democracy to come will have to be unpacked. The democracy to come yields two irreducible results. First, through the temporal models of the "to come" of the promise and the spatio-temporisation of différance, all politics is arch-structured by the undecidability of the double bind of possibility and impossibility. Second, such undecidability articulates limits of possibility and impossibility, and such limits, though seemingly contradictory, make evident an aporia that is structured into politics. This aporia shows that if we are to have any-

---

[5] Richard Rorty, "Remarks on Deconstruction and Pragmatism" in *Deconstruction and Pragmatism* (ed.) Chantal Mouffe (London: Routledge, 1996), p. 17.

[6] Jacques Derrida, *"Signature événement contexte"* in *Marges* (Paris: Minuit, 1972) p. 377.

[7] Jürgen Habermas claims that Derrida is so faithful a reader of Heidegger that Derrida falls into the Heideggerian legacy of *Seinsmytizismus* Habermas remarks, "Derrida's grammatologically circumscribed concept of an archwriting whose traces call forth all the more interpretations the more unfamiliar they become, renews the mystical concept of tradition as an ever *delayed* event of revelation." *The Philosophical Discourse of Modernity* (tr.) F. Lawrence (Cambridge, MA: MIT Press, 1987), p. 183.

[8] Many American thinkers have insisted on the need to think politics outside of a metaphysical framework, including Hilary Putnam and Stanley Cavell. Exemplary in this attack of metaphysics is Rawls. See his "Justice as Fairness: Political not Metaphysical" in *Philosophy and Political Affairs*, 1985; 14, 223-251.

[9] Derrida *De la grammatologie* (Paris: Minuit, 1967), p. 227.

thing like, for example, political friendship, based on hospitality, justice and responsibility, we must recognise the very nature of the limits that these constituents of political friendship entail.[10] Traditional notions of democracy rooted in friendship, justice, hospitality and responsibility contain "within" themselves their very own radically absenting and annihilating limits, namely, the enemy, inhospitality, injustice and irresponsibility. The aporia consists in the fact that the limits which make politics both possible and impossible are simultaneously playing themselves out. Many critics have charged that the aporia of undecidability qua politics renders Derrida's political attempts futile, for the instant we try to think or act politically, our decisions and acts become undone and annihilated through the impossibility contained in the double bind. For Derrida, the limits of the double bind that make politics undecidable do not absolutely stymie political thinking and acting. Rather, if anything the limits encourage us to act again and again.[11] For example, the absences in justice, hospitality, friendship and responsibility, that is, injustice, inhospitality, the enemy, and irresponsibility, again and again require through the injunction of the promise and the repetition of différance to try and make present, even though we know we can never do so fully, a politics rooted in friendship, justice, hospitality and responsibility—a democracy to come which we always desire to make possible but which is impossible to bring about fully. The Derridean democracy to come is a useful or pragmatic political circle.

At this point, I would like to propose a thesis that will serve to structure this paper: Various authors have explored the pragmatic implications of Derrida's political thought.[12] This paper also wishes to bring to the fore some interesting pragmatic consequences of Derrida's thought, especially concerning time. Time is given little consideration in pragmatic treatments of Derrida's work, and this paper seeks to assist in filling out this important area of consideration. What are some of the pragmatic consequences of the Derridean undecidability of the democracy to come within a temporal framework? First, Rorty's definition of

---

[10] Derrida treats these themes in his works: *Politiques de l'amitié, De l'hospitalité, Spectres de Marx* and in his latest work just published called, *Voyous* (Paris: Galilée, 2003). In this text Derrida argues that sovereignty includes the abuse of power, that is, both sovereignty and the abuse of power are co-constitutive of one another. Because of time and space limitations, I will not explicitly treat here these themes.

[11] Simon Critchley, *The Ethics of Deconstruction* (Cambridge: Blackwell, 1992).

[12] Chantal Mouffe (ed.) *Deconstruction and Pragmatism* and Jim Vernon, "The People Have Spoken(?) Derrida, Democracy and Reciprocal Affirmation" in *International Studies in Philosophy* 34:2, 2002, pp. 115-131.

politics as making "short-term" reforms and compromises is subject to the same undecidability that would structure any kind of metaphysical account of presence. A short-term response does not necessarily guarantee an effectively pragmatic or more effective response to political situations. Pragmatically, it is wise not to think that short-term responses are more effective because they are temporally shorter. Whether short-term or long-term, time is the "source" of undecidability. The spatio-temporisation that is différance and the temporal model of the promise are arch-structuring, and hence, if we are to think and act politically, especially if we are mining Derrida for pragmatic possibilities, we must be aware of the undecidability of such a spatio-temporal arch-structure. In short, our political planning and decision-making must take undecidability into account. Second, Derrida's articulation of the democracy to come can serve as an "hypothesis" pragmatically "structuring" the way we are to bring about the reforms and compromises that Rorty sees as belonging to the nature of political thought and acts. This is evidenced in the viable uses of the Derridean democracy to come. To use an expression of William James, the "cash-value" of Derridean political thinking is threefold. First, it helps us think through and bring to the fore the limits that structure any political discourse. Second, it is a prophylactic in the sense that the democracy to come can "prevent", if one tries to live it, radical democracy from lapsing into a totalitarianism of the masses, something which Plato feared in his criticism of democracy. Derridean democracy could be seen as facilitating a radical pluralism. Finally, the democracy to come would help us understand what is entailed by making a political decision.

What "Is" the Democracy To Come?

In Spectres de Marx, Derrida makes explicit the relation between time and the democracy to come.

> Above and beyond the regulative idea in its classical formulation, the idea, if it still is an idea, of the democracy to come, its "idea" as the event of a launched injunction that commands to make come that which will never present itself in the form of a full presence, this is the opening of the gap between an infinite promise (at least always untenable because it calls for the infinite respect of singularity and the infinite alterity of the other, including a compatible equality, calculable and subject-able (subjectale), in the midst of anonymous singularities) and the determined forms, necessary but

necessarily inadequate to those who must measure themselves in relation to this promise.[13]

The democracy to come is the special articulation, just as writing is the species of the genus communication,[14] of the more general arch-structure Derrida calls différance. Différance is that which makes the fully present an impossibility. The spatio-temporisation, that is, the delay or deferral of the non-originary origin of all communication and experience as well as the concomitant differentiation that happens through repetition and intervalling, irreducibly structure the way we are to do and think politics. I shall briefly examine how Derrida can make such a claim by first examining what Derrida has to say about the sign and its delay, which results in an indirect representation of the signified. Second, I shall examine how differentiation contains within itself absence. Finally, I shall examine how reiteration implies a non-return or non-identical repetition. In addition to the temporal model of différance, a model that Derrida developed early on in his career, his more recent writings employ another temporal model, namely, that of the promise, which serves to concretise what Derrida means by the *à venir*, the to come. In short, if we are to understand what Derrida means by the democracy to come, we have to understand the temporality of différance and of the to come of the promise. Let us proceed in the following manner. First, I will sketch, and quite rapidly here, two key temporal structures associated with the democracy to come, namely, the spatio-temporisation that is différance and the to come of the promise. Second, I will discuss what Derrida entails by the term democracy. Finally, I will give a fuller discussion of the nature of the democracy to come and the undecidability that is contained within its structuralising force.

Différance is defined by Derrida as that double movement that, first, delays or defers an origin, which can never come to any presence because that which is originally present has to be represented by some sign, and second, as that movement which constantly differentiates the various elements within any kind of significative chain, be it experiential or communicative. The reason that the origin can never come to presence again is that in the repetition or iterability that is required in order for there to be anything like a chain of communication or experience, the various elements of the chain are constantly differentiating them-

---

[13] Jacques Derrida, *Spectres de Marx* (Paris: Galilée, 1993) p. 111. Translations are mine unless otherwise specified.

[14] *Marges,* pp. 373-74.

selves. The elements need to differentiate themselves in order for the elements to stand out as individual elements within the chain. An element can be an element unto itself if and only if it is simultaneously distinguished radically from itself. Its radical other is the element's radical absence.[15] In playing itself out an individual element of a communicative or experiential chain will come into some form of delayed presence only if it distinguishes itself from itself by positing its own radical absence. But each time it reiterates itself, the element is not identical to its previous saying, for the previous saying has been erased and there is yet an even further delay of the "originally" signified. All that is left is a trace that points back to a non-originary origin that can never come back to any presence—a trace that continually undoes itself.

The undecidability that stems from the playing out of différance is two-fold. First, there is the undecidability of the origin that never comes to presence. We know there is an origin which is constantly represented in linguistic and graphic communication, but because the signs delay the origin, the origin itself can never be brought to presence as it is in its presence, or in Husserlian terms, as *lebendige Gegenwart*. Second, as the repetition and intervalling result in a constant differentiation of elements that constantly erase themselves while striving to come to presence (the logic of the trace), not only is the origin undecidable, that is we do not know what it is presently, but the various elements or signs by which we refer to the origin themselves are not identical with the origin. Rather, they are constantly differentiating themselves through their very attempts to come to presence and their simultaneous erasure. The double bind of possibility and impossibility come into play in différance in that it is possible to speak of an origin, but it is impossible to know what it is. Moreover, the possibility of signifying that origin is certainly there, but because there is constant differentiation that happens in repetition, the signs themselves are quite impossible to fix with absolute sense/meaning, that is, it is hard to make the full sense of the communicative signs present or completely present.

Let us move to the temporal model of the promise. The second temporal model that Derrida develops in order to explain and articulate what he conceives non-originary originary time to "be" is that of the promise. Key in this metaphor is the notion of the "to come." In

---

[15] In *"Signature événement contexte"* Derrida demonstrates how the radical absence of the writer/receiver of texts/experiencer is necessary in order for writing, speech, communication and experience to exist. He does this by employing the works of Condillac, Austin and Husserl. See *Marges*, pp. 365ff.

French, the to come translates *l'à-venir*, which also means the future (*l'avenir*). The to come, however, is not to be understood simply as the future, as simple protention or as simple futurity, for the to come has within its structure the double bind of being haunted by a past that had already been and the present that never comes to present itself fully.[16]

The to come contains within itself both the possibility of an open-ended temporal horizon and the impossibility of anything coming to full presence in such an horizon. The promise, then, is that model which concretises the temporisation of the double bind of the possible and the impossible, ultimately yielding Derridean undecidability.[17] Derrida says that the promise contains within itself a "yes".[18] The "yes" that Derrida describes the to come as being is a consent, a consent that there is a possibility of the opening of an horizon, an horizon of futurity. The promise contains within itself the logic of différance, but it also empha- sises the possibility of a futurity, the possibility of an horizon, that can never make fully present its "contents." The "yes" of the model of the promise is analogous to the repetition or iterability that is necessary for there to be any kind of movement or flow that is communication, ex- perience or writing. The promise needs that iterability if it is to continue to flow or move as a promise. That is, some kind of temporal extension or horizon has to be given if the promise is to be articulated "again and again" as a promise that requires an extended or future time in order to be fulfilled. There is also a temporal delay contained within the model of the promise. The object promised is always represented in experi- ence or consciousness through communication. And the communica- tion is a sign of the thing originally promised that never comes to full and immediate presence as "living present" in consciousness. The promise itself is a delayed or deferred representation/sign of a more original reality. This delay makes what was originally promised impossi- bly present. Moreover, in the temporal horizon that is the futurity of the promise, that futurity requires repetition. This repetition is interval- ling and differentiating such that in order for the promise to be a prom- ise it continually differentiates itself, thereby bringing to the fore the

---

[16] *Spectres de Marx*, p. 60.

[17] Silvano Petrosino, *Jacques Derrida e la legge del possibile: Un'introduzione* (Milano: Jaca, 1997), p. 221.

[18] *"L'affirmation de l'à-venir, donc: ce n'est pas une thèse positive. Ce n'est rien d'autre que l'affirmation même, le "oui" en tant qu'il est la condition de toute promesse ou de toute espérance, de toute attente, de toute performativité, de toute ouverture à l'avenir, quel qu'il soit, pour la science ou pour la religion."* Jacques Derrida, *Mal d'archive* (Paris: Galilée, 1995), p. 109. The consent to a possibility of an opening horizon harkens back to Merleau-Ponty's *Bejahung*.

constantly differentiating sense of the promise within its own spatio-temporisation. As time inevitably progresses, the meaning of the promise will take on altering and differentiating senses, thereby making the sense of the "original" promise impossibly fully present, one or absolute. The communicative flow or movement that is guaranteed by repetition or the "yes" of the promise opens up an horizon of possibility, but what is promised in the flow is always delayed and differentiating, and hence what is originally promised can neither come to full presence nor can its sense be absolutely fixed, that is, come to be absolutely fulfilled as a promise. An absolute sense of what is promised is impossible. Hence, the double bind of possibility an impossibility of the promise folded into the concept of the "to come."[19]

Having unfolded the two temporal structures of the democracy to come, ultimately showing how they bring undecidability into play, let us turn to a more specific treatment of democracy. What does Derrida entail by democracy? Speaking at an international philosophy colloquium in April 1968, Derrida maintained that democracy was the form that such colloquia were to take. He also maintains that democracy must be the organisational political form of society.

It is necessary that democracy be here the form of political organisation of society. This means that at least:

> 1. National philosophical identity is placed together with non-identity. Philosophical identity must not exclude a diversity relative to and that comes with the language of such diversity, that comes eventually as a minority...Concerning the fact that the totality of this diversity be exhaustively represented, this cannot but remain problematic...

> 2. So that philosophers will not identify with one another, the philosophers present here must not assume the politics of their own countries. It should be permitted here that I should be able to speak in my own name. I will not do otherwise than in the measure where the problem posed to me refers back in truth to an essential generality and it is in the form of this generality that I wish to articulate it.[20]

---

[19] Derrida describes the to come as possessing three traits: It is not fully knowable (connaissable) as the to come; it is to be seen as messianic (distinguished from messianism); and it is radically ascribed to functioning within the parameters of an injunction. These traits are vital to the Derridean understanding of the promise and the to come, but because of space limitations, I will simply mention them here as I will make allusion to them in the paper.

[20] Marges, p. 134. Note that society here is a double entendre. It refers both to society in general but also to the French Society of Philosophy. Here, we have a formulation

For society to have a democratic political form, it must meet two fundamental conditions. First, for a national philosophical identity to exist, that is, to exist democratically, all that is non-identical must come to have a voice; it must be represented in the politically temporalised sense. All diversity must be allowed to articulate itself within a democracy, problematic as that may be. Obviously, what Derrida means by the demos of democracy is not the German notion of Volk, but more the popular notion of people as individuals dwelling together. Until the fullness of diversity is articulated, a true democratic form of political organisation is not able to realise itself fully. We see in this first condition an intimation of the to come. Why? Derrida wants all diversity to come and articulate itself, but if we take seriously his claim about spatio-temporisation and the force of the to come, this democratic articulation of fullness will never come to any kind of full presence. Moreover, it is undecidable at best and uncertain. Yet, the injunction of the to come as assured by iterability means that any political discourse or experience will require a continual playing out of différance and the double bind. Hence, we continue to strive to achieve this goal of full expression, knowing that we can never achieve it,[21] but our failure to achieve this full democratic articulation of individual differences calls us to responsibly try and make it "present" again and again (*l'injonction/itérabilité*).

The second condition is that all nationalist political platforms ought to be dropped. That one should speak in one's own voice, in one's own name. We see in this condition the emphasis on each individual, each differentiated individual, articulating her own self. If we line up each of these conditions and have them stand together, they form a kind of antinomous notion of democratic nationhood. On one hand, a democratic nation can only be philosophically democratic if it allows all diversity to come to the fore. On the other hand, while it simultaneously allows all diversity to come to the fore, it must not nationalise such diversity. One must be allowed to speak in one's own name. A nation is only democratically national when it cultivates diversity and yet it can make no claim to national identity based on such diversity.

---

that is seemingly and irreducibly decided in that democracy is selected as the form of political organisation, ultimately bringing into question the force of Derrida's claim of undecidability. Why Derrida chooses to call his politics a democracy to come as opposed to a communism to come or a liberalism to come is a huge question. Roughly, democracy is a logical choice for Derrida in that it best can account for the structure of plurality while avoiding *"fusion communitaire"*, which other forms of political organisation stress.

[21] To claim to achieve something and achieve it fully is to make a metaphysical claim for Derrida.

Given the analysis above, one could see democracy within the framework of différance. Democracy has as its enacting subject that individual person that comes to differentiate herself from the other (through ruptures of intervals),[22] and yet who, at the same time, makes no claim to possess totally or absolutely that difference even when one properly speaks in one's own name. The philosophical subject can never fully present to herself. Moreover, her decisions, conventions and political opinions are all signs of a non-originary origin that is delayed. It would seem that Derrida is advocating a kind of having an identity while simultaneously losing or depossessing it.[23] Concretely, then, one could claim, for example, that one is not only a Torontonian, but one is also "not only" a Frenchman, an Italian, etc. This double motion is what Derrida described earlier when he described the promise as infinitely untenable because of the double call for the infinite respect of the singularity of the individual and the infinite alterity of the other.

Democracy to come, then, is that arch-structure of différance or the double bind of the promise that conditions and structures all temporalised politics as irreducibly undecidable. That is, if we are to think politically or if we are to do politics, then we have to allow or be mindful of the delayed non-originary origin of politics, namely, the democracy to come. Democracy to come understood as a condition for the possibility of politics consists of two components. First, a democratic subjectivity,[24] as outlined above, has to be concretised. Second, this can only be achieved through the temporisation of différance and through the to come of the promise. The simultaneous affirmation and erasure of difference as one's own happens not because we will it but because it sim-

---

[22] *"Le propre d'une culture, c'est de n'être pas identique à elle même."* Jacques Derrida, *L'autre cap* (Paris: Minuit, 1990), p. 16.

[23] If the possibility of a democratic culture is to exist, then its identity is structured by a simultaneous possession and depossession of identity, that is, the double bind of possibility and impossibility comes into play. "Le propre d'une culture, c'est de n'être pas identique à elle-même. Non pas de n'avoir pas d'identité, mais de ne pouvoir prendre la forme du sujet que dans la non-identité à soi ou, si vous préférez, la différence avec soi. Il n'y a pas de culture ou d'identité culturelle sans cette différence *avec soi*...Cela peut se dire, inversement ou réciproquement, de toute identité ou de toute identification: il n'y a pas de rapport à soi, d'identification à soi sans culture, mais culture de soi comme culture de l'autre, culture de *double génitif* et de la *différence à soi*. La grammaire du double génitif signale aussi qu'une culture n'a jamais une seule origine. La monogénealogie serait toujours une mystification dans l'histoire de la culture." *L'autre cap*, p. 16.

[24] Subjectivity is my descriptive term. Derrida is reluctant to use the term subjectivity because of its metaphysical legacy. I use it, mindful of the double bind that structures it, to denote both the embodied agent necessary for any kind of politics to happen.

ply is an extension of the irreducible arch-structure Derrida calls dif-férance. It is something that is given (*la donation*).[25] The moment we try to de-structure this irreducible structure of différance is the moment we fall into the traps of a political thinking which is saturated by a meta-physics of presence.

Rather, political thinking must be aware of its conditions of possibil-ity, for these conditions colour the temporalised affairs of *le politique* or the way we run and manage our present-day political economy. To this end, politics is conditioned deeply by the to come and temporis-ing/differentiation of time, for time shows us the possibility and impos-sibility contained within an horizon but also the delay and differentiation that happens in temporising. The disjunction of the present comes to the fore.[26] The democracy to come is that injunction to make present that which will never be fully presentable. The unpresentable present that is commanded to be made present but never is made fully present because of differentiation and delay haunt political thinking and will al-ways be a source of binding tension. Derrida is quick to note that pre-sent day political structures, in so far as they are the "heritage" of our "epoch" "within" which we operate, will be necessary but inadequate.[27] Reforming present day structures such as the daily temporised version of parliamentary democracy that Derrida criticises in *L'autre cap* would consist of trying to become more aware and creating more political space such that democracy to come can articulate itself fully.[28]

Pragmatic Possibilities

Richard Rorty sees politics as a series of short-term compromises. If Derrida's thesis is true about the nature of time as irreducibly bringing undecidability into play, the effectiveness of short-term "deals" and po-

---

[25] *Spectres de Marx*, p. 56.

[26] 'La disjoncture dans la présence même du présent, cette sorte de non-contempo-raineté du temps présent à lui-même (cette intempestivite ou cette anachronie radicales à partir desquelles nous essaierons ici de *penser le fantôme*), la parole d'Anaximandre, selon Heidegger, la "dit et ne dit pas".*Spectres de Marx*, p. 52.

[27] If democracy to come is understood as this arch-structure that makes politics undecidable, then it can come into contact with the heritage of our epoch's political or-ganisation and thinking. It can deconstruct the view of presence that is contained in Marxism and Western liberal democracies—a deconstruction that happens in *Spectres de Marx* where Derrida critiques both Fukuyama's and Marx's thought.

[28] *Spectres de Marx*, p. 111. More can be said about "heritage" and the shortcomings of parliamentary democracy as Derrida sees it, but space limitations prevent a more sus-tained discussion here in the context of this paper.

litical compromises comes into question. The short-term or brief, efficient and "cash-value" pragmatism that Rorty advocates does not un-
dermine Derrida's insights. Though Rorty criticises Derrida for being
too "sentimental"[29] in that Derrida longs for metaphysical explanations
that Derrida himself admits are impossible, Derrida's accounts must not
be understood as metaphysics. Rather, Derrida is giving an account of
how we experience, communicate and write the way we do, which is not
fixed, absolute and unmoving. Rather, human experience *generaliter* is in
flux, constantly differentiating itself and is, ultimately, undecidable.
Politics, insofar as it is part of human experience *generaliter*, is irreducibly
structured by the temporal models discussed. The pragmatic approach
to politics, if anything, still claims to make things present, albeit for the
short-term. The Rortyan short-term view of temporality is useful in that
it does not fix matters as absolute and universal, *sub specie aeternitatis*.
Yet, it may give the false impression that the best that politics can do for
the short-term is a short-term series of compromises and reforms. This
excludes the possibility that long-term solutions may be more feasible
and it tries to make present the most useful or effective short-term solution, which may ultimately eclipse the force of undecidability that haunts
even short-term compromises and reforms. In short, Rorty's pragmatic
approach absolutises the short-term compromise and reform, making it
present—a presence that Derrida claims is impossible given the temporal structures discussed above. If undecidability is eclipsed within the
model of short-term pragmatic compromises and reforms, what is to
prevent short-term political absolutes and short-term totalitarianism?

Rorty believes that political thinking, in part, is constituted by hypotheses. Derrida's democracy to come can only be understood in
terms of an hypothesis, that is, as something that is both possible but
uncertain or perhaps impossible. With this in mind, what can the double bind structure of the democracy to come contribute to political
thinking *generaliter*? I venture three main contributions.[30] First, the dou-

---

[29] Jacques Derrida, "Remarks on Deconstruction and Pragmatism" in *Deconstruction
and Pragmatism* (ed.) Chantal Mouffe (London: Routledge, 1996) p. 77.

[30] Jim Vernon discusses three consequences of Derridean undecidability in light of the
Bush/Gore "tie" in the American presidential election. First, "The refusal, by the representatives, to declare their *determinate* legitimacy, or the *final* acceptance of their proposed
mandate, on the basis of an electoral result." Second, "The recognition and affirmation,
by both the people and the representatives, of the unconscious influence the marks of
the other in the manifestation of voter intention." Finally, "Both the people and their
representatives must incessantly enact the erosion of the border between the private and

ble bind conditions the way we view decision-making as decidability and undecidability come to the fore as capital in the political decision-making process. This would help us plan, organise and strategize such that every decision, convention and political thought has to take account of the simultaneous possibility and impossibility (radical absence) that are constitutive of political experience in general. This process would only stop when human experience stops or when iterability ceases to play itself out. For example, when we think politically about justice, we must not think solely about justice *in se*. Neither ought we to think justice apophatically, that is, what justice is by describing what it is not. In such accounts, the emphasis is still on making justice present, not yielding to the radical absence that is injustice, thereby giving injustice its own proper force. Rather, for justice to "exist", for it to individualise itself, it must consider as co-constitutive injustice.[31] Injustice, then, shows the limits of justice, where it is absent and vice versa. But Derridean justice also calls for the preservation of the irreducibility of différance, that is, avoiding the legacy of a metaphysics of presence. This is an iterable process—a process calling for the constant redefinition of justice and injustice, mindful that no definition can ever fully come to presence. We are *semper tendens*, to borrow a mediaeval turn of phrase. I will show how this dynamic can play itself out by examining the case of capital punishment. Second, it would allow for a radically pluralist democracy, a democracy that would provide space and time for all different individuals to speak in their own name while simultaneously allowing such a speaking not to silence or do violence to the speaking/experiencing other. The democracy to come could be a useful prophylactic against the tendency of democracies to lapse into a totalitarianism of the masses, including a blind majority rule. Finally, the double bind of the democracy to come would help us perceive political limits. Such limits would help us make political and social decisions. They would also help structure our political organising according to the exigencies of such limits while rendering us cognisant of the constant need to infinitely and possibly tend to surpass such negating or absenting limits through the logic of the to come of the promise and the double bind.

public spheres." Jim Vernon, "The People have Spoken?" Derrida, Democracy and Reciprocal Affirmation" in *International Studies in Philosophy* 34:2, 2002, pp. 115-131.

[31] See Jacques Derrida's *La force de loi* (Paris: Galilée, 1994).

Let us turn to the first contribution. For Derrida, the double bind structures all political decisions in that both decidability and undecidability are "irreducible" in all responsible decisions.[32] Decisions only arise or have to be made when something presents itself as undecidable and when there is a call for such undecidability to be made decisive. The openness of the temporal horizon of the promise along with the delay of temporisation ensure that such decisions are never fully present, and hence the need to rethink constantly the decision that is always eliciting a response because it is inherent to the very structure of decidability itself.

> Conflicts of duty—and there is only duty in conflict—are interminable and even when I take my decision and do something, undecidability is not an end. I know that I have not done enough and it is in this way that morality continues, that history and politics continue. There is politicisation or because undecidability is not simply a moment to be overcome by the occurrence of the decision. Undecidability continues to inhabit the decision and the latter does not close itself off from the former. The relation to the other does not close itself off, and it is because of this that there is history and one tries to act politically.[33]

Political decision-making is possible only because of its own impossibility. Its own impossibility creates a need for the decision to be made. This decision making is never fully present and continues to be haunted by its own impossibility. Pragmatically, this means that any political decision should never be conceived as absolute. And more importantly, all political decisions must somehow make space for that ambiguity that arises from the structure of the double bind enacting itself.

The classic example of an application of this double bind structure would be to capital punishment. Derrida has been an avid advocate of the banning of the death penalty in the United States.[34] Sentencing a

---

[32] Jacques Derrida, "Remarks on Deconstruction and Pragmatism" in *Deconstruction and Pragmatism* (ed.) Chantal Mouffe (London: Routledge, 1996), p. 86.

[33] Jacques Derrida, "Remarks on Deconstruction and Pragmatism", p. 87. See also, Chantal Mouffe, "Conclusion" in *Deconstruction and Pragmatism,* p. 136.

[34] M. Abu-Jamal, *En direct du couloir de la mort* (tr.) J.M. St. Upéry avec un préface de Jacques Derrida (Paris: La Decouverte, 1999). See also Derrida's speech at the acceptance of the Adorno Peace Prize in *Fichus* (Paris: Galilée, 2002). This speech indicates a definitive commitment on the part of Derrida to peace. His stance against capital punishment and his commitment to peace along with his commitment to the *villes-refuges* indicate Derrida's taking on of a definite or decisive political position, especially in terms of social justice. Such decisive actions, however, seem to be disjointed with Derridean undecidability.

criminal to die is a political act. It is political because citizens consent to a system that will hand out the death penalty as punishment for the violation of certain legal and social norms of the polis. The sentence of death is absolute. It maintains that one is guilty of one's crime and therefore is subject to death, which can be said to be absolute because, as Heidegger notes, death in itself contains no other possibility, it is that radical impossibility that is *das Nichts*. The sentence is a decision that reduces the person to an object of presence. The person is identified with his crime and is reduced to it, whereas a Derridean democratic subjectivity would suggest that the person is larger than his crime. The democracy to come would bring into play the undecidability that structures the present and guilty verdict that bears the absolute punishment of death. If this is the case, then we have a responsibility to let all the personal differences come to the fore as opposed to limiting the person to one difference, namely, his crime. The person is more than his crime, and as such should be responsible for his crime but should also be allowed to maximise all of his other differences as well. Hence, the decision to execute is a decision of full presence that ignores the undecidability that is articulating itself. There still arises the undecidability of personal differences that exceed the person being reduced to his crimes. Moreover, the decision to execute cannot possibly account for the impossibility of responsibility that haunts the decision of the criminal's responsibility. In other words, though a criminal may be responsible for his crime, he alone may not be solely responsible. There are innumerable social, genetic and environmental reasons why the person may have committed a crime— a crime he may have never had full control over although it may appear that way. Given this undecidability and given the undecidability of differences that is the person sentenced to death, it would be a matter of Derridean justice to avoid lapsing into a metaphysics of presence by enforcing the full and absolute presence of a death sentence.

But the pragmatist would respond, and justly so, if undecidability structures all political acts, then any judicial sentence could be seen as "metaphysically present" because the criminal is always reduced or presently identified with his or her crime, thereby seriously challenging any possibility of handing out sentences for what the state considers to be criminal. Derridean undecidability seemingly precludes any possibility of handing out definitive criminal sentences. A Derridean may respond by saying that the death penalty is not like any other sentence because it is so absolute and extreme. In executing a criminal, repetition and the horizon of the promise are absolutely and unilaterally closed. That is, the possibility of the double bind that is undecidability is wilfully and politically eliminated absolutely and forever. Furthermore, one could certainly give sentences, for that is always a possibility, but such sentences would have to ensure that the criminal is never reduced absolutely and constantly to his criminality, especially, of course, if the criminal decides to reform his or her ways. Practically, that means, that criminal records should not perpetually come to define a person. Second, and more concretely, there would be a responsibility on the part of society, if we believe in Derridean democracy to come, to help reform the criminal, to help the criminal differentiate herself or himself such that the criminal is not reduced to an identity of criminal. In other words, we would try and help the person's diversity and differences "to come" to the fore, always making sure that the criminal is not absolutely reduced to his or her personal differences, including that of criminal difference.

The second contribution of a democracy to come is its radically pluralist vision. Why pluralism? A pluralistic democracy would be desirable because it would make space for the maximisation of the naturally occurring differences of each individual. The corollary of such a pluralism is the injunction to not absolutise or totalise, to use a Levinasian expression, such differences as one's own or as those of the other. This double bind of democratic subjectivity would result in an ethos of responsibility bent on simultaneously maximising and preserving differences, thereby avoiding the potential of a democratic totalitarian state.[35] Given that we are anthropologically arch-structured as different, and undecidably so, such a political structure of pluralistic democracy would best suit this anthropological reality.[36] Pragmatically speaking, a political structure works best if it best approximates the needs and existential re-

---

[35] A democratic totalitarian state is possible when one has majority rule in all levels and branches of government. For example, the control of both houses of the Canadian parliament by the Liberal Party has raised this very question of democratic totalitarianism. One wonders whether the Derridean approach, because of its universal (irreducible) applicability (that is, the democratic injunction), could be seen as applicable to the globalising world, especially when it comes to the question of individual human rights. For an interesting discussion of globalisation and human rights in general, see Caroline Bayard, "Droits humains et mondialisation" in *Carrefour* 2000 22(1), pp. 29-48.

[36] "Derrida has repeatedly insisted that, without taking a rigorous account of undecidability, it is impossible to think of the concepts of political decision and ethical responsibility."
Chantal Mouffe, *The Democratic Paradox* (London: Verso, 2000), p. 135.

ality of its subjects, which in today's North American context is pluralistic. The Derridean "hypothesis" concerning the maximisation of difference while simultaneously negating any absolute claim to such a differentiated identity could be seen as possibly working within our present day political world.[37]

Finally, democracy to come contributes to our recognising the political limits imposed on us by the structure of the double bind. The "constitutive outside" that Mouffe speaks about, that is, the double bind of possibility and impossibility, and decidability and undecidability, can aid us in structuring our polis and the laws and political decisions we make. "...[A]ny social objectivity is constituted through acts of power. This means that any social objectivity is ultimately political and has to show the traces of the acts of exclusion which govern its constitution; what following Derrida, can be referred to as its "constitutive outside'."[38] How does democracy to come structure our social objectivities? Negatively, there is an injunction not to reduce social objectivities and decision making to a matter of full presence. In other words, we should avoid onto-theological thinking. Positively, we should structure our laws, conventions and institutions along the political arch-structural movements of the democracy to come, which includes the democratic ethos and heritage of friendship and hospitality rooted in responsibility.[39] Furthermore, repetition guarantees that there will be a constant playing out of the double bind, which means that every absence will have to be attempted to be filled, even though it will never be done fully and absolutely. Each political thought to each political action, though possible, will never be complete. Like Rorty, Derrida can account for the need for constant reform insofar as the absence contained in impossibility requires possibility to exist and vice versa. Again and again, we are called to try and fill that gap that is caused by constitutive impossibility. That is, again and again we are called to fill in the gap, to re-form the political qua act and qua thought.

Derridean Limitations?

---

[37] Certainly, such a position is challenged by other political theories that maintain identity as central and defining, including Liberal and phenomenological accounts of the state.

[38] Chantal Mouffe, *The Democratic Paradox*, p. 21.

[39] See Derrida's treatment of friendship and responsibility in *De l'hospitalité* and in *Politiques de l'amitié*.

If one is to keep within the spirit of deconstruction, Derrida must show forth his own limits and inadequacies. Again, space and time limit the full articulation of the pragmatic limitations of the foregoing discussion. Nonetheless, there are three limitations that can be touched upon. First, if politics is really undecidable, then why bother engaging in politics if the end result will always be irreducibly undecidable? If we know the conclusion, why bother attempting to bring about concrete and pragmatic political solutions? Derrida would argue that the absences that come to the fore in iterable differentiation make a certain "demand" upon us in that there is an injunction contained in such absences.[40] We see this claim articulated in Derrida's reading of Levinas. But given the dynamic of human freedom, one could simply reject and refuse the injunction. There can never be a guarantee that an absence will be filled, but even a shrewd pragmatist will have to concede that there are no guarantees when it comes to human political action, despite one's best intentions. A pragmatist can plan and make short term concessions and reforms, and yet, people can still refuse to participate and follow the plan despite everyone's good intentions.

Second, how could Derrida's political philosophy give any concrete account of the singularity of political events when they seem to be irreducibly arch-structured by the two models of temporality discussed above? In other words, all political events suffer form the same irreducible logic of the double bind, making all political events ultimately undecidable. On Derrida's view, the singularity or unicity of any political event, including the great political events that have shaped our contemporary world, namely, the American, French and Russian Revolutions concomitant with the fall of the old Soviet Union, would be undecidable. Derridean impossibility understood as radical absence would undo the unicity of such events. Yet, practically and empirically speaking, the above-mentioned events continue to play themselves out and structure world politics to this day. Alain Badiou has remarked in his work that there is a fidelity to such political events in that we keep referring to such events, and they are singular even though their multiple meanings keep changing through time.[41]

Finally, pragmatically speaking, is this whole project unnecessarily frustrating, endlessly and "metaphysically" or "romantically", to borrow from Rorty, raising points that in the end will yield no definite or deci-

---

[40] See Jacques Derrida, *Foi et savoir* (Paris: Seuil, 2000).

[41] See Alain Badiou's treatment of the event and the temporal intervention required to bring about such events in *L'être et l'événement* (Paris: Seuil, 1988).

sive results, which are necessary if we are to do and think politics? Derrida's project is frustrating, but this is the nature of reality. Reality is constantly in flux and we find ourselves "within" such flux. Both the pragmatist and the deconstructionist can agree on this point. What Derrida tries to do is to be faithful to the force of such flux by trying to give an account of it and by trying to urge us to structure our lives and politics "within" the flux by recognising its undecidable structuring force. But structuring our lives and politics according the undecidable flux we find ourselves "within" is only one response. We could just as well try to resist the flux as much as we can, knowing that our efforts will always be imperfect but doing what we can do best within such limits. Hence, we can see a space where the pragmatist approach of short-term reforms and compromises could articulate itself as an act of resistance to the flux we find ourselves within.

ANNE URBANCIC

THE FRANCISCAN MAGIC
OF TOMIE DE PAOLA

ABSTRACT. Children's stories unabashedly transgress boundaries; in them, the simple and the playful become profound. This is the storytelling technique of de Paola (b. 1934), an award winning author and illustrator of children's books. It is also the tradition attributed to St. Francis of Assisi. My paper shall examine how de Paola reveals St. Francis' simplicity of style and profundity of intent.

In the preface to his 1982 book for children, *Francis the Poor Man of Assisi* (New York: Holiday House), Tomie de Paola wrote:

> Very few characters in history have captured the imagination as much as Francis of Assisi and his companion, Clare. They captured mine when I was very young and first heard stories about them. In 1956, after I graduated from art school, I took a trip to Europe. While in Italy, I traveled to Assisi. It was then and there that I was determined, some day, to recount the tales, in words and paintings, of the two saints. Not an easy task!.... I have tried to give you at least a glimpse of their lives; a glimpse into the essential Franciscan spirit--simplicity, joy, the love of nature, and the love of Lady Poverty."(Preface)

It would seem to me, as a long time reader of de Paola, that he himself espouses (and I am aware of the pun here) that same Franciscan spirit, and that he does so despite his personal rejection of ritualized religious tradition. In this paper I would like to take a closer look at de Paola; my purpose is not to focus on why this author has justifiably become as well known and well loved as he has, but to show instead how his life's work has required him to make choices that have demanded from him an awareness of the boundaries to be crossed in his life and his work.

Boundaries demand that we accept their divisive binary status. They comprise a here and a there; between them is a gap or crisis which exists in that moment of realization that we are neither here nor there. This moment can be spatial or it may be temporal; it can also be both. It is

Limina: Thresholds and Borders - A St. Michael's College Symposium
Joseph Goering, Francesco Guardiani, Giulio Silano eds. Ottawa: Legas, 2005

the moment that contemporary philosopher Jacques Derrida would call the impasse or aporia. Furthermore it is also the moment that profoundly changes us as we cross from one side of the threshold to the other. Jung would call this the instance of individuation; it is that realization that

> a force compels individuals to break away from the assumptions learned from family and society and to develop a unique way of looking at and living out their lives....If the individual is both brave enough to break away from the group consensus and strong enough to accept who s/he really is, an authentic personality is created. (McMichaels 1997: 2)

Individuation in Jungian terms does not comprise a rejection of one's social position. Such a position is merely a starting point and, at first, conformity is a necessary status. We must accept our own place in society before we cross the boundary beyond it. In this acceptance we can discover the intensive inner work that results in the transformation of our outer world perspective. We find there empathy without judgement, spontaneity without self-consciousness; it is essentially an attitude that may be described as warmly emotional rather than coldly rational (McMichaels 1997: 70).

I would like to argue that despite the centuries and the miles that separate them, St. Francis and de Paola have shared a similar process of individuation.

We do need some perspective here. Francis of Assisi is a saint who has entered the hagiographic tradition where legend, fact and interpretation of divine elements co-exist. De Paola, on the other hand, is well rooted in our own contemporary world and, ironically, if there is to be any hagiographic element about him, it will surely proceed from the marketing machine that has been developed to promote him. Yet, as does Francis, so does de Paola stand out as an individual, external to the impetus, divine or mass mediatic, that would make either man the stuff of legend.

Stories and legends about the Poor Man of Assisi existed even prior to their recording by early biographers, Thomas of Celano and Bonaventure. In the first case, Brother Thomas, who knew Francis, nevertheless already had to rely on the stories that were being recounted of Francis' early life, since he "could not have spent too much time in the company of St. Francis" (Habig 1983: 185). The biography written by Bonaventure dates to the directive for a *Legend of St. Francis* which was given in 1260; the text itself was approved three years later, in 1263, almost four decades after the death of Francis in 1226. However the facts may have become elaborated, the image of Francis that we have received in our own time is captured best, I feel, in the one offered to us by G.K. Chesterton. In his study of the saint of Assisi, Chesterton seizes the image of the troubadour and confronts it with that of the tumbler, whom he calls the *jongleur*. Francis was both. Born of and nurtured in the environment of the troubadour tradition (and much has been made of the Provençal roots of Madonna Pica, Francis' mother), he and his fellow *Tripundanti* celebrated the secular and sacred events of Assisi. (McMichaels 1997: 35). In answering his call to God, Francis crossed over the boundary of how his society extolled the virtues and beauty of Love, and consciously and carefully chose a different path. Chesterton has him become the tumbler of God, a fool of sorts, but a fool operating with the understanding that his attitude embodied self-liberation and love of God. Chesterton comments that

> the jongleur was properly a joculator or jester; sometimes he was what we should call a juggler.... Sometimes he may have been even a tumbler....In the ordinary way, we may imagine, the troubadour would exalt the company with earnest and solemn strains of love and then the jongleur would do his turn as a sort of comic relief....Somewhere in that transition from the ambition of the Troubadour to the antics of the Tumbler is hidden, as under a parable, the truth of St. Francis....The jester could be free when the knight was rigid; and it was possible to be a jester in the service which is perfect freedom. (Chesterton 1934: 78).

The knight could not declare his love but to a lady of virtue and of noble birth. The jester could love whomever he chose, including, as in the case of Francis, the Lady Poverty.

In transgressing the boundary between between troubadour and jongleur, between knight and fool, Francis opened himself up to new possibilities and new attitudes; these served to make him stand out among his contemporaries. "He took his unique relationship to his inner truth out into the world, " writes Susan McMichaels. "He accepted the reality of his world, but he believed it could be tranformed by an infusion of interior values" (McMichaels 1997: 135).

Those objects or signs that served to witness his transformation included, among the many, the repairing of the church of San Damiano, his meeting with the dreaded leper and his receiving of the stigmata. As Susan McMichaels asserts, we express these signs today through sacred terminology and call them miracles. In secular terms, McMichaels refers to them as 'magical' (McMichaels 1997: 86). In post-structuralist terms, we have in the miracles or the magic the realization of the gap because over and beyond their categorizations as miracle or magic, these signs are also the demarcation of a threshold. Accepting the miracle or the magic involves a profound change in our inner Self in addition to an understanding (can it be called faith?) that there is some element on the other side of the threshold which will deeply and radically change our worldview.

McMichaels has argued that the magic of St. Francis may be ascribed to those signs that we, in our contemporary society, understand in terms of Jungian individuation. In de Paola, these signs are to be seen not in extraordinary events but in his words and in his images, and in the way his words and images point to his individuation.

De Paola, born in 1934, is an American of Irish and Italian descent. He began his writing and illustrating career in 1965 after a brief stint as a professional tapdancer. To date he has illustrated over two hundred books; he has also provided the text for about half of them. Working from his New Hampshire studio, de Paola has authored picture books, storybooks and just recently (1999) he has begun a series of chapter books intended for children who are already independent readers. He has been the recipient of numerous accolades and awards, including degrees *honoris causa* from various American academic institutions.

De Paola is not an ascetic; furthermore he is well versed in how to market his talent to his best advantage. He is, however, a deeply and openly spiritual man who, as a child, was completely enchanted by the rituals of the Catholic Church, and by the stories of saints. He was especially attracted by examples of simple and pure faith (Elleman 1999: 19). Writing about him in *Books & Religion*, artist Mary Zeman has commented that his voice is that of

> a receptive man, whose approach to his work betrays what Thomas Merton once described as the willingness of saints 'to answer the secret voice of God calling--to take a risk and venture by faith outside the reassuring and protective limits of our five senses'. (Quoted in Elleman 1999: 20)

As in Francis, we have in de Paola an artist whose particular focus is, from the outset, that of transgressing socially prescribed and accepted boundaries. And as with Francis in the cave, de Paola too had to undergo a personal transformation in order that the troubadour might become a jongleur. His moment of introspective threshold crossing took place in the more typical 20th century milieu of a therapist's office. As an artist, de Paola felt that he had reached a critical impasse; he thought his work had become stale and unimaginative and he believed there was no fresh creative aspect to his art. His therapist suggested that he "get in touch with the child in himself", a clichéd phrase perhaps, but the advice helped him across the impasse. In his reflection on that moment of aporia, he says: "I had totally fallen for that old line 'Don't be childish' and I had smothered my childlikeness; I had to like that child again" (Elleman 1999: 20). The therapist agreed to be paid through his pictures in order to facilitate the transition. At about the same time a second transition took place; after a Pentecostal liturgy held in his home, de Paola realized that the dove, the symbol of the Holy Spirit had, unconsciously for him, held a prominent place in his art work. In mythology the dove had often been employed as a messenger between the gods and humans; as such it had often crossed the boundaries understood to exist between sacred and secular. De Paola decided to appropriate the symbol for his own and to make it a deliberate component of most of his drawings, in addition to naming his business Whitebird. "I know I get my inspiration from a higher source, and what better symbol for an artist, especially for me?.... It's my way of acknowledging the source of my talent", he has told his biographer (Elleman 1999: 20). The dove became for him a symbol of crossing from one point to another.

I am struck by how, first, the realization of the need to cross a threshold and secondly, the actual crossing of that boundary, have produced a similar instatiation of joy in both the Poor Man of Assisi and the savvy artist from New Hampshire. The joy is accompanied by a sense of play and fun. There exists in de Paola's words and pictures an echo of Admonition XXI of Francis: "Blessed that religious who finds all his joy and happiness in the words and deeds of our Lord and uses them to make people love God gladly" (Habig 1973: 93). While for de Paola that sense of joy does not have strictly religious overtones, it cannot be ignored as a fundamental characteristic of his work. Nor can we ignore that the framework within which it operates belongs indubitably to the late 20th century and its attraction is more likely explained in terms of post-structuralism and psychological process-to individuation.

I would like to offer some examples of how this joy, this Franciscan magic, defines the works of de Paola.

It has already been pointed out that the journey to individuation begins with an acceptance of self. This is the point of departure for de Paola as well. His home life as a child was not always a happy one his biographer tells us; she then deftly glosses over the strained relationship between the older brother Buddy and Tomie, and his sorrow over the fact that he barely knew his younger sister, born many years after the first three children. De Paola uses his personal pain in these and other situations to allow his own vulnerability to come to the fore and it is clear that this self truth is an attraction for his readers, children and adults alike. Here he transgresses the boundary between author and persona. From a Jungian perspective, persona (from the Greek for mask), "is a compromise between individual and society as to what a man should appear to be," as Susan McMichaels reminds us in speaking of Francis of Assisi's coming to self (McMichaels 1997: 24). After his liminal experience in the therapist's office, De Paola no longer has any commitment to such a mask--he can simply be Tomie. We can follow this process to individuation from as early as 1973, the year in which his confidence in his self as author and person, not persona, first appears in print in *Andy, That's My Name* and *Nana Upstairs and Nana Downstairs*. In the former story Tomie has yet to use his own name; he chooses Andy instead. But this simply told tale, ostensibly about letter recognition by the very youngest of his readers, teaches all children the importance of names, their names, in affirming their selfhood. (Tomie's own name was given to him because of his mother's suggestion that baby Thomas, still in utero, would be famous one day and his uncle's reply that in that case an unusual spelling of his name was required as a distinguishing feature. This story is not dissimilar to the one of the naming of Francis). In *Andy*, a young boy wheels the letters of his name in a wagonload of alphabet blocks. He hopes to join older kids in their games but they reject him and go so far as to rearrange the letters of his name. But Andy stands up for his identity, his Self. He angrily picks up his letters and wheels them away with the assertion that "I may be little, but I'm very important". In a later story entitled *Oliver Button is a Sissy* (1979), the little boy Oliver/Tomie is taunted for the fact that he prefers dancing to sports. De Paola clearly depicts how the rejections that children suffer at the hands of their playmates are actually his own rejections and he portrays them truthfully and unabashedly. In yet another example from *The Art Lesson* (1989), the protagonist (now significantly called Tomie) suffers the unsympathetic judgement of a school teacher. He re-enacts from his perspective the devastating situation that many young children feel as they begin going to school. Tomie shows that dealing with such rejection, and showing forgiveness for it, is part and parcel of our individuation process.

The process of attaining selfhood is far more obvious in de Paola's semi-autobiographical books, those that I will refer to as "culturally correct". These include the previously mentioned *Nana Upstairs and Nana Downstairs* (1973), *Watch Out for the Chicken Feet in Your Soup* (1974) and

Tom (1993), as well as *The Baby Sister*(1996). They are culturally correct because they reflect honestly and without bias some of the experiences that children with racial or ethnic backgrounds outside of the perceived 'mass' population undergo. In *Watch Out...* the protagonist is torn between his love for his Italian grandmother and the fear that she will act in her customary way in front of his friend Eugene, who comes for a visit. Tomie dreads the possibility that grandmother will pinch Eugene's cheeks, or offer him strange food (including broth made from chicken feet), or speak in her broken English. Eugene, however, is enchanted by the elderly lady, by the new and mysterious culinary experience and especially by the warm, uncompromising welcome he receives from her. Grandmother loves Tomie, but he is often afraid of her and feels her disapproval, as he describes in *The Baby Sister.* She is so un-American, so different, that the boy must struggle to return her love. At first, there is no common ground between them: she refuses to discuss the impending arrival of the new baby, is constantly comparing him negatively to his older brother and often deliberately excludes him by speaking Italian so that he cannot understand. But at the point where the story could merely play itself out as the foreign other versus the little American boy, de Paola adds an interesting 'human' twist. Forgiveness enters into the story and plays a not unimportant role in helping the boy cross the threshold from being ashamed of his grandmother to accepting and valuing her. And the initial rejection of Nana, shown explicitly in the child's refusal of the food she cooks, is cancelled beautifully by a series of vignettes showing the boy in front of his plate of (disappearing) spaghetti. Forgiveness helps the boy cross the threshold from being ashamed of his grandmother to accepting and valuing her.

In *Nana Upstairs and Nana Downstairs* the young Tomie has to come to grips with death. I think there will be much agreement that death is not a usual theme in children's books.

Nana Upstairs is his Irish great-grandmother who is confined to her bed on the second floor of her house while her daughter, Nana Downstairs, lives on the first floor. Watching the daily rituals that Nana Downstairs performs for Nana Upstairs, Tomie is left with the memory of happiness and love. Three poignant symbols mark the author's acceptance of death, and mark also steps in de Paola's journey to individuation: the empty bed that definitively signals to the little boy Tomie the absence of Nana Upstairs, the move of Nana Downstairs to the second floor, and two falling stars. The first star the boy Tomie attributes to a kiss falling from heaven and sent by Nana Upstairs. At the end of the story, the grown up Tomie sees another falling star. He remembers Nana Downstairs and he reflects that now both of his grandmothers are Nana Upstairs. There is no saccharine or sentimental scene, only the acceptance that death is a necessary passage in life. And again in this, there is a similarity in attitude between Francis and de Paola.

Tom is also a story that is culturally correct. It recounts the special relationship that existed between the young Tomie and his Irish grandfather who loved to tell silly stories and whose sense of humour leads to trouble for the young boy. Grandfather, a retired butcher, teaches the boy to manipulate the tendons of chicken feet. Tomie paints the claws with nail polish and proceeds to create havoc at school, involving even the teacher. A stern note from the principal of the school ends the prank, but with no blame being assigned to the child. It is the grandfather who recognizes the boy's need for unwavering acceptance despite his indiscretion. "We'll just have to think of something else to do. Don't you think?" The adult Tomie acknowledges this criss-crossing between adult approval and disapproval and comments that "[h]aving a grandfather who got you into that kind of trouble at school was, actually, wonderful"(quoted in Elleman 1999: 37).

For a child, normally preoccupied with maintaining the status quo in order to gain the acceptance of his peers, and quickly assigning blame should that status quo be threatened, de Paola's wink-wink/nudge-nudge remark to his young readers is a simple but viable act of forgiveness.

These few examples from the 'culturally correct' stories are, under closer scrutiny, quite transgressive in the same way that the actions attributed to Francis were transgressive. They switch easily between the troubadour, the one who acts within accepted societal parameters, and the jongleur, the one who does not. The secular magic of Tomie de Paola is not all that far removed from the the miraculous attributed to St. Francis. I am struck by how the artistry of de Paola goes far beyond the words and the pictures and results in a childlike portrayal of forgiveness and embrace of the Other. This becomes clearer when we consider how Francis also forgave and embraced the Other, the unwanted one, in total and unconditional love, and how he professed the joy that sprang from this act. Jacques Derrida has put his finger on a similar problematic in his discussion of host and guest found in the essay *Of Hospitality* (2000). The host is such only because the guest has literally crossed the threshold into his house and has been accepted:

the awaited guest is not only someone to whom you say "come" but "enter", enter without waiting, make a pause in our home without waiting, hurry up and come in, "come inside", "come within me" not only toward me, but within me: occupy me, take place in me, which means, by the same token, also take my place, don't content yourself with coming to me or "into my home". Crossing the threshold is entering and not only approaching or coming. Strange logic, but so enlightening for us, that of an impatient master awaiting his guest as a liberator, his emancipator. (Derrida 2000:123)

In de Paola this occurs with the crossing of the guest, represented by the child Tomie, into the psyche of the adult Tomie; it is a crossing that brings precisely the self confidence of individuality and liberation. De Paola's biographer has noted this by pointing out that

deceptively simple, his books often contain layers of meaning....young readers gain satisfaction from seeing the littlest (themselves) rising to face the adult world. At the same time, adults enjoy the stories from the vantage point of both the children they once were and the adults they have become. It is to de Paola's credit that he is able to encompass both audiences. (Elleman 1999: 26)

Even when de Paola withdraws himself as a character in his stories, the sense of welcome and love nevertheless remains. I shall propose as my examples two of his religiously themed books: *Mary, the Mother of Jesus* and *Francis, the Poor Man of Assisi*. *Mary* was published in 1995 as a "praise of Mary, the Mother of Jesus," according to de Paola's preface. He draws and comments 14 events from Mary's life, from her birth to her Assumption into heaven. What is most striking as we read the book is that 13 of the 14 illustrated pages show scenes of unconditional welcome, either Mary being welcomed or in the act of welcoming. The enactment of crossing this threshold, as Derrida would have it, is depicted in the simplest of ways through outstretched arms and/or acts of embrace. But the drawings reveal an artistic sophistication far beyond the simple lines and muted colours. In his earlier work, *Francis* (1982), there is a similar attitude. Basing his own pictorial understanding of the life of Francis on the frescoes by Giotto, de Paola has been able to capture the seminal moments of the life of the Poor Man of Assisi; again his pictures show in their simple lines and muted colours (with delightful touches such as the illuminated first letter of each page) the joy of welcoming and of being welcomed, a joy that occurs only when the guest crosses the boundary into our home, or when the troubadour becomes the jongleur. I was especially touched by the representation of this attitude in the painting depicting Francis' acceptance that he was now the jongleur, God's fool, and no longer the troubadour. Francis is alone. He is dancing. His open arms embrace and welcome the whole city around him, extending into the vignette on the opposite page. This is Francis' moment of individuation, of becoming Francis of God.[1] What de Paola does not explicitly show but intimates through his art is that it is also a moment of transgression and of acceptance. Francis is no longer one of the "socially accepted" members of his town. He is an outcast. Yet he has forgiven the townspeople and in his embrace we can feel the joy of that act. De Paola has gone beyond the mere cultural correctness of depicting 13th century Assisi appropriately, which he undoubtedly does, to arrive at the sophistication of depicting the human condition.

The Franciscan magic of Tomie de Paola is best exemplified in his Strega Nona series. Justifiably this is the collection of books that has earned him his greatest accolades. Strega Nona, or Grandma Witch, is an elderly lady who lives in Calabria, where de Paola's ancestors came from. From her little house, where all are welcomed, she dispenses sage advice and potions for headaches and husbands and warts. "Although all the people of the town talked about her in whispers, they all went to see her if they had troubles. Event the priest and the sisters of the convent went because Strega Nona did have a magic touch (*Strega Nona*, 1975: 1).

Her magic is not born of hocus pocus or sleights of hand. Strega Nona works hard, is honest and open, and non-judgemental. She accepts all who need her: the bumbling Big Anthony (who never listens and causes untold trouble as a result), the overworked and talented Bambolona, the baker's daughter, and even her own flamboyant alter-ego, Strega Amelia (who prefers the magic produced by new technological inventions). Many of the main characters are social outcasts, unappreciated by the people around them. Big Anthony, for example, is unable to keep a job because he simply cannot follow directions. The disastrous results that ensue make him an unwanted element in his town. His family sends him away "out into the world and [to] earn his fortune....Before he ruins ours" say his Papa and Nonna Graziella (*Big Anthony His Story*, 1998). Always well intentioned, as is shown in his attempts to straighten the Tower of Pisa (ibid), he finds acceptance only

---

[1] I am grateful to Professor Giuseppe Mazzotta for reminding me that the moment of Francis' passage from troubadour to jongleur has been noted and admired by numerous authors and film makers who have recognized its profound importance. Space does not allow for a fuller discussion of these, nor of de Paola's story in *The Clown of God* (New York: HBJ, 1978).

when he arrives at the little house of Strega Nona in Calabria. She accepts his foibles, although not without allowing just punishment. When he steals her pasta pot in order to show off, and almost drowns the town in pasta, she forgives him, but makes him eat the leftover pasta. When he tries on her ring which turns him into a handsome dandy and he cannot get it off, she helps him but only after he has come to the realization, having been endlessly pursued by the town's ladies, that physical beauty also has its disadvantages. Bambolona is also a social outcast and particularly when she enrages her father as he engages in open discrimination. She too, finds acceptance at the home of Strega Nona who takes her in as an apprentice Strega. The acceptance does not, however, exempt her from hard work. Strega Amelia is also an outcast, even among her fellow streghe, because she is determined to go against tradition and use only the latest technological innovations along with some rather savvy marketing techniques. But again Strega Nona is patient and accepting. Strega Nona herself feels at times that she is an outcast. Particularly poignant is her loneliness in *Merry Christmas, Strega Nona* (1986). But as de Paola says, "Christmas has a magic of its own", and the townspeople are the ones who open their arms to welcome their Strega with a special feast. The culturally correct touches of the presepio (the manger scene), the baccalà (the salted codfish) and the pastries make it an Italian story, and a story about Italian culture clearly, but with a lesson far beyond.

De Paola's biographer has observed that in Strega Nona we have de Paola the adult. I would venture to add that in Strega Nona is also the fictionalized embodiment of the author's transformation, his crossing to individuation. Jung, basing himself on a text of alchemy from the 1500's, repeats that

> he who would be initiated into this art and secret wisdom (ie of individuation) must put away the vice of arrogance, must be devout, deep-witted, humane toward his fellows, of a cheerful countenance and a happy disposition and respectful withal. Likewise he must be an observer of the eternal secrets that are revealed to him (quoted in Sharp, 1991: frontispiece)

McMichaels also quotes this passage but in reference to Francis. It can just as easily be applied to Tomie de Paola. *Strega Nona* shows us what it means to be 'initiated into [the] art and secret wisdom' of individuation. She is, as the alchemist would want, humble, devout, deep witted, humane and embodies contentment with self and internal happiness. Beyond the thoughtfulness, the well-crafted story and the fun pictures of the Strega Nona stories, there is a profound lesson to be learned. Not uncoincidentally it is the same lesson that Francis had to learn in order that that troubadour might become a jongleur. The lesson is that the transformation cannot take place without love. "For that is the INGREDIENTE SEGRETO, LOVE. It is the same with all your magic. Always Love!" (*Strega Nona, Her Story*: 1996) Tomie de Paola claims that his work points to a need for "being happy with oneself, the need for generosity and the importance of love" (Elleman 1999: 93). Such an assertion can only come from one who has crossed the threshold beyond ego and beyond the merely sensorial and is able to welcome and love unconditionally the new person he or she has become. This is that secret ingredient. This is also the Franciscan magic that de Paola offers his readers.

WORKS CITED

Chesterton, G. K. *St. Francis of Assisi*. London/Toronto: Hodder and Stoughton, [1934].

Derrida, Jacques. *Of Hospitality*. Anne Dufourmantelle invites Jacques Derrida to Respond. Translated by Rachel Bowlby. Stanford, CA.: Stanford UP, 2000.

De Paola, *Tomie. Andy, That's My Name*. New York: Prentice-Hall, 1973.

_____. *The Art Lesson*. New York: Putnam, 1989.

_____. *The Baby Sister*. New York: Putnam, 1996.

_____. *Big Anthony, His Story*. New York: Putnam, 1998.

_____. *Francis, the Poor Man of Assisi*. New York: Holiday House, 1982.

_____. *Mary, the Mother of Jesus*. New York: Holiday House, 1995.

_____. *Nana Upstairs and Nana Downstairs*. New York: Putnam, 1973 (new edition: Putnam, 1998).

_____. *Oliver Button is a Sissy*. New York: HBJ 1979.

_____. *Strega Nona*. New York: Prentice-Hall, 1975.

_____. *Strega Nona, Her Story*. New York: Putnam, 1996.

_____. *Watch Out for the Chicken Feet in your Soup*. New York: Prentice-Hall, 1974.

Elleman, Barbara. *Tomie de Paola. His Art and His Stories*. New York: G. P. Putnam's Sons, 1999.

Habig, Marion A. *St. Francis of Assisi. Writings and Early Biographies*. English Omnibus of the Sources for the Life of St. Francis. Chicago: Franciscan Herald Press, 1973.

McMichaels, Susan. *Journey Out of the Garden. St. Francis of Assisi and the Process of Individuation*. New York/Mahwah, N.J.: Paulist Press, 1997.

Sharp, Daryl. *C.G. Jung Lexicon. A Primer of Terms and Concepts*. Toronto: Inner City Books, 1991.

Robert Sweetman

Haunting Conceptual Boundaries: Miracles in the *Summa Theologiae* of Thomas Aquinas

ABSTRACT. Thomas understands our creaturely being under two contiguous categories: nature and grace, or the natural and the supernatural. In this two-fold understanding of the creaturely whole, miracle names a reality that haunts the boundary between. Is the result seamless harmony? Or seismic activity?.

1. Introduction

Miracles and the miraculous only became a primary theme of theological and philosophical reflection late in the game. You could say that "miracle" came into its own in the eighteenth century and in response to the skeptical criticism leveled against it by David Hume among others.[1] In the long preceding centuries, Christian discussions of miracle occurred within the context of what were thought of as other, more elemental themes: providence, grace, justification, Christology, the sacraments. Moreover, if one thinks about the thirteenth century, these more elemental themes are themselves perhaps best pictured as the distillate of attempts to plumb theoretically the allegorical or theological meaning of scriptural "things" or *res*.[2]

---

[1] The course of miracles as a theological *locus* in its own right is well surveyed in Colin Brown, *Miracles and the Critical Mind* (Grand Rapids, MI: Eerdman's, 1984). For philosophical and theological responses to Hume's arguments in particular see David Johnson, *Hume, Holism and Miracles* (Ithaca NY: Cornell University Press, 1999); and with greater spleen John Earman, *Hume's Abject Failure: The Argument Against Miracles* (Oxford: Oxford University Press, 2000).

[2] The formulation of an allegorical meaning to scriptural things could be said to take its provenance in the Latin tradition from Augustine's sacred semiology in *De doctrina christiana*. The sense of theological *loci* as collated and discussed in Peter Lombard's *Sentences* and in commentary upon their four books as the allegorical sense of scripture *in*

Limina: Thresholds and Borders - A St. Michael's College Symposium
Joseph Goering, Francesco Guardiani, Giulio Silano eds. Ottawa: Legas, 2005

We do well to remind ourselves of this thirteenth-century situation. The term "miracle" was used in formal theological discourse to name above all a determinable subset or category of scriptural "things." As a result, miracle impressed itself upon theological minds in the interpretive struggle to understand the "things" there encountered *in their pointing beyond themselves* to Christ and the church.[3] We do *well* in this, for it provides us an illuminating context for examining the appearance of miracle within the *Summa theologiae* of Thomas Aquinas.[4]

Of course, I am suggesting we do more than map the word "miracle" onto the blandly bureaucratic term "category." That is, I do not want us to deal with miracle as if it were an organizational container meant to hold in well-marked and cross-referenced locales certain bits of reality.[5]

---

nuce see John Van Engen, "Studying Scripture in the Early University," in *Neue Richtungen in der hoch- und spätmittelalterlichen Bibelexegese*, ed. Robert E. Lerner and Elisabeth Müller-Luckner (Munich: Oldenbourg, 1996) 17-38; and Robert Sweetman: "Beryl Smalley, Thomas of Cantimpré, and the Performative Reading of Scripture: A Study in Two *Exempla*," in *With Reverence for the Word: Medieval Scriptural Exegesis in Judaism, Christianity, and Islam*, ed. Jane Dammen McAuliffe, Barry D. Walfish and Joseph W. Goering (Oxford: Oxford University Press, 2003): 256-275.

[3] The classic study of the four senses of Scripture remains Henri De Lubac, *Exégèse médiévale: Les quatre sens de l'Écriture*, 4 vol. (Paris: Aubier, 1959-1964); but, see, also, Beryl Smalley, *The Study of the Bible in the Middle Ages* 3rd edition (Oxford: Basil Blackwell, 1983). For Thomas' understanding of the allegorical sense see Thomas Aquinas, *Summa theologiae* 1.1.10.resp.. There Thomas identifies the allegorical sense with the capacity of the "old law" to act as signifier of the "new law." But he goes on to sum up that sense of scripture as "ea quae in Christo sunt facta, vel in his quae Christum significant" before moving on to identify the moral sense of Scripture with what within those allegorical things signify in turn what we should do. So while I am claiming that "miracle" as it comes to be thematized by scholastic theologians does so primarily as scriptural "res," I acknowledge that Scripture was not the only source from which the thirteenth-century theologian drew. Miracles clustered around the saints and their posthumous *relicta*, and wherever one encountered the spectre of martyrdom and its aura of sanctity (e.g., in the context of the Crusades). See in this regard, Benedicta Ward, *Miracles and the Medieval Mind: Theory, Record and Event, 1000-1215* (Aldershot: Scolar, 1982).

[4] The most recent treatment of the theme in Aquinas is Gilles Berceville, "L'étonnante Alliance: Évangile et miracles selon saint Thomas d'Aquin," *Revue Thomiste* 103 (2003): 5-74. Berceville is a student of Jean-Pierre Torrel and represents as a result his newer and revisionary approach to reading Thomas. For older neo-scholastic treatments, see Vladimiro Boublík, *L'Azione divina «praeter ordinem naturae» secondo S. Tommaso d'Aquino* (Rome: Libreria editrice della pontificia università lateranense, 1968); and Alois Van Hove, *La doctrine du miracle chez saint Thomas et son accord avec les principes de la recherche scientifique* (Wetteren: Meester en Fils, 1927).

[5] Descriptions and criticisms of "container logic" are characteristic of the work of George Lakoff. See his *Women, Fire and Dangerous Things: What Categories Reveal about the Mind* (Chicago: University of Chicago Press, 1987) and more recently with Mark John-

Rather I am suggesting that those bits are recalcitrant and so can only be contained under constraint. They resist such housebreaking, for there is something altogether different, even spooky, about the bits we would consign to this category.

Moreover, the category itself turns out to be a trickster. That is, miracle is profitably imagined as hiding behind the corners of Thomas's conceptual edifice. It seems intent upon jumping out at unsuspecting readers to bellow its characteristic, "Boo!" Indeed it is a spectral presence within the world of Aquinas' *Summa theologiae*, one that confounds a certain conceptual *ductus* or flow that is equally native to the text.[6] As such, it opens the text up to the what-must-be-said about the world revealed in the scriptures, but which is nearly impossible to say within the limits of Thomas's chosen discourse.

2. Nature and Grace in the World of Creatures

So we ask of Thomas and his *Summa*: what is this world opened up by the scriptures? The answer is deceptively simple: it is a world of creatures. But what is *this* world? It is a God-made harmony or order of beings which harmony or order can be distributed across two ontological fields: nature and grace—the latter in and through its chief created effect, the supernatural. Thomas understands each of these fields to be a gift of God. In both of these gifts, God gives what God has to give: nothing less than God's self, *esse*, albeit ecstatically and proportionate to the natural or supernatural entity in question. The model here is Christological, i.e., the Incarnation, *kenosis*, God's self-emptying by which God-in-Christ descends to join those creatures that are most damaged in a sin-soaked world. This should not surprise. The *Summa* is perhaps best understood as an attempt to prepare Dominican friars for their apostolate *ad extra* via the location of a precise understanding of virtue, vice and Christian living within a systematic, theological, indeed Christological order, which order was associated by scholastic theologians or masters of the sacred page with the allegorical sense of Scripture, that is, as said, the meaning of scriptural "things" as they point beyond themselves to Christ and his church.[7]

---

son, *Philosophy in the Flesh: The Embodied Mind and Its Challenge to Western Thought* (New York: Basic Books, 1999).

[6] For the notion of literary *ductus* see Mary Carruthers, *The Craft of Thought: Meditation, Rhetoric, and the Making of Images, 400-1200* (Cambridge: Cambridge University Press, 1998), especially 77-81.

[7] This way of understanding the *Summa* presupposes Van Engen's understanding of the development and purpose of the *Sentences* of Peter Lombard as school text in theol-

So both nature and grace can be seen as gifts of God but gifts given unto distinguishable ends. Nature is given so as to make something of or to give substance to all of us creaturely nothings, indeed, to creation itself. And grace is given to draw what we nothings-made-somethings are forward toward what we are meant to be. Thomas establishes this way of looking at the creation most clearly with respect to the human creature.

In 1.94.1, he asks whether the First Human was created in grace. One can, Thomas admits, find strong arguments in the tradition against such a notion. He cites Augustine's *City of God,* however, as the frame for his magisterial response: God established nature and simultaneously (*simul*) gifted it with grace. Thus, there never was a time in which Adam was without grace. Thomas elaborates his subsequent response in terms of what he understands to be a normatively hierarchical ordering of the human person: reason is to be subject to God, the lower psychic powers to reason, and the body to the soul. But, this right ordering is not natural, for had it been, it would have survived Adam's fall into sin. Consequently, the right ordering of the human person is an effect of grace.

Thomas goes on to explore the implications of such a position. What passions would have been present in a right ordered human person (1.94.2)? What virtues (1.94.3)? The first question demands that one define passion. On the old stoic definition, there would have been no passions at all in the right ordered person.[8] But if passion is taken as a synonym for appetite, there would have been present in the First Human every passion that is properly subjectible to truly God-subject reason. The second question leads to the conclusion that the theological as well as the cardinal virtues were present in the First Human, even before the fall.

So if the world of creatures is constituted by both nature and grace, how are these two ontological fields to be understood in relation to each

---

ogy, Leonard Boyle's work on the setting of the *Summa*, and Jean-Marc Laporte's work on the Christological order of the *Summa*. It puts these sources together to draw conclusions that the sources' authors would undoubtedly not have foreseen. For Van Engen see note 2 above. For Boyle, see Leonard E. Boyle, *Facing History: A Different Thomas Aquinas* (Louvain-la-neuve: Fédération Internationale des Instituts d'Études Médiévales, 2000) especially 64-106. For Laporte's work see "Christ in Aquinas' *Summa theologiae:* Peripheral or Pervasive?" *The Thomist* 67 (2003): 221-248.

[8] For the Stoics and the passions see Martha Nussbaum, *The Therapy of Desire: Theory and Practice in Hellenistic Ethics* (Princeton: Princeton University Press, 1994) especially 316-483; and Richard Sorabji, *Emotion and Peace of Mind: From Stoic Agitation to Christian Temptation* (Oxford: Oxford University Press), 2000.

other? Here, of course, one can point to Thomas's oft-repeated maxim: grace does not destroy but rather perfects nature (*In Boethii de trinitate* 2,3). Grace is, in this sense, nature's (proximate) end or term. Nature enjoys its perfection if and only if it is graced, one could say. And because this is so, grace acts upon nature as a final cause acts upon its effect. Final causes, it is to be remembered, are first in the order of causation. Consequently, grace can be said to call nature into being, to rule and measure its stuff, its movements, its intelligible patterns by imbuing each with purposiveness. I should quickly add that it does so unto glory; its perfecting of nature is itself ruled to the final causality of glory.

Such a conception of nature and grace can entail no disharmony. Because nature is ruled to grace, it is conformed and fitted to grace from its very inception. The creation story reveals God's judgment upon the fit: "it is very good," we are told. One must, however, draw a further implication. Pure nature without the structuring dynamic of grace is impossible; without grace there is no nature.

But here we must pause, for such a position does not accord with a venerable interpretation of Thomas on the fall. The position goes something like this: When Adam sinned, grace and its salubrious effects were withdrawn from him, leaving him in the vulnerable and diminished state of pure nature, a state slowly but progressively bent and wizened by subsequent sinful acts and the vicious habits they engendered.[9]

---

[9] This way of interpreting Thomas has its roots in the sixteenth-century reflorescence of Thomism. It takes its cue from the insistence upon an irreducibly duplex end of human living and flourishing apparent in the work of Cajetan and others. See, Thomas de Vio Cajetan's commentary on *Summa theologiae* 1.23 and 1-2.85.1 in *Divi Thomae Aquinatis doctoris angelici ordinis fratrum Praedicatorum totius theologiae summa, in tres partes digesta, et ad Romanum exemplar collata, cum commentariis R.D.D. Thomae de Vio Caietano*, (Venetiis: apud Francescum de Franciscis Senensem , 1596). For the notion of *natura pura* as it came to be developed at one end of this revival, see the article "Natura pura" in *Enciclopedia cattolica* 8: 1689-1691. For twentieth-century proponents of the interpretation I am opposing here see Giacomo Crosignani, *La teoria del naturale e del soprannaturale secondo s. Tommaso d'Aquino* (Piacenza: Collegio Albernoni, 1974) especially 15-32; and Jean Baptiste Kors, *La justice primitive et le péché original d'après s. Thomas* (Paris: J. Vrin, 1930) especially 120 and again 161-163. It must be said that both of the latter theologians acknowledge the incoherence of "pure nature" and yet their account of the fall continues to oppose nature to grace dichotomously and so to act as if "pure nature" were in fact a Thomistic possibility, at least for the purposes of dealing with the effects of original sin. Finally see the fine historical overview provided by Henri de Lubac in his *Le surnaturel: Étude historique* (Paris: Aubier, 1946), i.e., his justly (in)famous revisionary reading of Thomas and the tradition. I find myself deeply indebted to De Lubac in my own ongoing attempts to understand the Angelic Doctor on nature and Grace.

Thomas trains his whole eye upon what he calls "the good of nature" in his discussion of original sin and its effects. In 1-2.85.1, he asks whether the good of nature is diminished by sin. In the next article he asks whether the whole good of nature can be borne away in sin. He answers the first question by distinguishing three ways of understanding what constitutes the good of nature. In the first place, the good of nature can refer to the principles or constitutive elements of nature, inclusive of the properties they entail. In the second place, the good of nature can refer to the inclination to virtue that is a human being's natural disposition. In the third place, the good of nature refers to the gift of original justice. In Thomas's view the third of these goods is an effect of grace and so is taken away by sin. The first good is constitutive of nature itself and therefore cannot be taken away without the annihilation of that nature. Finally, the second good of nature is diminished but cannot be eradicated by sin, for it is rooted in nature, though it only achieves its perfection as an effect of grace.

Since the diminution of nature's good is only meaningful in the second way of speaking of nature's good, Thomas denies the eradicability of the good of nature in 1-2.85.2. He then uses the remaining articles to explore the implications of a proper concept of the diminution of nature's good, exploring seriatim nature's wounds (1-2.85.3), privations (1-2.85.4), and death (1-2.85.5). He concludes his *quaestio* by asking whether and in what sense all these implications can meaningfully be called natural (1-2.85.6). The point is that grace *is* nearly absent from his discussion of the effects of original sin. Moreover, in speaking of the removal of original justice in sin, Thomas accounts for the removal precisely *because it is an effect of grace*. It is easy to see how one could understand Thomas's *quaestio* on the effects of original sin to imply that the gift of grace is withdrawn from human nature. Indeed, this withdrawal is precisely original sin's chief effect. All else, i.e., everything discussed in the articles of the *quaestio*, is, in such a view, the implication of the withdrawal of grace from human nature. It is in effect another way of naming the diminution of nature's good.

Such a way of interpreting the effects of original sin is defensible, provided the *quaestio* is thought of in isolation from other sections of the *Summa*. Nevertheless, it is difficult if not impossible to square with grace's relationship to nature as a final cause to its effect. Moreover, Thomas does not in fact state that grace is withdrawn from humankind as a result of original sin but that its supernatural effect upon human nature is interrupted. A new and handicapped order emerges in the human person via the rupture caused by sin. And yet, though the good of nature is diminished, it is not wholly taken away. This entails the continued presence of grace as structuring dynamic, for no grace, no nature; final causes are first in the order of causation. So grace remains even in the ambivalent order emergent within a postlapsarian world. Its structuring dynamic continues to operate within nature so that it remains structurally whole, though no longer lifted toward its perfection. In other words, by the hidden presence of grace, nature remains what it was always meant to be as a barest beginning. But by the very hiddenness of grace its elevating excess, its supernatural or perfecting effects are removed; nature is unable to become all that it was meant to be in the end or indeed what it had been in its prelapsarian condition. And so its good, i.e., its orientation toward its end, is diminished and right living becomes a difficult thing, wrested, you might say, from the cold hard ground by the sweat of our brows.

3. Miracle in Relation To Nature, Itself and Grace

In the *Summa,* the incarnational pattern of *kenosis* forms the template for all God's interaction with the world of creatures. This is also true of the acts called miracles. Miracles accompany scriptural revelation about God's providence for creation (1.105.6-8). They mark an instrumentality God assigns to angels and saints in the execution of divine care (1.110.4; 1.114.4). They can accompany and hence provide an important perspective from which to examine the justification of the impious (1-2.113.10). They constitute a special gifting of the prophet within the communal life of faith (2-2.178). They punctuate the life of the Saviour, witnessing to the truth of his teaching (3.43-45). Finally, they signify even as they confer the outpouring of grace in the sacraments (3.75-77).

Miracles are events that work palpable effects on the world of creatures. One need only remember the wonders of the world-made-right envisioned by Isaiah (Is. 35, 5-6), recited by Jesus to John the Baptizer's disciples (Mt. 11, 1-6): the blind see, the deaf hear, the lame walk, the dumb speak. And so a question arises that seems hard to avoid when considering the world of creatures as Thomas understands it, dispersed as it is across the ontological fields of nature and grace: to what field does miracle belong?

As soon as one has asked the question, one wishes one had not. For the uncomplicated image of nature and the supernatural sketched out above begins to change before our eyes. Nature and grace go all fuzzy and out of focus. We might imagine whimsically if a bit invidiously that in the presence of miracle our clear-eyed Dominican becomes afflicted with double vision. Whatever the case, miracle as it is thematized in Thomas's *Summa* cuts an eerie figure. Indeed, as promised, it confounds the serene *ductus* or flow of Thomas's story of nature and grace by doubling both protagonists, and itself in the process. It disturbs the simplicity of their interaction by generating the uncanny presence of not one, not two, but three *doppelgänger*. Shelley smiles; what conceit!

Let us look our uncanny doubles right in the face. We begin with the field or order of nature and Thomas's discussion of divine governance. In the course of his examination of God's power to change creatures, Thomas asks whether God can do anything outside of the order intrinsic to things (1.105.6); whether all God's works outside of the natural order of things are miracles (1.105.7); and whether there is a proper gradation of miracles along the continuum of greater and lesser (1.105.8).

In the first of these articles, Thomas begins by observing that the effects of a given cause are subject to an order derived from the cause itself. Moreover there are as many such orders as there are causes, and just as causes are themselves subject to an order along the continuum of superior to inferior, so too are the orders derived from them. He offers as example that the domestic order and its causal paterfamilias depends upon the civil order and its causal rector that in turn depends upon the royal order and its causal king. So if the order of things is to be considered as derived from and dependent upon the first cause, absolutely speaking, God cannot act against the order of things. If however the order of things depends upon a cause among secondary causes, then God can act outside of the order of things. For God is not subject to such an order; rather, it is subject to God.

Thomas does not choose between these two ways of understanding God's relationship to the order of things. Both capture something true about the ways of God in the world. Already one sees a doubling of vision. Nature itself is doubled and therefore miracle is legitimately understood to have an ambivalent relationship to it. Miracle is properly understood as something that has a cause hidden pure-and-simple and to everyone (1.105.7). God is that cause, and God acts so whenever God acts outside of the order of causes known to us.

This latter description however is still too broad. Creation and the justification of the impious are also enacted by God and outside of the created or secondary causes known to us. Yet they are not miracles, strictly speaking, for they do not pertain to the order of nature in that they cannot be caused by any secondary cause. Consequently, they are not enacted outside of the order of nature. This understanding of miracle, of course, presupposes the order of nature as an order of secondary or created causes. Miracles are those creaturely possibilities that God enacts outside of the order of created natures to which miracles belong. But, since the order of nature is legitimately viewed, absolutely, i.e., as derived from God as first cause, it can also be said that no natural phenomenon is a miracle; for nothing is done outside of the power of God (1.105.8). It is in this light that I claimed that, in the *Summa*, nature is doubled in the face of miracle, though asymmetrically, as miracle can only appear with respect to the one order and not the other.

Another doubling occurs with respect to miracle itself, though in this case the double image is symmetrical. For just as miracle is properly identified with respect to the created order of nature, there are equally phenomena of the field of grace that are properly called miraculous. There is of course an affinity between miracle and grace; grace too names God's immediate action within the world of creatures. What differentiates miracle from grace, however, is that miracle effects changes upon things normally effected by secondary or created causes. Grace works otherwise. God works grace immediately and only God can. Nevertheless, grace too acts as cause. It causes those creaturely events, virtues etc. that are properly called supernatural, and these manifest an order that determines or grounds legitimate theological expectation. However, God can and does at times work outside of this supernatural order. When this happens a supernatural occurrence properly associated with grace is also called miraculous. Paul's conversion on the road to Damascus, because it is a turning from unbelief to mature or perfect faith in a twinkling instead of in a staged process of maturation or sanctification provides Thomas a case in point (1-2.103.10).

Finally, grace is itself doubled in the context of miracle. For, its supernatural effects are divisible into the miraculous and the non-miraculous. Moreover, miracle understood as an effect of grace extends beyond supernatural miracle to include miracle as it relates to the order of nature. That is, grace can also be divided between what effects recreation unto the perfection of nature and what does not. Indeed, unbelievers and demons alike behold Christ's miracles and remain miscreant (3.43)

4. Concluding Metaphor

What are we to make of all this doubling? Are we to accuse Thomas of a magician's prestigeneration? There are perhaps multiple ways in which we can account for what we have noticed. I will conclude with just one suggestion. I wonder if Thomas is well served by conceiving of nature and grace as the structural harmony of a thing and its final cause? I admit that *he* does not seem to have felt constrained by this concept. But it does set up expectations of an elegant fit that is called into question by all these doublings. So, maybe, if we are to deal with the complexity we have observed Thomas acknowledging in the *Summa*, we do well to leave Aristotle and his physics behind, and experiment with a different conception altogether, even at the risk of anachronism? Maybe we should imagine Thomas's nature and grace as tectonic plates floating on the molten core of mystery that is God's abiding and active presence within the creation and its creatures? Since tectonic plates float, such a concept entails an expectation of movement. In such a view nature and grace can be counted on to shift shape and position in the unfolding of time. Occasionally, these plates will collide; one passing its edge under the other. When this happens, seismic activity will be set off on the surface of things, transforming the landscape in which they exist. Maybe one better understands the function of miracle in Thomas's *Summa* as the landscape transforming seismic activity revealed by scripture in its allegorical sense, an activity set off by the flotation of nature and grace upon the mysterious liquid of the Creator's care.

Of course, the anachronism is real. In my mind's eye I imagine Thomas throwing up his hands like the German university administrator Paul Gooch is reputed to have once taken around the University of Toronto so as to explain its lushly complex governance. I can imagine Thomas too uttering in wonderment—"Well, that may work in practice, but it will never work in theory." Only too true I suppose. For, as I said at the beginning, in the *Summa*, miracle is that kind of trickster. Boo!

FRANCESCO GUARDIANI

The West Shall Shake the East Awake
MATTEO RICCI (1552-1610)
A JESUIT IN CHINA

ABSTRACT. The first Westerner to set foot in mainland China with the declared intention to change its millenary culture was a man of faith, not only a Christian faith, but a faith in the egalitarian, democratic principles of modernity, inspired by the Gutenberg revolution. The rather cryptic, prophetic quote from Joyce (*Finnegans Wake*, 473) appears well apt to describe the epic adventure of Matteo Ricci in China as the very beginning of a process of cultural globalization in which we are still immersed today.

Behind every paper there is a story, and this paper is no exception. However, it is exceptional and no doubt surprising for the colleagues who know me, and know of my interest in Petrarch, the Baroque, and love poetry in general, that I should become interested in the works of a Jesuit priest, a missionary who arrived in China in 1583 and died there twenty-eight years later. This paper should clarify the whys and hows of this interest of mine, but its main purpose here is a personal challenge. Will I be able to communicate the admiration that I have for Matteo Ricci and his works? Will I be able to show how profoundly inspiring his life and writings can still be today for the great humanistic and humanitarian generosity of his mind and soul? This is the challenge that I have in front of me today.

Let me say, at the outset, that after reading just a few passages of Ricci's *Commentaries* and a few of his wonderful *Letters*, I was struck by the strong impression that he deserves to be acclaimed among the greatest writers and philosophers of his time. The end of the sixteenth and the beginning of the seventeenth centuries were turbulent times – times of accelerated cultural transformation all over Europe – times that were shared by Shakespeare and Francis Bacon in England, Campanella, Bruno, and Galileo in Italy, Cervantes, Lope de Vega, and Góngora in

Limina: Thresholds and Borders - A St. Michael's College Symposium
Joseph Goering, Francesco Guardiani, Giulio Silano eds. Ottawa: Legas, 2005

Spain – in short, by the founding fathers of what we have come to call Modernity.

Matteo Ricci was born in 1552 in Macerata, in central Italy, and died in 1610 in Beijing, China. He is not usually found in annals of Italian literature, not even among the numerous "minor authors" of his time. The simple but problematic reason for his absence is in his being a Jesuit. He belonged to the religious world that, in the cultural historiography of an openly anti-clerical modern Italy (i.e. after the unification of 1861), was considered anti-Italian, anti-patriotic. This historiographic perspective has been variously criticized and modified, and certainly with the figure of Matteo Ricci, something more could be done to this effect. My intention, however, is not to focus on the poor critical fortune of this writer or his absence from the canon of Italian literature, but rather on the exceptional dimension of his cultural adventure which allows us to place him among the most innovative thinkers of his time.

In order to introduce the works of Matteo Ricci, a word must be spent on how they got to us. It is an interesting story, and there is no need for a philological analysis to appreciate it. Ricci wrote his major work, *Della entrata della Compania di Giesù e del Cristianesimo in Cina*, between 1609 and 1610. The title literally means, "On the Entry of the Society of Jesus and of Christendom in China," but this work is more commonly known as the *Commentaries on China*. Ricci died in Beijing at the age of fifty-eight, just when he was about to complete the work in Italian. The *Commentaries* constitute a comprehensive synthesis of all of Ricci's previous works, of various kinds (religious, philosophical, and scientific treatises, letters and reports) and in various languages (Italian, Chinese, Portuguese, and Spanish). Because of this comprehensiveness that is proportionate to its voluminous size, the *Commentaries* are considered Ricci's major work, and a truly monumental masterpiece.

With the death of the author, the Italian manuscript fell into the hands of Father Nicolas Trigault, a Belgian Jesuit and historian. Trigault translated it into Latin with a few touch-ups and some addenda, publishing the volume with a frontispiece and an introduction indicating that the work, though based on Ricci's diaries, was in fact his own. This piece of pious collaboration was ·published five years after Ricci's death with a new title – *De christiana expeditione apud Sinas [The Christian Expedition to China]* – and was enormously successful. It was translated into many languages, including Italian (by Antonio Sozzini da Sarzana in 1622, who didn't even make the attempt to check the original "diaries" by Ricci). Ricci remained in the background of Trigault's book for centuries. It was, in fact, only in 1911 that another Jesuit, Father Pietro Tacchi-Venturi, found and published the original manuscript with the title *Historical Works of Father Matteo Ricci*. But for a truly reliable and well-restored text, we have to wait for another Jesuit and a scholar in the Chinese language, Father Pasquale D'Elia, whose superb critical edition of Ricci's work was published in several volumes from 1942 to 1949. All new editions of Ricci's works, including the latest from Quodlibet in 2001, depend on D'Elia's text.

Trigault, Tacchi-Venturi, and D'Elia were all Jesuits, which simply means that Ricci's critical fortune has remained within the confines of his Order. Recently, thanks to the interest of the Bishop of Macerata, the process of the beatification of Matteo Ricci was initiated, and it is very possible that, with the favour of the present Pope, he might soon be venerated as a saint. Now, I believe that together with the religious merits of this remarkable man, we should also give relevance to his civic virtues. As an Italianist and a historian of culture, I feel compelled to speak of Ricci's spectacular cultural openness, his egalitarian perception of all mankind, his active apostolate, and his lack of even the slightest expectation of ecclesiastical advancement or temporal fame for the investment of his entire life as a teacher of science and Christian doctrine.

But before continuing with other comments, let me give you some information on Ricci's formative years. He remained in his native city until the age of sixteen, studying in the newest school of the new order of the Jesuits. Among his teachers and friends were Alessandro Valignani, Roberto Bellarmino, and Rodolfo Acquaviva, all of whom had a major influence on his life (as I will clarify further). Inspired by them, he entered the novitiate of the Jesuits in Rome where, at the Collegio Romano (the Jesuit university), he studied with Father Christopher Clavius. He remained in Rome until the age of twenty-five, when he was called to the Asian missions. Ricci rushed to the Portuguese city of Lisbon without even stopping to see his family. He didn't want to miss a moment of his missionary life which, he soon learned, necessitated a great deal of patience and plain hard work. To begin, he had to learn Portuguese, the official language of the Portuguese ports of Goa and Macau, where Jesuits had established their first missions. In Goa and Cochin (in India), the young novice taught in a seminary for natives. He was finally ordained a priest and destined to China by the Father Superior of all Asian missions, the so-called *Padre Visitatore*, Alessandro Valignani. Father Valignani was an immensely talented man who understood that to enter China – an accomplishment that had been denied to

St. Francis Xavier – one had to learn the culture and acquire the language of the Chinese. And that is exactly what he ordered Matteo Ricci to do. The young priest, who had been waiting for just such an opportunity, immersed himself in the culture of the Chinese and was able to master the language in a relatively short period.

Ricci entered mainland China in 1583, a date that four hundred years afterwards would be celebrated by the People's Republic of China by the issuing of an official commemorative stamp and the restoration of Ricci's tomb in Beijing (which had been vandalized by the nationalistic excesses of the Red Guards). Why were the Chinese so appreciative of the memory of Matteo Ricci, although realistically, nothing was left of his religious apostolate there? Perhaps a simple list of his non-religious works in Chinese – works that have been continually in print from the sixteenth-century to today – would suggest an answer:

1584 – *Geographic Map of the Mountains and of the Seas*

1600 – *Essay on the Four Elements* [there were five for the Chinese]

1601 – *Treatise on the Constellations*

1601 – *The Mysterious Visual Map of the Entire World*

1603 – *Mappamondo, or, World Atlas*

1601 and 1607 – *Lunar and Solar Discs*

1607 – *Astronomical Sphere with Figures and Comments*

1607 – *Elements of Geometry* [a Chinese translation of the first six books of Euclid]

1608 – *Eight Songs for Western Harpsichord*

1609 – *Treatise of Iso-Perimetric Figures*

Posthumous – *Treatise of Arithmetic*

Posthumous – *Theory and Method of Measurement*

Posthumous – *Western Art of Memory*

(from "Bibliografia ricciana," in Ricci, *Della entrata...*, pp. xli-xlii)

Many ideas come to mind just from reading these titles. First of all, they constitute a complex of works reflecting perfectly the didactic *cursus* of the *Quadrivium*, the four traditional scientific disciplines of arithmetic, geometry, music, and astronomy. Ricci obviously felt the pressure and responsibility of scientific teaching, and he performed using the most organized and systematic *curriculum studiorum* he knew.

Some may ask, "but who published all these works for Ricci in China, in several successful and successive editions?" In the fourth chapter of the first book of his *Commentaries,* entitled, "Of the Mechanical Arts of This Land," Ricci spoke of the printing press in China. One could write an entire essay on this description, not for its extension, but for the symbolic and practical value that this art had for Ricci in China. In brief, he indicated that although the Chinese had invented the printing press five hundred years before, they did not use it to its full potential as a European like himself could do only one hundred and fifty years after Gutenberg. Ricci assumed this medium of communication with enthusiasm, energy, and a civic faith in its positive emancipating effects. Ricci's first books in Chinese were done in his own house with the help of servants who, with sharp chisels, engraved the wood to create the matrix for the printed sheet. The Chinese ideograms allow the use of wood rather than lead, Ricci explained, which greatly simplified the work of the printing shop.

Coming now to the central part of my discussion, I would like to focus on the generosity with which Ricci gratified his attentive audience teaching astronomy, geometry, trigonometry, and so on; a generosity which appears excessive if one accepts the common opinion of the Jesuit critics that have dealt with Ricci's works. For them, Ricci's scientific teaching was some sort of trick devised to appeal to the curiosity of the Chinese intellectuals and then convert them to Christianity. We must stress the fact that Ricci's conversions were not over-abundant in number – only two thousand, a good number but disappointing for someone who had entered China with the intent of converting the entire empire of millions. What, then, motivated this person and gave him strength to continue his difficult apostolate in a distant country? Fillipo Mignini, introducing Ricci's *Letters*, gives us a list of the primary elements of his motivation:

> The love of God, Father of all men . . . the desire to transmit the revealed truth . . . the Jesuit legendary obedience . . . the desire of martyrdom . . . all of these explain, in part, the human experience of Matteo Ricci.
> (Mignini, in Ricci's *Lettere,* p.xiii. Translation mine, here and below)

The list is obviously insufficient if Mignini himself continues:

> There were two other factors in Ricci's experience: a natural inclination of his character to people of foreign culture, and an authentic feeling of equality, a perception of the very equal dignity of every human being. (*Ibid.* p.xii)

This is where I wanted to arrive, to focus on Ricci's religious virtues as civic virtues, soon to become a mental state, a basic condition of the modern, emancipated, democratic societies. Matteo Ricci was a man of great faith. As the first Westerner to set foot in continental China with the intent of changing its culture, he was not only a man blessed with Christian faith, but also a visionary armed with the egalitarian principles inspired by the Gutenberg Revolution, of which the Jesuits were principal supporters and promoters.

The Jesuits were a relatively new ecclesiastical order at the time of Matteo Ricci. Their founder, Ignatius of Loyola (1491 – 1556) was still alive when Ricci was born. Actually, observing with a bit of attention the dates of the important events of the time, we notice that the year in which Ricci was born – 1552 – was the same as that of Francis Xavier's death. Xavier was, of course, the trusted friend of Ignatius and the first Jesuit missionary in Asia. He desperately tried to enter China, but that was continually denied to him, and he died right at the port of entry of the most populous country on earth, the country with more souls to save than any other. The dream of converting it was passed to Matteo Ricci. And so when Ricci, at the end of his life, wrote the *Commentaries*, or rather, *On the Entry of the Society of Jesus and of Christendom in China*, he was in fact celebrating the triumph of the Society, an event that associated him directly with Francis Xavier and Ignatius. That was the celebration of a triumph of an ideal and of a method, a Christian conversion of the world with a common respect for the different local cultures.

To this extraordinary Christian faith, as I was saying, a civic faith corresponded on the equal dignity of all mankind. The strength of this belief in Ricci is illustrated by a particular episode in his life in Goa, on the Indian subcontinent, where he spent some years teaching in a Jesuit seminary for natives. In this seminary, some faculty members (including the Father Superior) refused to teach philosophy and theology to native students, claiming that if they mastered these disciplines, the Indians would become as knowledgeable as the Europeans, and this would make them arrogant. Ricci saw a great contradiction in this blatant example of colonial anxiety; the gift of culture and emancipation was being blocked by an action that denied culture and emancipation, to say nothing of brotherhood. So he wrote to the General of the Order, Father Claudio Acquaviva, who was uncle to one of Ricci's greatest influences. Rodolfo

Acquaviva (1550 – 1585) was a fellow Jesuit and Asian missionary of Ricci's own age who found martyrdom in Persia. Ricci, in his letter to Rodolfo's uncle, made his point with the eloquence of a great advocate of human right. I'll skip the text of the letter here, because it is very long, but I would like to translate the last few lines. Ricci wrote:

> I realized that I might have gone overboard with my limited judgement, young age [he was twenty-nine], and lack of experience…, but I am sure you will understand me in the right way. (*Lettere* p. 29-30)

I am focusing now on the closing of the letter, which is not rhetorical at all, since Ricci knew that Claudio Acquaviva would understand him "in the right way." The Acquavivas were from Atri, a municipality in Abruzzo, in central Italy, not far from Ricci's hometown of Macerata, which is in the bordering region of Marche. There was an extraordinary "modern" understanding between Ricci and Acquaviva, which was strengthened by their common provincial and aristocratic background from the same area in Italy.

It should not be forgotten, in the same context, the common background of Alessandro Valignani of Chieti, also in Abruzzo; he was the Jesuit superior of all Asian missions, who sent Ricci to China together with Father Michele Ruggieri (1543 – 1607). Valignani was the first to understand the necessity of a perfect knowledge of the Chinese language and culture for all missionaries to Asia, as it has already been said, so he freed Ricci and Ruggieri of any other commitments for two years in order for the two to study and prepare themselves to enter the continent. Ruggieri eventually returned to Italy and died in Salerno, but the return was denied to Ricci (who never requested it), by the emperor Wanli and his ministers, because they believed that a man of Ricci's intelligence must have learned so much of China that he could, if he turned against them, prove a great danger to the Empire. Ricci knew that he would die in China. With the occasional sense of melancholy, his letters are nevertheless replenished with a sense of euphoria, of training for the great moment – the conversion of the Emperor. This is never explicitly stated in the letters, but the hope of it is very clear, and with it, of the reversal of the coolness, indifference, and even hostility demonstrated by the Chinese to the idea of conversion. The break that Ricci pursued at all levels of Chinese hierarchy, leading to the chief mandarins and to the emperor himself, would never take place, and yet, when Ricci was finally received by the Emperor, he had, for a moment, the illusion of the greatest of all conquests. In fact, he was never received personally by Wanli – only by an empty throne, a feature of Imperial etiquette. The

Emperor, however, was so curious regarding Ricci that he ordered a full-figure painting of the missionary in order to see him.

Ricci's trust in the administrative and political hierarchy of China, his open dialogue with the Imperial astronomers and scientists, were not a result of Ricci's personal attitude, but rather of a well-planned strategy of conversion; namely, to deal with the heads of governments instead of the poor and disadvantaged – working from the top down. The first Jesuit missionaries in Japan, including Ricci's mentor Alessandro Valignani, had encountered this objection from the "wise men" of the land: "All our beliefs and our ancient traditions derive from China. When China becomes Christian, so will Japan." The entering of China, therefore, was particularly significant to the conversion of Asia as a whole. This is why Francis Xavier interrupted his work in Japan and tried to enter China. If China is the head of Asia, the Emperor is the head of China, and Ricci aimed to convert him from the moment of his entrance into the country.

Ricci classified the existing religious "sects" of his China into two groups: Buddhism/Taoism and Confucianism. He accepted the latter as a possible basis for Christianity, but rejected the first. The difficulty with Buddhism, he clarified, is the absence of a transcendental entity identifiable as a "person." According to Ricci, there is no personal God and no personal spiritual link with mankind in Buddhism. In contrast, he found Confucianism to be more of a tradition than a religion, based on the cult of ancestor worship. The figure of Christ and the teaching of the Gospels could be integrated with Confucianism without drastic contrasts or contradictions. This very modern position – so modern that it has been inserted in the Directive for Missions of the Second Vatican Council – created quite a controversy after Ricci's death, and contributed to the isolation of the Jesuit missionaries. Father Niccolò Longobardo (1565 – 1655), Ricci's successor as superior of the missions in China, did not have his vision or faith, and was uncomfortable accepting Confucian beliefs in the Christian doctrine. Without the protection of the Jesuits, and with the Franciscans and the Dominicans pressing for an official Church position equating Confucianism with paganism, Ricci's position was rejected with an official decree of Pope Urban VIII. The most enlightened among the Jesuits reacted by launching "an investigation into the true tenets of Confucianism," led by the brilliant Father Martino Martini, who finally obtained a reversal of the papal decree. But this is a story for another paper, and we have to leave it at that. I will only say that, after Ricci's death, and with the controversy going on, there were only few Chinese conversions. Other events made the situation even worse, among them the death of the emperor Wanli, and soon after, the end of the Ming dynasty. The new expressions of nationalism that followed multiplied the difficulties for Jesuits in Asia, who nevertheless remained the only teachers and mediators of Western culture in China until the order was abolished in 1773.

If the religious apostolate of Ricci did not satisfy all expectations, his scientific apostolate produced extraordinary fruits for the Chinese culture. Ricci has become part of China's cultural history, and today his books are still reprinted there. In certain aspects, he was a startlingly modern writer. In a new detailed list of all elements of modernity present in his *Commentaries*, the most important that I have found are clocks, calendars, spiritual exercises, geographical maps, the glass prisms of Venice, the printing press, and the ladder of Roberto Bellarmino.

Clocks and the measure of time, calendars, and astronomy were real obsessions of the cultured Chinese. Ricci, who had studied at the Collegio Romano under Christopher Clavius (who had been recruited by Pope Gregory XII for the reform of the calendar), could certainly satisfy their intellectual curiosity. He built solar, water, and mechanical clocks, he corrected the lunar calendar of the Chinese to the more precise Gregorian, and was able to forecast lunar eclipses with a precision that astounded the imperial astronomers. He also created the first maps of China and a large world atlas, or *Mappamondo*, that became the most desired Western artefact of the intellectual Chinese.

Ricci's culture was systematic, based on analytical notions kept together in a linear chain of cause and effect with an inductive logic that constitutes the foundation of the modern age. He was not affected by the controversies that poisoned the Italian academia a few years after his death. In his time, the Jesuits were the *avant-garde*, the true protagonists in the pursuit of modern science. They did not (yet) have positions to be defended. Father Roberto Bellarmino was another Jesuit (later canonized as a saint) that Ricci must have met in his early years. Bellarmino's treatise *La scala per salire con la mente a Dio (The Ladder with Which to Ascend with the Mind to God)* is, in essence, a series of spiritual exercises combining theology and science without contrasts. It is a beautiful example of the Jesuits' approach to modernity: dividing knowledge into small particles, to be studied individually and systematically. Note that the division of light that appears from exposing the glass prisms of Venice to the sun was something enchanting to the Chinese. In the fascination that Ricci's audience felt for this modest toy of Western ingenuity, one can perhaps see a more complex admiration for a form of knowledge that gives relevance to an analytical perception of reality, one divided into its atomic components, each studied separately. Using the prisms of Venice as a metaphor for this kind of perception, we can see that each coloured ray of light corresponds to a step in the ladder of Bellarmino, or a unit to be remembered in the vast *Palace of Memory* that Matteo Ricci introduced to the Chinese, or a minimum square of his world atlas, drawn by meridians and parallels, or a fixed thought of a mental exercise extracted from the spiritual exercises of St. Ignatius of Loyola, or one small lead character representing the printing press of the Western world.

These are also the signs and the symbols of modernity that captured the curiosity of the Asian minds of which Ricci became the generous teacher. This is how the treatises of arithmetic and geometry were born, and this is the key to the *Mysterious Map of the Entire World* or of the *Treatise on Theory and Method of Measurements*. There is a euphoric spirit in the Chinese lessons of Ricci that is born out of his Christian feeling of being in the right. It is a moment in which militant Christianity and scientific *avant-garde* are perfectly combined to become, in the apostolate of this missionary, one and the same. It is a moment of profound faith, which opened the road to an effective emancipation of human consciousness by means of love – fraternal love.

WORKS CITED

Ricci, Matteo. *Della entrata della Compagnia di Gesù e del Cristianesimo in Cina*. Ed. Maddalena del Gatto. Project directed by Piero Corradini; Introduction by Filippo Mignini. Macerata: Quodlibet, 2000.

_____. *Lettere*. Ed. Francesco D'Arelli. Project directed by Piero Corradini; Introduction by Filippo Mignini, and with an essay by Sergio Bozzola. Macerata: Quodlibet, 2001.

D'Elia, Pasquale S.J. *Storia dell'introduzione del cristianesimo in Cina scritta da Matteo Ricci; nuovamente edita e ampiamente commentata col sussidio di molte fonti inedite e delle fonti cinesi da Pasquale M. D'Elia*. Roma: Libreria dello Stato, 1942-1949. 3 Vols. ("Fonti ricciane. Edizione nazionale delle opere edite e inedite di Matteo Ricci S.J.").

Trigault, Nicholas. *De Christiana expeditione apud Sinas suscepta ab Societate Jesu. Ex P. Matthaei Ricij comentarijs, libri V.; in quibus Sinensis regni mores, leges atque instituta et novae illius ecclesiae difficillima primordia accurate et summa fide describuntur, auctore P. Nicolao Trigautio.* Augustae: apud Christoph. Mangium, 1615.

Trigault, Nicholas. *Entrata nella Cina de' Padri della Compagnia del Gesù. Tolta dai Comentarii del Padre Matteo Ricci [...] opera del Padre Nicolao Trigarici. Volgarizzata dal Signor Antonio Sozzini da Sarzana.* In Napoli: per Lazzaro Scoriggio, 1622.

Tacchi-Venturi, Pietro. *Opere storiche del Padre Matteo Ricci.* 2 Vols. Macerata: Stabilimento Tip. Giorgetti.

GIULIO SILANO

POSTLIMINIUM: REFLECTIONS IN MARGIN TO JUSTINIAN'S DIGEST 49.15

To Francesca

ABSTRACT. Boundaries as places at which rights were gained and lost, and obligations assumed and shed, were of some relevance to the Roman jurists of the classical age. The analysis of the institute of *postliminium* constituted a specific occasion for their reflection on these issues. It may be that our contemporary language of liminality is indebted to those jurists' reflection as it is preserved in *Digest* 49.15

Since Arnold van Gennep first proposed the language of liminality for the examination of rites of passage, and after Victor Turner refined this language with ever happier results, liminality has proven immensely attractive and fruitful in a variety of approaches to cultural studies whose focus might be said to reside in the relationship of centre and periphery.[1] The more recent application of liminal language to literary studies is

---

[1] Piety seems to require that discussions of liminality always begin by referring to Arnold van Gennep, *Les rites de passage*, translated by Monika B. Vizedom and Gabrielle L. Caffee, with an introduction by Solon T. Kimball, *The Rites of Passage*; at pp. 10-11 of the English translation, we read the following: "I have tried to assemble here all the ceremonial patterns which accompany a passage from one situation to another or from one cosmic or social world to another. Because of the importance of these transitions, I think it legitimate to single out *rites of passage* as a special category, which under further analysis may be subdivided into *rites of separation, transition rites,* and *rites of incorporation*. These three sub-categories are not developed to the same extent by all peoples or in every ceremonial pattern. ... Thus, although a complete scheme of rites of passage theoretically includes preliminary rites (rites of separation), liminal rites (rites of transition) amd postliminal rites (rites of incorporation), in specific instances these three types are not always equally important or equally elaborated." This

Limina: Thresholds and Borders - A St. Michael's College Symposium
Joseph Goering, Francesco Guardiani, Giulio Silano eds. Ottawa: Legas, 2005

perhaps not yet as powerful and arresting as its use in the anthropo-logical analysis of cultural regeneration.[2] And yet the notion remains beguiling that the wilful assumption of a liminal state promises a broader and deeper grasp of human realities than is vouchsafed to those who hanker to remain firmly fixed in a certain place.[3]

These are sublime, even ineffable, topics. They are not the ones which shall exercise us. Our limited aim is to engage in what might be termed the archeology of ideas of liminality by retracing for the uninitiated the evolution of the Roman juridical institute known as *postliminium*. Aside from the intrinsic interest of this institute and its development over the long history of Roman law, it seems probable that, despite van Gennep's silence on the matter, his adoption of terms of liminality to describe a process of separation from the community, a transitional period, and re-integration into the same community owes something to Roman juridical reflection on these matters, particularly by reference to *postliminium*. Our aim, then, is to relay something of the complex and very specialized reflection on *postliminium*, in the hopeful expectation that contemporary usage of terms of liminality can be enriched by an awareness of their long history.

The jurisprudence of *postliminium*, like so much else in Roman law, found its most elegant summation in the *Corpus iuris civilis*, produced at

---

brief passage appears to mark the beginning of the modern tradition of reflec-tion on liminality. Much greater sophistication to the reflection was brought by Victor Turner, who first broached the subject in "Betwixt and Between: The Liminal Period in Rites of Passage," *The Forest of Symbols*, pp. 93-111; a fuller and more magisterial exposition followed in *The Ritual Process: Structure and Anti-Structure*.

[2]For a range of examples of the application of ideas of liminality to literary endeavours, see Manuel Aguirre, Roberta Quance, Philip Sutton, *Margins and Thresholds. An Enquiry into the Concept of Limitality in Text Studies*; Isabel Soto, *A Place that is not a Place. Essays in Liminality and Text*.

[3]For the hope that the lessons taught by the anthropologists regarding liminality can find broad and fruitful application in the attempt to find deeper meaning in one's own existence, see Timothy L. Carson, *Liminal Reality and Transformational Power*. Franco Rella, *Limina. Il pensiero e le cose*, p. 9, with the authority of Simone Weil, suggests that a conscious choice in favour of *atopy*, or placelessness, may hold the key to a fuller perception of place by the internali-zation of boundary (*limite*); in this perspective, fuller understanding follows the de-bounding of space and the re-situation of bounds away from their defensive function to an inner dimension.

the commission of Emperor Justinian in 529-533. In the *Digest*, the largest and most complex part of this greatest of legal compilations, Justinian's commissioners excerpted the opinions of the great jurists of several centuries earlier. It is in margin to the opinions of some of these jurists that we undertake our reflections on our topic.

Postliminium has been somewhat dismissively defined as "basically the recovery of certain legal rights by a Roman who had been taken prisoner by the enemy and who returned home without dishonor. *Postliminium* is simply a part of internal Roman law."[4] While it is not wholly unjust to hold this definition as adequate for much of Roman history, it is not at all peaceful that the restriction of the operation of *postliminium* was always limited to situations of war, even in earliest times.[5] On the other hand, that war had come to be the ordinary condition for its operation is made clear by the fact that the compilers of Justinian's *Digest* place their title on *postliminium* just before three other titles expressly concerned with military matters; furthermore, they join their treatment of *postliminium* to their discussion of captives and those who have been redeemed from the enemy.[6]

The ordinary connection of *postliminium* with war is certainly assumed by the exquisitely technical opening excerpt of our *Digest* title:

> That for which the slave of a person who has been captured by the enemy subsequently stipulates, or any legacy which may come to his slave after he has passed into the hands of the enemy, shall be the property of his heirs because, if he had died in the course of his captivity, it would have been acquired by the heir.[7]

---

[4] Alan Watson, *International Law in Archaic Rome*, p. xii.

[5] Various disputed opinions regarding this and other matters are lucidly outlined in Maria Floriana Cursi, *La struttura del 'postliminium' nella Repubblica e nel Principato*, pp. 1-7. The most vigorous recent restatement of the view that *postliminium* is tightly bound to capitivity is A. Maffi, *Ricerche sul 'postliminium'*.

[6] The Latin text of the *Digest* is quoted from the edition of Mommsen and Krueger, in *Corpus Iuris Civilis*, v. 1 (henceforth *Digesta*); English renderings of the *Digest* are taken from Alan Watson, ed., *The Digest of Justinian* (henceforth *Digest*). References to the *Digest* shall be by book and title, which are uniform in both versions. The title in which *postlimium* is treated is 49.15 and it bears the rubric: *De captivis et de postliminio et redemptis ab hostibus*. It is followed by the following titles: 49.16: *De re militari*; 49.17: *De castrensi peculio*; 49.18: *De veteranis*.

[7] *Digest*, 49.15.1. *Digesta*, 49.15.1: "Marcellus 22 dig. Quod servus eius, qui ab hostibus captus est, postea stipulatus est, aut si legatum sit servo eius, postea-

Curiously, this opening excerpt of our title does not seem to have attracted the attention of the specialists on *postliminium*. Or perhaps its neglect is understandable, since it has so little to say about the institute, failing even to mention it. Indeed, the situation which the excerpt contemplates is one in which *postliminium* has failed to occur. And yet, this text effectively reveals the assumption of Justinian's commissioners that war is the ordinary condition in which *postliminium* has the chance to apply.

But it may be that the excerpt fittingly belongs at the opening of the presentation of *postliminium* because it reveals also a deeply rooted anxiety which must always have surrounded the (possible) application of this institute, particularly when it concerned a *paterfamilias*. The absence of such a person from within the bounds of the Roman state, in situations which made it impossible for him to exercise his authority over those subject to him, combined with the possibility of his return and consequent restoration of the *status quo ante*, created not only a familial rupture, but also a wider one because it put in doubt a great number of rights and obligations of those subject to him and of all those who might in turn have dealings with them.[8] So prominent to Justinian's

---

quam ille ad hostes pervenit, hoc habebunt heredes eius, quia et si captivitatis tempore decessisset, adquisitum foret heredi."

[8]The jurist Tryphoninus adverts to the many difficulties in *Digest* 19.15.12: "1. Should someone be captured by the enemy, those whom he had this power are in an uncertain state, whether they become *sui juris* or are still to be reckoned as sons-in-power; for on his death in enemy hands, they will be considered as *patresfamiliarum* from the date of his capture or, should he return, as never having ceased to be in his power. Therefore, it has been debated whether, if, when the father has not returned, it should happen that others have been instituted heirs to all the estate ([the *sui*] being disinherited by the will) or to part of it, those things that [the *sui*] acquire meantime by stipulation, delivery, or legacy (for they cannot [do so] by inheritance) are part of the captive [father's] inheritance which falls under the *lex Cornelia*, or become their own property. The latter is true; and it is different in the case of those things which are acquired through slaves, and rightly so; for the one class were [part of his] property and continue to be so, while the others are understood to be *sui juris* from then on and for that reason to have acquired on their own behalf. ... 3. A son who was in the power of someone [now] a captive can in the meantime marry a wife, although his father cannot consent to the marriage; for by the same token [he cannot] refuse consent. An acknowledged grandchild, therefore, will be in the power of the returned captive, as his grandfather, and *suus heres* to him, even though it was to some degree against his will, because he did not give consent

commissioners was this feature of these situations of liminality that, in the *Institutes* which they compiled as part of the *Corpus juris civilis* for the instruction of beginning law students, they presented *postliminium* not under its own title, but under the rubric of the ways in which the power of a *paterfamilias* is dissolved. That text is worth quoting because, among other things, it includes a definition of *postliminium* which Isidore would not have been ashamed to offer:

> Again, capture of the father by the enemy makes him a slave of the latter; but the status of his children is suspended by his right of subsequent restoration by *postliminium*; for on escape from captivity a man recovers all his former rights, and among them the right of paternal power over his children, the law of *postliminium* resting on a fiction that the captive has never been absent from the state. But if he dies in captivity the son is reckoned to have been independent from the moment of his father's capture. So too, if a son or a grandson is captured by the enemy, the power of his ascendant is provisionally suspended, though he may again be subjected to it by *postliminium*. This term is derived from *limen* and *post*, which explains why we say that the person who has been captured by the enemy and has come back into our territories has returned by *postliminium*: for just as the threshold forms the boundary of a house, so the ancients represented the boundaries of the empire as a threshold; and this is also the origin of the term *limes*, signifying a kind of end and limit. Thus *postliminium* means that the captive returns by the same threshold at which he was lost. A captive who is recovered after a victory over the enemy is deemed to have returned by *postliminium*.[9]

---

to the marriage. Nor is this surprising, since the situation and the exigency of that time brought it about, and the social utility of marriage required it. 4. But the wife of a captive, however much she may wish it and although she may live in his house, is not in the married state. ... 6. A person's other legal rights, after he has returned with *postliminium*, are considered just as if he had never been in enemy hands." Tryphoninus, in the same place, goes on at length in his discussion of the many complications which arise from both the application and the failure of *postliminium*; what we have quoted may be thought sufficient to confirm the point that anxiety was bound to be great in situations where the institute might apply.

[9]Moyle, *The Institutes of Justinian*, 1.12.5; the text may be conveniently consulted at *http://members.aol.com/hsauertieg/institutes/book1.htm* The Latin original is in Kruger, *Institutiones*, 1.12.5, where the passage reads as follows: "Si ab hostibus captus fuerit parens, quamvis servus hostium fiat, tamen pendet ius liberorum propter ius postliminii: quia hi qui ab hostibus capti sunt si reversi fuerint, omnia pristina iura recipiunt. idcirco reversus et liberos habebit in

The priority here belongs clearly to the suspensive effects of *postliminium* which have as a consequence the placing in a liminal or uncertain state not merely of the person who may exercise the right of return, but also of all those who are dependent on him. But the pedagogical purposes of the work make room for erudition to break out at the end of the paragraph to offer an archaic-sounding rendering of the institute. With its reliance on etymology, the definition of *postliminium* here tendered seems to have the effect of making the crossing of boundaries the essential element in the re-assumption of juridical personality within the Roman state on the part of one whose same personality had entered into a suspended state by virtue of his having been placed outside those boundaries against his will. Perhaps the desirable possibility of drawing an analogy between house and empire proved too tempting to Justinian's commissioners, to the point of making them forgetful of the great space which, as we shall have occasion to see, the jurists of old had gradually asserted for the subjective state of the returnee as determinant for the application of *postliminium*. At the same time, they would have had the greatest difficulty to prove their blithe assumption that those same ancients had been clear about the clarity and role of boundaries in the definition of the empire.[10] For example, with two exceptions, one looks in vain among the rich dossier of texts gathered in our title of the *Digest* for any mention of the actual crossing of boundaries as being relevant to the operation of *postliminium*; over and over again, those texts keep referring to return by right of *postliminium*, without ever mentioning

---

potestate, quia postliminium fingit eum qui captus est semper in civitate fuisse: si vero ibi decesserit, exinde, ex quo captus est pater, filius sui iuris fuisse videtur. ipse quoque filius neposve si ab hostibus captus fuerit, similiter dicimus propter ius postliminii ius quoque potestatis parentis in suspenso esse. dictum est autem postliminium a limine et post, ut eum qui ab hostibus captus in fines nostros postea pervenit postliminio reversum recte dicimus. nam limina sicut in domibus finem quendam faciunt, sic et imperii finem limen esse veteres voluerunt. hinc et limes dictus est quasi finis quidam et terminus. ab eo postliminium dictum, quia eodem limine revertebatur, quo amissus erat. sed et qui victis hostibus recuperatur, postliminio rediisse existimatur."

[10]Cursi, *La struttura*, gamely makes the effort to show that, at least in ancient times, the crossing of the Roman boundaries had been the necessary prerequisite for the operation of *postliminium*; she purports to summarize the evidence for this point at pp. 327-330, but, in the end, is forced to argue the point principally from the technicalities of grammatical usage for dearth of actual examples of a crossing of boundaries, even from literary sources.

the crossing of boundaries as the moment at which such a return has occurred.[11]

One of the exceptions to which reference has been made is the concluding excerpt of the title, which gathers together views of the jurists Labeo and Paul. In the first part of the excerpt, Labeo states:

> If a thing of ours which the enemy captures is of such a kind that it can return by *postliminium*, then as soon as it has escaped from the enemy for the purpose of returning to us and has begun to be within the boundaries of our empire, it is to be reckoned as having returned by *postliminium*.[12]

Although Labeo here allows importance to beginning to be within the boundaries of the empire (notice that this very expression seems to suffer from uncertainty as to what it might take to be fully within the boundaries!), the mention of 'purpose' in this text itself introduces a subjective dimension into the operation of *postliminium* which is lacking from the *Institutes*'s definition. But this exception to the jurists' general failure to mention boundaries is further qualified by the second half of the excerpt within which it is contained:

> Paul: Not always. When the slave of a Roman citizen, after capture by the enemy, escapes from thence and is in the city of Rome, but in such a way that he is neither in the power of his master nor serving anyone else, it is to be reckoned that he has not yet returned by *postliminium*.[13]

Paul's mention of the city of Rome, coupled with his reference to a returned slave, is particularly effective in pointing out how comparatively irrelevant, in the view of the jurists, the actual crossing of boundaries has become to the operation of *postliminium*. One who has come to the city of Rome has crossed a whole series of boundaries, including the most venerable ones of all, whose crossing by Remus had lead Romulus to the commission of fratricide. And yet, even the crossing of these boundaries, and even on the part of a slave, is not sufficient to bring about the restoration of prior rights by *postliminium*; it is only the actual

---

[11]See, e.g., *Digest* 49.15.4, 5, 12, 22, 23.

[12]*Digest* 49.15.30. *Digesta* 49.15.30: "Labeo 8 pith. a paulo epit. Si id, quod nostrum hostes ceperunt, eius generis est, ut postliminio redire possit: simul atque ad nos redeundi causa profugit ab hostibus et intra fines imperii nostri esse coepit, postliminio redisse existimandum est."

[13]*Digest* 49.15.30. *Digesta* 49.15.30: "paulus. immo cum servus civis nostri ab hostibus captus inde aufugit et vel in urbe roma ita est, ut neque in domini sui potestate sit neque ulli serviat, nondum postliminio redisse existimandum est."

submission of the slave to the authority of his master, or to his servile condition, that will reactivate the suspended relationship of ownership. So prominent has the voluntaristic element become in the thought of the jurists that, in effect, even a slave needs to intend to return to his prior state of dependency, if he is to be said to have returned to his master by right of *postliminium*.

Intentionality, just like the exclusive application of the institute in situations of war, had not always clearly defined *postliminium*, and the jurists knew it. The nice balance between practice, which witnessed the use of *postliminium* most usually in war, and the memory of the possibility that it could be invoked even in peace is elegantly expressed in the comprehensive definition of our institute offered by the same Paul, whom we have just seen defend the relevance of the intention even of a returning slave to the operation of the institute. Paradoxically enough, it is in his definition that we seem to find the second exception to the general failure of the jurists to consider the effect of the crossing of boundaries. Paul's definition reads as follows:

> PAUL, *Sabinus, book 16: Postliminium* is the right, established by customs and laws between ourselves and free peoples and kings, of recovering from a foreigner property which has been lost and restoring it to its former condition. For what we have lost in war, or even short of war, if we recover it again, we are said to recover by *postliminium*. And this was introduced by natural justice, so that a person wrongfully detained by foreigners might, when he had returned to his own country, recover his former rights. ... 2. Persons captured by pirates and brigands continue to be freemen. 3. A person is seen as having returned with *postliminium* when he enters our territories, just as he was lost when he went outside them. However, if he comes to an allied or friendly *civitas*, or to the court of an allied or friendly king, he is forthwith seen as having returned with *postliminium*, because it is there that he first, by the authority of the state, begins to be safe. 4. There is no *postliminium* for a deserter to the enemy; for the man who with evil counsel and a traitor's intention has left his *patria* is to be counted among [our] enemies. This though is the legal position in the case of a free deserter, whether a woman or a man. ... 7. Again, a son-in-power who is a deserter cannot return with *postliminium*, not at least while his father is alive, because his father lost him in the same manner as did his country, and because military discipline was, for Roman parents, a more ancient tradition than love of children. 8. A deserter, however, is taken to be not only someone who goes over to the enemy in time of war but also someone who goes over after accepting a promise during a truce to [a people] with whom Rome has no friendship. ... 10. *Postliminium* is for people whatever their sex or status; nor does it make a difference whether they are freemen or slaves.

For those who return with *postliminium* are not only persons capable of fighting, but all who are of such a character that they can be of use, whether by giving advice or in other ways.[14]

A cursory, or perhaps even a careful, reading of the translation of Paul's definition may not readily reveal the extent to which he has retained firm memory of a time when the crossing of boundaries might have been thought to be entirely relevant, perhaps even sufficient, apart from any other considerations, to the operation of postliminium. Rare mistranslations, in an otherwise admirable rendering of a very challenging text, appear to be responsible for the difficulty. The expression in the prologue to the definition, "when he had returned to his own country," serves to translate ubi in fines suos redisset, which would more fairly be rendered as "when he had returned within his own boundaries." And in § 3 of the definition, the phrase "A person is seen as having returned with postliminium when he enters our territories, just as he was lost when he went outside them," renders the original's Postliminio redisse videtur, cum in fines nostros intraverit, sicuti amittitur, ubi fines nostros excessit. Again, a more adequate rendering of

---

[14]*Digest* 49.15.19; *Digesta* 49.15.19: "Paulus 16 ad sab. Postliminium est ius amissae rei recipiendae ab extraneo et in statum pristinum restituendae inter nos ac liberos populos regesque moribus legibus constitutum. nam quod bello amissimus aut etiam citra bellum, hoc si rursus recipiamus, dicimur postliminio recipere. idque naturali aequitate introductum est, ut qui per iniuriam ab extraneis detinebatur, is, ubi in fines suos redisset, pristinum ius suum reciperet. ... 2 Paulus 16 ad sab. A piratis aut latronibus capti liberi permanent. 3 Paulus 16 ad sab. Postliminio redisse videtur, cum in fines nostros intraverit, sicuti amittitur, ubi fines nostros excessit. sed et si in civitatem sociam amicamve aut ad regem socium vel amicum venerit, statim postliminio redisse videtur, quia ibi primum nomine publico tutus esse incipiat. 4 Paulus 16 ad sab. Transfugae nullum postliminium est: nam qui malo consilio et proditoris animo patriam reliquit, hostium numero habendus est. sed hoc in libero transfuga iuris est, sive femina sive masculus sit. ... 7 Paulus 16 ad sab. Filius quoque familias transfuga non potest postliminio reverti neque vivo patre, quia pater sic illum amisit, quemadmodum patria, et quia disciplina castrorum antiquior fuit parentibus romanis quam caritas liberorum. 8 Paulus 16 ad sab. Transfuga autem non is solus accipiendus est, qui aut ad hostes aut in bello transfugit, sed et qui per indutiarum tempus aut ad eos, cum quibus nulla amicitia est, fide suscepta transfugit. ... 10 Paulus 16 ad sab. Postliminium hominibus est, cuiuscumque sexus condicionisve sint: nec interest, liberi an servi sint. nec enim soli postliminio recipiuntur, qui pugnare possunt, sed omnes homines, quia eius naturae sunt, ut usui esse vel consilio vel aliis modis possint."

this phrase would read: "A person is seen to have returned by postliminium when he has entered within our boundaries, just as he was lost when he went outside our boundaries." Of course, the allusion to the importance of the crossing of the boundaries is quickly qualified by a host of examples in which the crossing will not achieve the operation of postliminium because of other, primarily subjective, elements which will not allow the returnee to claim restoration to his or her previous status. But the allusion remains striking as evidence that Paul, more than most, had retained a firm grasp of the historical evolution of postliminium and knew that the elements which he was outlining had emerged gradually at the hands of the jurists in order to modify an institute which may have been relatively simple and uncomplicated in earlier times.[15]

Paul's definition is notable for a number of reasons. Its placement of *postliminium* firmly among those legal institutes which have their origins in international relations squarely challenges Watson's definition of it as "simply a part of internal Roman law."[16] It remains valid to say that *postliminium* is concerned with the effect within the Roman legal order of the absence and then the return most usually of a citizen, or the absence and then the return of persons and goods subject to the authority of such a citizen. But such an assertion fails to address the specific sorts of circumstances which give rise to the possibility of *postliminium*, and these tend not to be internal to the Roman legal order. Paul's definition makes clear that *postliminium* addresses the difficulties which originate in the citizen's inability to exercise his rights as a result of events which occur outside the ambit of the Roman state. Specifically, *postliminium* offers the possibility of restoration of his person and rights within the Roman state to one who has for a time, become subject to the authority of another state, whether in his person or in his goods. It is only when a person or thing has been taken out of the Roman community to be taken into another recognized community that the question of restoration into the original community acquires relevance and *postliminium* may offer itself as the legal fiction by which the restoration occurs. Hence both the relevance of boundaries and the resistance of the jurists to regard these

---

[15]For the antecedents to Paul's definition, in particular his familiarity with and reception of the definition of *postliminium* by the grammarian Aelius Gallus, see Cursi, *La struttura*, pp.121-122; for Aelius Gallus' definition and its importance and difficulties of interpretation, see Cursi, *La struttura*, pp. 13-26 and passim.

[16]See above, at n. 4.

same boundaries as some kind of magical instrument by the crossing of which return by right of *postliminium* occurs. Indeed, it seems probable that of more relevance to them are the other boundaries, the ones of the receiving community which mark the entry into a liminal state of the possibility of the exercise of specifically Roman rights and obligations. It seems equally probable that this greater relevance of the other community's boundaries and a greater interest in defining them clearly, as opposed to marking clearly the points of exit for members of the Roman community, is a long-standing feature of the Roman approach to boundary-crossing.

Paul's definition of *postliminium* links its origins firmly to injury sustained by Romans because of the detention of things at the hands of foreigners within the bounds of a foreign, but acknowledged, state; it seems to be Paul's view that, while the institute of *postliminium* was originally established by customs and laws to enable the restoration of things to their lawful Roman owner, as if there had been no rupture in the owner's rights, the extension of its application from things to persons had been the fruit of natural justice. The aspect of the definition which concerns things and their return as the first field of application of *postliminium* has plausibly been thought to call to mind an ancient ceremony by which formal request was made for the return of things injuriously detained within the bounds of another state.[17] This ancient ceremony, by which a *rerum repetitio* occurred, was called *clarigatio* and was described by Livy in the following terms:

> Numa had instituted religious observances for times of peace, he would hand down the ceremonies appropriate to a state of war. In order, therefore, that wars might be not only conducted but also proclaimed with some formality, he wrote down the law, as taken from the ancient nation of the Aequicoli, under which the Fetials act down to this day when seeking redress for injuries. The procedure is as follows: The ambassador binds his head in a woollen fillet. When he has reached the frontiers of the nation from whom satisfaction is demanded, he says, `Hear, O Jupiter! Hear ye confines' naming the particular nation whose they are – `Hear, O Justice! I am the public herald of the Roman People; rightly and duly authorised do I come; let confidence be placed in my words.' Then he recites the terms of the demands and calls Jupiter to witness: `If I am demanding the surrender of those men or those goods, contrary to justice and religion, suffer me nevermore to enjoy my native land.' He repeats these words as he crosses the frontier, he repeats them to whoever happens to be the first person he

---

[17]Cf. Cursi, *La struttura*, pp. 313-314, and the authorities there cited.

meets, he repeats them as he enters the gates and again on entering the forum, with some slight changes in the wording of the formula. If what he demands are not surrendered at the expiration of thirty-three days – for that is the fixed period of grace – he declares war in the following terms: 'Hear, O Jupiter, and thou Janus Quirinus, and all ye heavenly gods, and ye, gods of earth and of the lower world, hear me! I call you to witness that this people' – mentioning it by name – 'is unjust and does not fulfill its sacred obligations. But about these matters we must consult the elders in our own land in what way we may obtain our rights.' With these words the ambassador returned to Rome for consultation.[18]

---

[18]Livy, *History of Rome*, tr. Canon Roberts, 1.32. Titus Livius, *Ab urbe condita*, 1.32: "ut tamen, quoniam Numa in pace religiones instituisset, a se bellicae caerimoniae proderentur, nec gererentur solum sed etiam indicerentur bella aliquo ritu, ius ab antiqua gente Aequicolis quod nunc fetiales habent descripsit, quo res repetuntur. [6] legatus ubi ad fines eorum uenit unde res repetuntur, capite uelato filo--lanae uelamen est--'audi, Iuppiter' inquit; 'audite, fines'--cuiuscumque gentis sunt, nominat--; 'audiat fas. ego sum publicus nuntius populi Romani; iuste pieque legatus uenio, uerbisque meis fides sit.' peragit deinde postulata. [7] inde Iouem testem facit: 'si ego iniuste impieque illos homines illasque res dedier mihi exposco, tum patriae compotem me nunquam siris esse.' haec, [8] cum fines suprascandit, haec, quicumque ei primus uir obuius fuerit, haec portam ingrediens, haec forum ingressus, paucis uerbis carminis concipiendique iuris iurandi mutatis, peragit. [9] si non deduntur quos exposcit diebus tribus et triginta--tot enim sollemnes sunt--peractis bellum ita indicit: 'audi, Iuppiter, et tu, Iane Quirine, dique omnes caelestes, uosque terrestres uosque inferni, audite; [10] ego uos testor populum illum'--quicumque est, nominat--'iniustum esse neque ius persoluere; sed de istis rebus in patria maiores natu consulemus, quo pacto ius nostrum adipiscamur.' ' cum †. . . . .† nuntius Romam ad consulendum redit." Both Latin text and English translation may be consulted at http://www.perseus.tufts.edu. Another and fuller description of the ceremony, which substantially conforms to Livy's, is offered by Dionysius of Halicarnassus and is conveniently translated in full by Watson, *International Law in Archaic Rome*, pp. 2-3; at p. 74 n. 1, Watson offers a very useful summary of the conjectures and bibliography regarding the fetials. It is the burden of Watson's entire fascinating little book to prove that, in passages like the one quoted above, we find Jupiter called to judge, and not to witness, the justice of the forthcoming Roman declaration of war; this appeal to the gods as judges of the justice of Roman claims and Roman wars is taken to be, at least until the end of the Republic, a constant practice that gives substance, and not only in Roman eyes, to the claim that they are the most pious of peoples, even in the conduct of wars which result in conquest.

Here, then, we have the description of a rite which is meant to bring about the sort of situation, whether in peace or by war, in which *postliminium*, perhaps first of things and then of persons, is originally supposed to apply. Here, we have also some mention of boundaries. Fascinatingly, it is not the boundaries of the Roman state which are in any way defined in the course of the ceremony, but those of the communities which are charged with detaining unjustly Roman goods and persons. These boundaries are themselves called upon to witness (or is it to judge?) the claim that an injustice has been committed by the detention of Roman goods and persons within those very boundaries. Apparently, justice will be achieved not when such goods and persons return within the Roman bounds, but when the boundaries which unjustly detain them leave them free to move to more friendly spaces, within which they may re-acquire their proper status in accordance with Roman law. This and like descriptions of *clarigatio* are consistent with what we have seen Paul say with regard to the spatio-temporal point of application of *postliminium*, namely either when the person enters into Roman territories, or when he enters into friendly territories, within which he may already safely act in accordance with his postliminal state.[19]

This marked disinterest to emphasize the importance of crossing Roman boundaries on the part of such disparate Romans (including, as we have seen, anyone from fetial priests to just about all the jurists quoted in our title of the *Digest*) might well be taken to flow from the nature of the issue which faces them, namely the removal of a bar upon the Roman juridical faculties of a citizen, either with regard to his person or to his property. If that is the problem, then the moment of liberation from the bar, wherever it may occur in space and time, can reasonably be postulated to be the point at which *postliminium* begins to operate. But it remains our conviction that something more significant is at work in the failure of the more ancient sources (indeed, of all of them, apart from the qualified assertion of the view in the *Institutes*) to mention the crossing of Roman boundaries as the moment when *postliminium* ought to begin to operate. Such a mention or requirement for the functioning of the institute would in turn have made it necessary for the Romans to mark clearly the boundaries of their state, and this they seem to have been unwilling to do.

---

[19]*Digest* 49.15.19.3, cited above at n. 13.

An interesting indication of this unwillingness can be found in the form of the celebration of the *Terminalia*, a feast in honour of the god Terminus, guarantor of the sacredness of boundaries. On this feast, held on 23 February, two forms of celebrations were held, one to safeguard private boundaries, the other to protect the public ones. As one would expect of such celebrations, the private one served to mark the bounds between neighbouring properties and so neighbours would offer sacrifices at the boundary stones. The public sacrifice, on the other hand, did not serve to identify the boundaries of the Roman state since it consisted in the offering of the sacrifice of a sheep at the sixth milestone outside the city on the Laurentine road. To choose a milestone rather than a boundary for the celebration of a feast intended to mark the sacredness of all boundaries can and has been understood to mean that, while private Roman boundaries are to be fixed and certain for the sake of peace and security, the boundaries of the Roman state are to be moveable and open-ended until the city and the world coincide:[20]

> There's a track that takes people to the Laurentine fields,
> The kingdom once sought by Aeneas, the Trojan leader:
> The sixth milestone from the City, there, bears witness
> To the sacrifice of a sheep's entrails to you, Terminus.
> The lands of other races have fixed boundaries:
> The extent of the City of Rome and the world is one.[21]

But if both the practice of the ancient fetials and the views of the much later Paul seem to show no particular concern with the definition and crossing of Roman boundaries for the application of *postliminium*,

---

[20] Dario Sabbatucci, *La religione di Roma antica*, pp. 74-75, with references to Ovid's *fasti* as one authority that makes many of these assumptions manifest. For a fuller discussion of the *Terminalia*, see Giulia Piccaluga, *Terminus*, pp. 265-285; in the same work, at pp. 286-292 and passim, fascinating things are said about Terminus' resistance to Juppiter's invasion of the Capitol. Piccaluga, at pp. 111-115, also points out the importance of the association in Roman ritual and language of *imperium* and *propagatio* of the public boundaries; in her view, there has been too much resistance, or too little attention, among specialists to the dynamic quality of Roman public boundaries and to the expectation that they would perennially grow.

[21] Ovidius, *Fasti*, 2.679-684, translated by A.S. Kline and available at www. tonykline.co.uk / Browsepages/Latin/Ovid FastiBk Two. htm#_Toc69367696, the Latin text may be consulted at www .intratext.com /IXT/LAT0537/_IDX-010.HTM.

and if Roman religious practice and poetic reflection seem averse to the very possibility of marking Roman boundaries, why would anyone ever have thought that such a moment might be determinant for the operation of the institute? A hint of an answer to this question might arise from our considering a final definition of *postliminium* occurring in our title and due to the jurist Pomponius. This definition, aside from confirming many of the elements we have identified in the texts considered earlier, offers a brief history of the development of *postliminium* by its reference to a number of ancient incidents which had allowed the importance of the subjective element to emerge more explicitly in its application. Pomponius' little treatise on *postliminium* reads as follows:

> POMPONIUS, Quintus Mucius, book 37: The right of postliminium applies both in war and in peace. 1. In war, when those who are our enemies have captured someone on our side and have taken him into their own lines; for if during the same war he returns he has postliminium, that is, all his rights are restored to him just as if he had not been captured by the enemy. Before he is taken into the enemy lines, he remans a citizen. He is regarded as having returned from the time when he passes into the hands of our allies or begins to be within our own lines. 2. Postliminium is also granted in peacetime; for if we have neither friendship nor hospitium with a particular people, nor a treaty made for the purpose of friendship, they are not precisely enemies, but that which passes from us into their hands becomes their property, and a freeman of ours who is captured by them becomes their slave, and similarly if anything of theirs passes into our hands. In this case also postliminium is therefore granted. 3. If, however, a prisoner of war is released by us and joins his own people, he is understood to have returned with postliminium if and only if he prefers to follow those [who are his own] rather than remain in our civitas. Accordingly, in the case of Atilius Regulus, whom the Carthaginians sent to Rome, the opinion was given that he had not returned with postliminium because he had sworn that he would return to Carthage and had not had the intention of remaining in Rome. And so in the case of a certain Menander, an interpreter, who was sent to his own people after he had been manumitted among ourselves, the law passed to cover him, that he should remain a Roman citizen, was not seen as necessary; for if his intention was to remain among his own people, he would cease to be a citizen, while if his intention were to return, he would remain a citizen; the law, therefore, would be entirely pointless.[22]

---

[22]*Digest*, 49.15.5. *Digesta*, 49.15.5: "Pomponius 37 ad q. muc. 1. In bello, cum hi, qui nobis hostes sunt, aliquem ex nostris ceperunt et intra praesidia sua perduxerunt: nam si eodem bello is reversus fuerit, postliminium habet, id est per-

In this definition, we see confirmed the main lines of *postliminium* as we have been discussing it on the basis of the opinions of the other jurists. Once more, the view is reiterated that need for it may occur in peace or in war, but war is treated as the ordinary context within which it may be useful. Once more, no requirement for the crossing of boundaries is mentioned; indeed, the assumption seems to be that most instances of return by *postliminium* will happen in military situations which may very well occur in areas not yet subject to Roman authority at all, so that both the liminal and postliminal events will take place outside the current boundaries of the Roman state. It is again the case that the juristic analysis is focussing closely on the bar to the exercise of juridical personality and to the removal of the same bar as the essential elements for the operation of *postliminium*. In effect, the best marker for Roman boundaries is treated as being not any physical sign, but the ability of the state to ensure the safety of its citizens and their full exercise of their rights.

Novelties for us in Pomponius' definition are presented in its third paragraph. It is here that we find fully and explicitly affirmed the view that the mere crossing of boundaries is not sufficient to bring about return by *postliminium*; the requirement is now expressly stated that the subjective intention of the returnee is determinant of whether or not *postliminium* will apply. But the terms of the definition make clear that the preponderant importance of the subjective element had not always been

---

inde omnia restituuntur ei iura, ac si captus ab hostibus non esset. antequam in praesidia perducatur hostium, manet civis. tunc autem reversus intellegitur, si aut ad amicos nostros perveniat aut intra praesidia nostra esse coepit. 2 Pomponius 37 ad q. muc. In pace quoque postliminium datum est: nam si cum gente aliqua neque amicitiam neque hospitium neque foedus amicitiae causa factum habemus, hi hostes quidem non sunt, quod autem ex nostro ad eos pervenit, illorum fit, et liber homo noster ab eis captus servus fit et eorum: idemque est, si ab illis ad nos aliquid perveniat. hoc quoque igitur casu postliminium datum est. 3 Pomponius 37 ad q. muc. Captivus autem si a nobis manumissus fuerit et pervenerit ad suos, ita demum postliminio reversus intellegitur, si malit eos sequi quam in nostra civitate manere. et ideo in Atilio Regulo, quem Carthaginienses Romam miserunt, responsum est non esse eum postliminio reversum, quia iuraverat Carthaginem reversurum et non habuerat animum Romae remanendi. et ideo in quodam interprete Menandro, qui posteaquam apud nos manumissus erat, missus est ad suos, non est visa necessaria lex, quae lata est de illo, ut maneret civis Romanus: nam sive animus ei fuisset remanendi apud suos, desineret esse civis, sive animus fuisset revertendi, maneret civis, et ideo esset lex supervacua."

evident throughout the course of Roman legal history; Pomponius cites two cases by reflection on which it was eventually agreed by the jurists that the subjective element was indispensable for the application of the institute.

Atilius Regulus was consul and Roman military leader in the first Punic war against Carthage.[23] After some bullying of the Carthaginians on his part and a haughty refusal to engage in a negotiated settlement with them, he did not do very well militarily against them and was himself taken prisoner by them. Having sworn an oath that he would return as a prisoner to Carthage if the negotiations were not successful, he was sent with an embassy to Rome to attempt once more the negotiation of a settlement. The late historians Dio Cassius, Zonaras, and Appianus all seem to agree that, in all he did at Rome, Regulus avoided acting as a Roman citizen and, perhaps most importantly from Pomponius' perspective, refused to cross the most ancient of the Roman boundaries, requesting that the Senate meet with the Carthaginian embassy outside that venerable boundary.[24] When the Senators met outside the *pomerium*, he appeared before them to tell them of the dismal conditions which he thought were afflicting Carthage and to discourage them from making peace. In accordance with his oath, he returned to Carthage where he

---

[23]The sources for the episode of Atilius Regulus are fully set out and well-exploited by Cursi, *La struttura*, pp. 41-45, on which we rely for what follows.

[24]Cassius Dio Cocceianus, *Dio's Roman History*, 11.26-27, describes the events in these terms: "They say that the Carthaginians made overtures to the Romans on account of the great number of the captives, among other causes; they wished most of all to see if they could make peace on some moderate terms, and if they could not do this, at least to get back the captives. It is said that Regulus, too, was sent among the envoys because of his reputation and valour. They assumed that the Romans would do anything whatever for the sake of getting him back, so that he might even be delivered up alone in return for peace, or at any rate in exchange for the captives. 27Accordingly, they bound him by mighty oaths and pledges to return without fail, in case he should accomplish neither of their objects; and they despatched him as an envoy along with others. Now he acted in all respects like a Carthaginian, and not a Roman. He did not even grant his wife leave to confer with him, nor did he enter the city, although invited inside..." The text of the *History* may be consulted at http://penelope.uchicago.edu/Thayer/E/Roman/Texts/Cassius_Dio/home.h tml For the additional contributions of Appianus and Zonaras, see Cursi, *La struttura*, pp. 43-44.

suffered an atrocious execution with great courage, so becoming a great example of Roman piety and virtue.

It is notable that none of the sources describing these events thought that *postliminium* had been an issue in the case of Regulus. Pomponius is the sole author to raise that possibility in an apparent gloss on Cicero's remarks about Regulus. In his *De officiis*, Cicero had pointed to Regulus as an example of great virtue and had briefly recounted the events that lead to his death. About the consul's behaviour during the embassy to Rome, Cicero said that he refused to participate in the deliberations of the Senate as a member of that body due to the oath which he had taken to the Carthaginians. And yet Regulus recommended that Rome not return its many Carthaginian prisoners, certainly not in exchange for himself, who was much older, and so less useful, than the prisoners. His advice was followed, and he returned to Carthage, in the awareness of the very severe sufferings that were to follow.[25]

Pomponius seems to report the conclusion of careful pondering in juridical circles of his own day as to what was implied in Regulus' denial of his ability to participate in the deliberations of the Senate as a member, as also perhaps about his refusal to cross the *pomerium* into the city; the conclusion of the jurists' pondering was that Regulus had intently been avoiding his resumption of his full rights and obligations by *postliminium*, which he could not do without remaining in Rome and so being in violation of his oath.[26] In other words, the possibility that the mere crossing

---

[25]Cicero, *De Officiis*, 3.27: "Itaque quid fecit? In senatum venit, mandata euit, sententiam ne diceret, recusavit; quamdiu iure iurando hostium teneretur, non esse se senatorem. Atque illud etiam, ("O stultum hominem," dixerit quispiam, "et repugnantem utilitati suae!"), reddi captivos negavit esse utile; illos enim adulescentes esse et bonos duces, se iam confectum senectute. Cuius cum valuisset auctoritas, captivi retenti sunt, ipse Carthaginem rediit, neque eum caritas patriae retinuit nec suorum. Neque vero tum ignorabat se ad crudelissimum hostem et ad exquisita supplicia proficisci, sed ius iurandum conservandum putabat. Itaque tum, cum vigilando necabatur, erat in meliore causa, quam si domi senex captivus, periurus consularis remansisset." The text is consultable at http://www.thelatinlibrary.com/cicero/off3.shtml#27

[26]We assume juristic debate and a resolution because of Pomponius' assertion, in § 3 of his little treatise, that "the opinion was given that he had not returned with *postliminium* because he had sworn that he would return to Carthage and had not had the intention of remaining in Rome." The expression 'the opinion was given,' or 'responsum est,' is a typical one by which to introduce the opinion of a jurist.

of a boundary might bring about *postliminium* is taken to be what Regulus is avoiding by his careful staging of his appearance in Rome, and this even though none of the sources which describe the events raises that possibility.

The suspicion is almost irresistible that no one, in fact, had ever raised the possibility that *postliminium* could be so automatic, and that the jurists, at least with reference to the Regulus case, raise it as a pedagogical device. They have become interested in clarifying more thoroughly the relevance of the subjective state of the returnee to the operation of *postliminium*, and the disparate details of the famous events surrounding Regulus are pulled together into a lesson about *postliminium*. It must be said that the import of the lesson as to boundaries is not entirely clear. As we have seen in Livy's description of the *clarigatio*, the *pomerium* is only the last and most intimate of the various sets of boundaries that might reasonably be said to enclose a political community. There is no obvious reason at all as to why it should become the boundary whose crossing determines the occurrence of *postliminium*. In effect, even if we think that *postliminium* is at all relevant to the Regulus episode, we might conclude that the protagonist here gets to decide which set of boundaries would have brought about *postliminium* so that he may avoid its crossing. More plausibly and in analogy with the Livy passage, we may take the episode as evidence of the obsessive concern of Roman protagonists to define their behaviour as pious in the oddest of circumstances, especially if these lead to war.

The Menander case is more compelling because it more fairly seems to spring from the view that the mere crossing of boundaries can bring about *postliminium*. The principal source of information regarding the case is Cicero. In a discussion of citizenship contained in his *Pro Balbo*, he sets out the impossibility of holding concurrent citizenship in Rome and in another state, so a Roman who acquires the citizenship of another state loses his Roman one, and this change can happen also by *postliminium*. To prove this point, he mentions the case of Menander, a Greek freedman who had been granted Roman citizenship and who had then been asked to serve as interpreter to Roman legates to Greece. On the supposition that, by crossing into his former country, he might reacquire his former citizenship by *postliminium*, a law was passed providing that, if he should reach his former home and then return to Rome, he would not be less a Roman citizen as a result. Cicero did not think that this step had been taken without cause.[27]

Once more, Pomponius' statement regarding Menander is compelling evidence of a subsequent debate among the jurists regarding the case. Despite Cicero's view that there might have been a point to the fear that *postliminium* might operate automatically, by the mere return of Menander to his former home, the jurists appear to have been unanimous in reaching the opposite conclusion. In their view, absent his intention to remain in his former home, Menander ran no risk of resuming his former citizenship by *postliminium* and so of losing his Roman one. If we can trust Cicero's report of a law having been passed in the Menander case, than this is the one bit of evidence that, at least at one point in Roman legal history, a number of people had been willing to consider the possibility that the operation of *postliminium* might be automatic and dependent on the crossing of a boundary. The doubt did not last. Perhaps this very exceptional case was responsible for the very modern view that liminality is largely a state of mind.

WORKS CITED

Aguirre, Manuel, Roberta Quance, Philip Sutton. *Margins and Thresholds. An Enquiry into the Concept of Liminality in Text Studies.* Studies in Liminality and Literature 1. Madrid: Gateway Press, 2000.

Carson, Timothy L. *Liminal Reality and Transformational Power.* Lanham MD: University Press of America, 1997.

Cassius Dio Cocceianus. *Dio's Roman History.* With an English translation by Earnest Car ; on the basis of the version of Herbert Baldwin Foster. 9 voll. London : W. Heinemann, 1914-27.

Cursi, Maria Floriana. *La struttura del 'postliminium' nella Repubblica e nel Principato.* Università di Roma 'La Sapienza', Pubblicazioni dell'Istituto di diritto romano e dei diritti dell'Oriente mediterraneo 73. Napoli: Jovene Editore, 1996.

---

[27]Cicero, *Pro Balbo*, 11.28: "sed etiam postliminio potest civitatis fieri mutatio; neque enim sine causa de Cn. Publicio Menandro, libertino homine, quem apud maiores legati nostri in Graeciam proficiscentes interpretem secum habere voluerunt, ad populum latum ut is Publicius, si domum revenisset et inde Romam redisset, ne minus civis esset." Watson, *The Law of Persons in the Later Roman Republic*, p. 241, as cited by Cursi, *La struttura*, p. 29, believes that the episode may have occurred either in 168 or in 146 b.C.

Krueger, Paul. *Institutiones.* In W. Kunkel, ed. *Corpus Iuris Civilis.* 19th ed. Vol. 1. Dublin and Zurich: Weidmann, 1966.

Livius, Titus. *Ab urbe condita.* Edd. Robert Seymour Conway and Charles Flamstead Walters. 5 voll. Oxford: Clarendon Press, 1914.

_____. *The History of Rome.* Tr. Canon Roberts. 6 voll. London: J.M. Dent, 1912.

Maffi, Alberto. *Ricerche sul 'postliminium'.* Università di Milano, Pubblicazioni dell'Istituto di diritto romano 29. Milano: Giuffré, 1992.

Mommsen, Theodor, and Paul Krueger. *Digesta.* In W. Kunkel, ed. *Corpus Iuris Civilis.* 19th ed. Vol. 1. Dublin and Zurich: Weidmann, 1966.

Moyle, John Baron. *The Institutes of Justinian.* 5th ed. Oxford: Clarendon Press, 1913.

Piccaluga, Giulia. *Terminus. I segni di confine nella religione romana.* Rome: Edizioni dell'Ateneo, 1974

Rella, Franco. *Limina. Il pensiero e le cose.* Milano: Feltrinelli, 1987.

Soto, Isabel. *A Place that is not a Place. Essays in Liminality and Text.* Studies in Liminality and Literature 2. Madrid: Gateway Press, 2000.

Turner, Victor W. "Betwixt and Between: The Liminal Period in Rites of Passage," *The Forest of Symbols,* pp. 93-111. Ithaca: Cornel University Press, 1967.

_____. *The Ritual Process. Structure and Anti-Structure.* The Lewis Henry Morgan Lectures/1966. Chicago: Aldine Publishing Company, 1969.

van Gennep, Arnold. *Les rites de passage; étude systématique des rites de la porte et du seuil, de l'hospitalité, de l'adoption, de la grossesse et de l'accouchement, de la naissance, de l'enfance, de la puberté, de l'initiation, de l'ordination, du couronnement des finançailles et du mariage, des funérailles, des saisons, etc* Paris: É. Nourry, 1909. Repr. New York: Johnson Reprint Corp., 1969.

_____. *The Rites of Passage.* Translated by Monika B. Vizedom and Gabrielle L. Caffe. Introd. by Solon T. Kimball. London: Routledge & Kegan Paul, 1960.

Watson, Alan. *International Law in Archaic Rome: War and Religion.* Baltimore and London: The John Hopkins University Press, 1993.

_____. *The Digest of Justinian.* 2 vv. Rev. ed. Philadelphia: University of Pennsylvania Press, 1998.

_____. *The Law of Persons in the Later Roman Republic.* Oxford: Clarendon Press, 1967.

Pauline A. Thompson

Contamination and Consent: The Illustration of an Augustinian Principle in Ælfric's Lives of Saints Agnes and Lucy

ABSTRACT. In Ælfric's *Life of St. Lucy*, Lucy's suitor/judge threatens to have her taken to a brothel in order that she will be forced to lose her virginity and, as a consequence, the Holy Spirit, who, she says, dwells in the bodies of those who preserve chastity. Lucy's response is to state the Augustinian doctrine that no one's body can be polluted unless the mind gives consent. The same idea, in a similar situation, appears, albeit more briefly, in Ælfric's *Life of St. Agnes*. But how can one demonstrate the truth of this statement? The *Life of St. Agnes* responds to this challenge by making Agnes's room in the brothel, brilliantly lit by the presence of an angel, symbolic of her body. He who crosses its threshold with evil intent and a refusal to be awed by the sanctity of the space is struck down, while she remains inviolate. Thus the episode in the *Life of St. Agnes* makes vivid in narrative form an important Augustinian doctrine.

Ælfric, the prolific writer of Old English homilies and saints' Lives, produced his *Lives of Saints* around the year 1,000 while he was a monk at Cerne Abbas in Dorset. The Lives were written at the request of two worldly-wise Anglo-Saxon noblemen, Æthelweard and Æthelmær. Since Dorothy Bethurum wrote her article in 1932 on Ælfric's saints' Lives, it has been widely understood that the main purpose of these Lives was to be entertainment for the devout. She says:

> [Ælfric] was interested in narrative in the Lives of Saints and very little in homiletic material.... [He] omits doctrinal matter, historical detail, and names that would be unfamiliar to his hearers. His avowed purpose was to tell the stories of the saints to laymen and he showed always the most courteous regard for what would entertain them (Bethurum, 519-20).

Ælfric's main teaching tools were, after all, his two series of Catholic Homilies. If one wanted to learn about doctrine, they surely are the

Limina: Thresholds and Borders - A St. Michael's College Symposium
Joseph Goering, Francesco Guardiani, Giulio Silano eds. Ottawa: Legas, 2005

works to devour. Recently, I have been taking a close look at a small subset of the saints' Lives, namely the Lives of the virgin martyrs, and finding embedded in the narrative line, in the images and metaphors, and in the speeches of the saints themselves, aspects of important Christian teaching. Usually this doctrinal material is present in the Latin originals from which Ælfric was working, and part of the pleasure of working in this area is to see how Ælfric treats the source material. Very often he abbreviates his source, sometimes quite drastically (as he does, for example, with the *Life of St. Cecilia*), but never to the exclusion of important doctrine. In the Lives I want to discuss here, those of Agnes and Lucy, Ælfric stays quite close to his sources, shortening the narrative somewhat from time to time, but capturing succinctly the important pedagogical themes.[1] From this we can assume that the Augustinian doctrine of consent and intention which appears in both these Lives was an important one for the period in which the Latin Lives were originally written (in the fifth and sixth centuries) and for Ælfric's own time (the end of the tenth century).

The narratives of the Lives of Agnes and Lucy share a similar moment: both saints are interrogated by pagan authorities with a view to having them change their minds about being Christians and virgins. Since neither will budge from their convictions, they are threatened with being sent to a brothel. The logic of this move is best spelled out in the *Life of Lucy*. Here, Paschasius, her judge, angry with Lucy because she talks so much, threatens her with a beating if she does not keep quiet (68-69). Lucy retorts that the words of the living God cannot be suppressed, nor put to silence. "What!" snorts Paschasius. "Are you God?" (72). Lucy replies that she is the handmaid of the Lord (a clear reference to Mary at the Annunciation, to which I will return later) and quotes the words of Jesus recorded in Matthew 10:20: "It will not be you speaking [when you are hauled up before the authorities], but the Spirit of your Father speaking in you." She also refers to 1 Corinthians 3:16, claiming that those who preserve chastity (i.e., those who do not defile the body) are God's temple and the dwelling place of the Holy Spirit (80). Seizing what he takes to be a golden opportunity, Paschasius says, "I shall

---

1 The closest Latin source for Ælfric's *Life of Agnes* is to be found in MS Cotton Nero E.i.(1), folios 114r-116v. It is in the BHL 156 tradition. The closest printed version is presented as a Ps. Ambrose *Epistola* in PL 17, 813-21. For the *Life of Lucy*, the closest Latin source is in MS Corpus Christi College Cambridge 9, pp. 437-40. This can be compared with the version in Mombritius, vol. 2, pp. 107-109 and is in the BHL 4992 tradition.

command my men to lead you straight away to the house of harlots, so that you may lose your maidenhood; then the Holy Spirit will flee from you when you are foully dishonoured" (81-83). It is at this point in the narrative that Lucy replies with the doctrine which I am particularly interested in examining here: "No one's body is contaminated," says Lucy, "unless it is with the consent of the mind" (84-85). She expands on this. Ælfric, staying fairly close to the Latin, can be translated as follows:

> If you were to lift up my hand to your idol, and so through me offer against my will, I shall still be guiltless in the sight of the true God, who judges according to the will and knows all things. If now, against my will, you cause me to be polluted, a two-fold purity shall be gloriously imputed to me. You cannot bend my will to your purpose; whatever you may do to my body, that cannot happen to me.[2]

The source of this doctrine is best expressed in Augustine's *City of God*, Book I, chapter 16:

> In the first place, then, let this be stated and affirmed: the virtue by which life is lived rightly has its seat in the soul; it directs the members of the body from there; the body is made holy by the exercise of a holy will; while this will remains unshaken and steadfast, nothing that another does with the body, or in the body, that the sufferer has no power to avert without sinning in turn, is the fault of the sufferer. *Not only the infliction of pain, but also the gratification of lust, is possible upon the body of another; but when anything of this kind is done, the chastity to which the most resolute soul holds fast is not struck down* [my italics] (*City of God*, 26).[3]

And again in chapter 18:

> No one, no matter how high-minded and modest, has power to control what is done to the flesh, *but only what the mind will consent to or refuse*. Who of sane mind, therefore, will suppose that purity is lost if it so happens that the

---

[2] Ne bið ænig gewemmed lichama to plihte gif hit ne licað þam mode. Þeah þu mine hand ahebbe to ðinum hæþengilde and swa þurh me geoffrige mines unwilles, ic beo þeah unscyldig ætforan ðam soðan gode, seþe demð þe þam willan and wat ealle þincg; gif þu me unwilles gewemman nu dest, me bið twifeald clænnysse geteald to wuldre. Ne miht þu gebigan minne willan to þe; swa hwæt swa þu minum lichaman dest, ne mæg þæt belimpan to me (*Life of Lucy*, 84-93).

[3] Sit igitur in primis positum atque firmatum uirtutem, qua recte uiuitur, ab animi sede membris corporis imperare sanctumque corpus usu fieri sanctae uoluntatis, qua inconcussa ac stabili permanente, quidquid alius de corpore uel in corpore fecerit, quod sine peccato proprio non ualeat euitari, praeter culpam esse patientis. Sed quia non solum quod ad dolorem, uerum etiam quod ad libidinem pertinet, in corpore alieno perpetrari potest: quidquid tale factum fuerit, etsi retentam constantissimo animo pudicitiam non excutit (*De ciuitate dei*, I.16, 8-17).

flesh is seized and overpowered, and another's lust exercised and satisfied on it? [my italics] (*City of God*, 27).[4]

The *Life of Agnes* makes use of the same doctrine, though the reference is more fleeting. When she too is threatened with pollution in a brothel, she says:

> I trust in Him [i.e. God] because He is to me a strong wall, and an unfailing defence, so that I need not sacrifice to your accursed gods; *nor by pollution from without [can I] ever be defiled among foul harlots* [my italics].[5]

Now, what I want to focus on is how this doctrine of "no contamination without consent" gets illustrated in the imagery of the narrative line of these saints' Lives. But at this point you may well be asking why it is important to illustrate it at all. My answer is that it seems to me that it is all very well to develop a doctrine like this, which was intended by Augustine to be a comfort to people.[6] But suppose you had a niggling doubt about its truth. Many a raped woman has probably felt this problem acutely, reassured somewhat by helpful pastoral counselling, but still struggling to feel uncontaminated and morally upright. How can the doctrine be shown to be true? The problem reminds me of the one faced by Jesus in the healing of the paralytic reported in Matthew 9. When he saw the man lying paralysed on his bed, Jesus said to him, "Take heart, my son; your sins are forgiven." The lawyers standing by accused him of blasphemy. Jesus asked them, "Is it easier to say, 'Your sins are forgiven,' or 'Stand up and walk'?" The answer, of course, is: "Your sins are forgiven" – anyone could *say* that! Then Jesus said: "But to convince you that the Son of Man has power on earth to forgive sins" – he turned to the paralysed man and said, "Stand up, take up your bed, and go home." And he got up and went off home (vv. 2-8). In other words, the much more risky statement "Take up your bed and walk" and the action which it produced demonstrated the truth of the earlier statement, "Your sins are forgiven," which is easy to say but hard to

---

[4] Nullus autem magnanimus et pudicus in potestate habeat, quid de sua carne fiat, sed tantum quid adnuat mente uel renuat: quis eadem sana mente putauerit perdere se pudicitiam, si forte in adprehensa et oppressa carne sua exerceatur et expleatur libido non sua? (*De civitate dei*, I.18, 5-9).

[5] Ic truwige on him forþan ðe he is me trumweall and unateorigendlic bewerigend, þæt ic ðinum awyrgedum godum ne ðurfe geoffrian, ne þurh ælfremede horwan æfre beon gefyled mid þam fulum myltestrum (*Life of Agnes*, 126-30).

[6] Nec tantum hic curamus alienis responsionem reddere, quantum ipsis nostris consolationem (*De civitate dei*, I.16, 7-8) 'But we are not here so much concerned to return an answer to outsiders as to bring comfort to our own people' (*City of God*, 26).

show to be true! In the case of Agnes and Lucy, the problem is one of verifying the truth of the doctrine of consent. It is easy to say that one's body is not polluted unless one gives consent, but how can it be shown to be true?

If I am right in thinking that the doctrine that one's body cannot be contaminated without the mind's consent is analogous to Jesus' claim to be able to forgive sins, then it is in some sense incumbent on the narrator of a saint's Life where the doctrine of consent is at issue to demonstrate the truth of the doctrine. Although the *Life of Lucy* gives the clearest statement of the doctrine, it is the *Life of Agnes* which supplies the most vivid demonstration of its validity. In the *Life of Lucy*, once Lucy has made her claim that she cannot be polluted without her consent, the authorities attempt to drag her off to a "house of lust," but are unable to move her. She is riveted to the ground. There are three attempts to move her: they fasten ropes to her, cast spells on her, and harness oxen to her, but all prove ineffective. Eventually, she is killed by a sword blow. So she never gets to the brothel, and the doctrine of consent gets no clear illustration in the imagery of immobility and force, since the doctrine seems to require an image of forceful or attempted threshold-crossing which does not in fact pollute. It is in the Life of Agnes where the doctrine receives figurative and narrative reinforcement.

As in the *Life of Lucy*, there are three images used in the narrative after Agnes claims that she cannot be defiled from without. But unlike the images in the *Life of Lucy*, these images are not about immovability, but about impenetrability. The first image comes as a result of the judge's decision to have her led stark naked through the streets to the brothel (*Life of Agnes*, 141-42). The removal of her clothes is obviously the first step in the process of her despoliation. Miraculously, as soon as her clothes are torn off, her hair grows thick and long and covers her on all sides (144-47); the result, the Latin Life assures us, was better than if she were still covered by her own clothes![7] No part of Agnes's body is visible. A second image is provided by an angel who is present in the brothel room to which Agnes is taken: Agnes is given a shining tunic, which fitted her exactly, itself shining with such brightness that men could perceive its divine origin. Clothed in it, Agnes has an aura of heavenly otherworldliness. This same angel is the source of a great light which surrounds Agnes in the room, so that no man could even look

---

[7] Statim autem ut spoliata est crine <soluto> tantam densitatem capillis eius gratia diuina concessit, ut melius eorum fimbri[i]s uideretur quam uestibus tecta (Cotton Nero E.i.[1], 115r).

upon her, much less touch her. The text presses the point home: "the more curiously someone wished to see, the more blunted was the sharpness of his vision" (153). Here then is the third image of impenetrability: a presence of light so dazzling that it effectively formed a barrier between Agnes and all others. The result is that the harlots' house is turned into a house of prayer: everyone who entered gave glory to God because of the great light, and left cleaner than they had been when they entered, a detail omitted by Ælfric, but present in the Latin original.[8] This detail is important because it underlines what has happened here: a place of shame, pollution and immorality has been transformed into a place a lot like heaven, a place of purity and light. Symbolically, it has become an image of the inviolability of the saint's body.

But it is the next incident which really brings home the truth of Augustine's teaching. The Prefect's son (who had originally been Agnes's suitor) arrives on the scene with his friends. Since Agnes has rejected and therefore humiliated him, he is now out to defile and humiliate her in as shameful a way as possible. First, he sends in his friends to have their way with her (165). But they have the same reaction that earlier onlookers had experienced: they are so astonished at the marvellous light that they retreat without attempting to enter the room where Agnes is. They make no attempt to violate her, so great is the sense that she is holy and protected. The fury of the prefect's son is aroused by their failure to defile her, and he himself boldly rushes in "with shameful intent" (170). He fails to acknowledge the light as of divine origin and as soon as he crosses the threshold, before he can so much as touch her hand, he falls prostrate before her, and expires. Agnes cannot be violated. She is now in control. In a final miracle, which proves her saintliness and overturns the accusation that it is as a harlot and witch that she has brought about the death of her suitor, she prays to God at the request of his father to raise the young man to life. Both father and son are converted to the Christian faith. Agnes's vindication is complete.

It is this three-fold image of impenetrability which offers to us visual and narrative verification of the validity of Augustine's doctrine of consent. Especially, it is the image of the brothel filled with awe-inspiring, well-nigh blinding light, to cross whose threshold without due reverence spells death, which makes this point. When those who approached did so with appropriate reverence and a recognition that worship was due to

---

8 ... et mundiores egrederentur foras, quam fuerant introgressi (Cotton Nero E.i.[1], 115r).

the true God, they chose not to enter the room, and so went away unharmed. They treated the room as symbolic of Agnes's own body, and just as they made no attempt to trespass into the room, so symbolically they made no attempt to violate her. When the prefect's son rushed into the room, without permission or respect, with the intention of raping Agnes, and with no sense of the sanctity of the place, he is rendered powerless and struck down. The two occupants of the room, Agnes and the angel, become symbolically aligned respectively with Agnes's mind (which did not give consent) and the Holy Spirit, whose temple Agnes's body is. Thus, the room is an image of the sanctity of Agnes herself: since she did not give consent to have the threshold of her body crossed by the prefect's son, either in marriage or in prostitution, she remains undefiled. Her chastity and sanctity are preserved by her non-consenting mind and by the presence of the angel of God as representative of God's spirit within her. As we saw earlier, Augustine would say, "The chastity to which the most resolute soul holds fast is not struck down."

There are two further points to be made. First, we might well ask why it is a brothel which is used to symbolise Agnes's body, rather than just a room without those sorts of associations? By taking her to a brothel, the magistrates symbolically attempt to pollute her by simply having her cross the brothel's threshold. As Shari Horner has put it: "A 'house of harlots' [is] a space which by its nature implies a penetration of the female body" (Horner, 34). The fact that, as soon as she enters it, it becomes a place of beauty, light and holiness, indwelt not only by Agnes but by the angel of God, reverses all our expectations and prepares us for the further exploration of the image which the text provides. Just so, it seems to me, did the story of the Incarnation, which begins in the most unlikely of places, a stable, and in so doing prepares us for the upsetting of so many of our expectations of kingship, power and authority. Thus, the author of the *Life of Agnes*, by writing a narrative which uses a glorified brothel room, a place of shame and humiliation turned into a place of light and glory, to symbolise the body of a saint who remains in her soul and body unpolluted, demonstrates the doctrine of Augustinian consent in a startling and vivid way.

The second point is that in denying consent to pollution, Agnes and Lucy in fact give their consent to sanctity. I mentioned earlier that Lucy informed Paschasius that she was the "handmaid of the Lord," words taken from Luke 1:38 which expressed Mary's consent to Gabriel's message. "As you have spoken, so be it," she continued, giving consent to have the threshold of her body crossed by the power of the Most High in order to become a temple of the Holy Spirit in a unique way, the shrine of the Christ-child. This reference to Mary in the *Life of Lucy*, veiled though it is, invokes the ideal of consent – consent to being the temple of the Holy Spirit, and sets it in stark contrast to the defilement which both Agnes and Lucy refuse. The presence of the angel in the brothel room, as representative of the Holy Spirit in Agnes, gives narrative and imaginative power to this concept.

That Augustine found it necessary to formulate this teaching as he says "to bring comfort to our own people" is indicative of the fact that this doctrine was born out of the exigencies of real life. This is no hypothetical morality, dreamed up in the cloister of a reclusive philosopher of religion. The Augustinian passage, *City of God* I.18, is echoed in the fifth century by Prosper of Aquitaine in Sentence 51 of his *Liber Sententiarum*,[9] and it is cited explicitly in Aldhelm's *De virginitate*, a seventh-century English work, together with an Epigram of Prosper of Aquitaine, who, as Aldhelm puts it, "sweetened" the idea by versifying it (Aldhelm, 319: 9-21). The locus in the *Life of Lucy* turns up in the works of Ado of Vienne (ninth century), in Rupert of Deutz and Gratian (both twelfth century), as well as in at least one other unidentified author.[10] Ælfric must also have been well aware of the practical ramifications of this doctrine. English history had been plagued for centuries by the incursions of raping and pillaging invaders. The future did not look particularly bright in Ælfric's own time: his king was Ethelred, colloquially known as "The Unready," and the throne was shortly to be taken over by the Danes and subsequently by the Normans. Times of uncertainty and times of war always bring with them the threat of violence, and the violence with which Augustine is concerned in Book one of *The City of God* is a particular concern for women. The Lives of Lucy and Agnes make this clear. It is perhaps telling that this doctrine does not receive illustration in a male saint's Life. Nonetheless, the principle applies to both sexes: if the mind does not consent to what the body is forced to, there is no sin. For Augustine in Hippo and for his audience in the West, as the Vandals and the Goths threatened the Empire; for the

---

9 Ita non amittitur corporis sanctitas, manente animi sanctitate, etiam corpore oppresso, sicut amittitur sanctitas corporis, uiolate animi puritate, etiam corpore intacto 'Just as the sanctity of the body is not lost as long as the sanctity of the soul remains intact, even though the body is overpowered, just so the sanctity of the body is lost when the purity of the soul is violated, even though the body is undefiled' (Sentence 51, p. 269).

10 *Vitis mystica seu tractatus de passione domini*, ch. 27, PL 184, 692B.

thousands of readers and hearers of the Lives of Agnes and Lucy throughout the long history of their popularity, especially in times of war and local persecution; and for Ælfric and his readers in England in the dying years of the first millenium, as Ethelred frittered away the country's strengths, the message must have been of some comfort. So, undoubtedly, has it also been in our own times, and in the intervening thousand years between us and Ælfric. The image of Agnes, clothed with her miraculous growth of hair, adorned with an angelic shift, and, above all, surrounded by a veritable "stockade" of light, has no doubt been carried in the imagination of many who have faced and endured various sorts of pollution of the body against their will.

WORKS CITED

Ado of Vienne. *Martyrologium.* PL 123, 413D-414A.

Aldhelm. *De virginitate. Aldhelmi opera.* Ed. R. Ehwald. Berlin: Weidmann, 1919.

Augustine. *De civitate dei, libri I-X.* CCSL 47. Turnholt: Brepols, 1955.

Augustine. *The City of God against the Pagans.* Ed. and trans. R.W. Dyson. Cambridge Texts in the History of Political Thought. Cambridge: Cambridge UP, 1998.

Life of Agnes. "Natale sancte Agnetis uirginis." Skeat, vol. 1, 170-94. Cited by line number.

Life of Lucy. "De sancta Lucia uirgine." Skeat, vol. 1, 210-18. Cited by line number.

Ælfric's Catholic Homilies: The First Series Text. Ed. Peter Clemoes. EETS ss. 17. London: Oxford UP, 1997.

Ælfric's Catholic Homilies: The Second Series Text. Ed. Malcolm Godden. EETS ss. 5. London: Oxford UP, 1979.

Bethurum, Dorothy. "The Form of Ælfric's *Lives of Saints.*" *Studies in Philology* 29.4 (1932), 515-33.

BHL. *Bibliotheca hagiographica latina antiquae et mediae aetatis.* Subsidia hagiographica 6. Brussells, 1898-1901. *Novum supplementum* (H. Fros). Subsidia hagiographica 70. Brussells, 1986.

Gratian. *Decretum Gratiani: concordia discordantium canonum. Pars secunda. Causa xxxii, quaest. v.* PL 187, 1484B.

Horner, Shari. "Reading the Bodies of Ælfric's Female Saints." *Violence Against Women in Medieval Texts.* Ed. Anna Roberts. Gainsville: University of Florida Press, 1998, 22-43.

Mombritius. "Passio sanctae Luciae virginis et martyris." *Sanctuarium seu vitae sanctorum.* Ed. Boninus Mombritius. Hildesheim: G. Olms, 1978, vol. 2, 107-109.

PL. *Patrologia cursus completus: series latina.* Ed. J.-P. Migne. Paris: Garnier, 1844-1864.

Rupert of Deutz. *De Trinitate et operibus ejus. Libri xlii in deutoronomium, I.xxi.* PL 167, 941C.

Skeat, Walter W., ed. and transl. *Ælfric's Lives of Saints.* EETS os. 76 and 82. London: Oxford UP, 1881, 1885. Rpt. as one volume, 1966.

Biblical quotations are from *The Revised English Bible with the Apocrypha.* Oxford: UP and Cambridge: UP, 1989.

MICHAEL VERTIN

AFFIRMING A LIMIT
AND TRANSCENDING IT

ABSTRACT. Do I ever genuinely know anything at all? Two historically significant answers
to that question are continuous with two opposed interpretations of Thomas Aquinas.
One of those answers presupposes that to affirm a limit is, in that very affirmation, to go
beyond the limit. The other has a different presupposition.

Do I ever genuinely know anything at all? Ordinarily this is not a question
that troubles us very much. Even our occasional moments of cognitional angst are usually – and thankfully – limited in scope. I may experience a moment of panic about my powers of discernment when I recognize that four times in a row I have made a mistake in adding the
same column of numbers, or that I am the only one in the room who
failed to get the joke, or that I have completely misunderstood what my
significant other has plainly been trying tell me. But even in such challenging and sometimes embarrassing circumstances, I do not seriously
doubt my ability to know at least some things passably well.

It remains that virtually all of us occasionally find ourselves struck by
what seems on the surface to be at least a conceivable possibility,
namely, that every one of our so-called cognitional acts is actually other
than it seems to be, that not a single one of them discloses reality as it
actually is. Some of us even go so far as to spend considerable time in-
vestigating this possibility and others like it, thus allying ourselves with
that long tradition of investigators who, though not necessarily deeming
themselves "wise," have been pleased to be known as at least "lovers of
wisdom."

The history of philosophy includes two main kinds of radical skepticism, two main types of thoroughly negative answers to the question, *Do
I ever genuinely know anything at all?* So-called "metaphysical" skepticism,
already emergent among early Greek philosophers, is the view that our
inability to know is a consequence of the character of reality itself: reality

Limina: Thresholds and Borders - A St. Michael's College Symposium
Joseph Goering, Francesco Guardiani, Giulio Silano eds. Ottawa: Legas, 2005

as such is so multiple and changeable, so diverse and unstable, that it is intrinsically unknowable. By contrast, so-called "epistemological" skepticism, more typically a modern phenomenon, is the view that our inability to know is the result of a constitutional incapacity in us as would-be knowers, a fundamental flaw with which we are afflicted that leaves us unable to perform genuinely cognitional acts.

If thoroughly *negative* answers to our key question express varieties of "skepticism," *affirmative* answers express varieties of what philosophers commonly have come to label "realism." And among prominent realists in the history of philosophy, surely one of the more notable is Thomas Aquinas.

Though his formal scholarly enterprise was theology, Aquinas took pains to spell out a detailed philosophical framework for his theological labors. That framework is so extensive in its scope and so profound in its depth that it has served as a major reference point for philosophers during the past 750 years, even those who dispute it in one way or another. Moreover, the realist character of that framework is not in doubt. For Aquinas is very far from being either a metaphysical or an epistemological skeptic. In his view, reality in itself is thoroughly knowable, for its radical ground and ultimate goal is an infinite being who is subsistent knowability. And we humans, for our part, are naturally able to reach some secure conclusions about reality, a natural ability that may be enhanced and extended by supernatural faith.

Still, if no one denies that Aquinas was a realist, there are diverse opinions among Thomist scholars about exactly how he understood his own realism to be justified. For example, in the terms of one conspicuous interpretational dispute that has emerged during the past century or so, did Aquinas view his realist stance as *the self-evidently valid starting point of all sane thinking*, or did he view it as *the consequence of something more basic?* Each side in this dispute has many able and prestigious exponents.[1] Moreover, given that the issue is philosophically so fundamental, the position one takes on it is bound to influence how one interprets Aquinas' views on many other issues. Hence, the significance of the dispute for Thomist scholarship in general is difficult to overestimate.

As it turns out, two of the most important participants in this dispute, one on each side, have links with St. Michael's College. Joseph Owens

---

[1] For brief but fairly representative versions of the respective positions in this dispute, see Etienne Gilson, *Réalisme thomiste et critique de la connaissance* (Paris: Vrin, 1939) [*Thomist Realism and the Critique of Knowledge* (San Franciso: Ignatius Institute, 1986)], Ch. V; and Joseph Donceel, "A Thomistic Misapprehension?", *Thought* 32 (1957), 189-98.

(1908 –), reportedly lauded by Etienne Gilson as the best student he had ever had, was a faculty member of the Pontifical Institute of Medi-aeval Studies for over forty years, until his retirement a few years ago in his late eighties. Works in which he takes an explicit stance on the grounds of Aquinas' realism include *An Elementary Christian Metaphysics* (1963), *An Interpretation of Existence* (1968), and numerous articles in scholarly journals. And Bernard Lonergan (1904-1984) taught at various institutions for about forty years, most notably for twelve years at the Gregorian University in Rome. However, for certain periods both be-fore and after his Roman sojourn he was associated with Christ the King Seminary – later Regis College – in Toronto, and during those periods he was a frequent visitor at St. Michael's. Works in which he addresses the issue of Aquinas' realism include *VERBUM: Word and Idea in Aquinas* (1946-49), *Insight: A Study of Human Understanding* (1957), *Method in Theology* (1972), and – like Owens – numerous articles.

At this point in my presentation, some of you may be muttering to yourselves, "What does all this talk about Aquinas and his interpreters have to do with the topic of our symposium?" My answer: *A certain fea-ture of thinking about a limit* can illuminate what I suggest is the funda-mental difference between the two contrasting traditions of Thomist interpretation – and, in particular, between Owens' account of Aquinas' realism and Lonergan's account. To spell out just what I mean by that statement, let me first sketch and then compare the respective answers given by Owens and Lonergan to two successive questions: (1) *What is the culminating act I experience myself performing whenever I APPARENTLY come to know a particular thing first-hand?* (2) *How, if at all, does that act meet the standard, satisfy the criterion, of GENUINE knowing?*

MY SUMMARY OF OWENS' ARGUMENT

1. The *culminating act* I experience myself performing whenever I AP-PARENTLY come to know a particular thing first-hand is *judgmentally intuiting* a particular intelligible content.

2. But *"judgmentally intuiting"* means *intellectually apprehending* and thus *cognitionally manifesting* a particular intelligible content's *concrete actual synthesizing* as *immediately given in the context of sense-experi-ence.*

A. Therefore, the *culminating act* I experience myself performing when-ever I APPARENTLY come to know a particular thing first-hand is *in-tellectually apprehending* and thus *cognitionally manifesting* a particular intelligible content's *concrete actual synthesizing* as *immediately given in the context of sense-experience.*

3. But a particular intelligible content's *concrete actual synthesizing* is *the culminating component* of a particular thing's *genuine reality.*

B. Therefore, the *culminating act* I experience myself performing whenever I APPARENTLY come to know a particular thing first-hand is *intellectually apprehending* and thus *cognitionally manifesting the culminating component* of a particular thing's *genuine reality* as *immediately given in the context of sense-experience.*

4. But *cognitionally manifesting the culminating component* of a particular thing's *genuine reality* as *immediately given in the context of sense-experience* is the basic meaning of *"an act of genuine knowing."*

C. Therefore, the *culminating act* I experience myself performing whenever I APPARENTLY come to know a particular thing first-hand is *an act of genuine knowing.*

MY SUMMARY OF LONERGAN'S ARGUMENT

1. The *culminating act* I experience myself performing whenever I APPARENTLY come to know a particular thing first-hand is *reasonably affirming* a particular intelligible content.

2. But *"reasonably affirming"* means *positing* and thus *cognitionally manifesting* a particular intelligible content as *part of the unlimited goal that by nature I cognitionally (and affectively) intend.*

A. Therefore, the *culminating act* I experience myself performing whenever I APPARENTLY come to know a particular thing first-hand is *positing* and thus cognitionally manifesting a particular intelligible content as *part of the unlimited goal* that by nature I cognitionally (and affectively) intend.

3. But the *unlimited goal that by nature I cognitionally (and affectively intend)* is *the totality of genuine reality.*

B. Therefore, the *culminating act* I experience myself performing whenever I APPARENTLY come to know a particular thing first-hand is *positing* and thus *cognitionally manifesting* a particular intelligible content as *part of the totality of genuine reality.*

4. But *cognitionally manifesting* a particular intelligible content as *part of the totality of genuine reality* is the basic meaning of *"an act of genuine knowing."*

C. Therefore, the *culminating act* I experience myself performing whenever I APPARENTLY come to know a particular thing first-hand is *an act of genuine knowing*.

Before offering some specific comments on these two arguments, I would ask you to notice four global features. First, the numbered and lettered steps in my summary of Owens' argument address more or less the same points as the corresponding numbered and lettered steps in my summary of Lonergan's argument. Second, the numbered steps are related to the lettered steps as premises are related to conclusions. What this means is that, if my logic is correct, the really significant steps are the numbered ones. The lettered steps simply make explicit what the numbered steps imply. Third, the final steps of each summary – the respective *Conclusions C* – are verbally identical. This is my way of highlighting that Owens and Lonergan, both of whom identify themselves as "Thomist realists," *agree* that one's careful acts of *apparent* knowing are indeed acts of *genuine* knowing. Nonetheless, the meaning of any conclusion is a matter not just of its words but of the premises that it expresses. And since Owens and Lonergan arrive at their ultimate conclusions via importantly different premises, the meanings of those verbally identical conclusions are importantly different. To pin down *precisely how* they are different, we must examine and compare the respective premises on which they depend. Fourth, the steps are expressed in first-person terms. This is my way of emphasizing that both Owens and Lonergan see themselves not as elaborating an *abstract theoretical hypothesis* but rather as providing a *concrete operational description*. The steps are cast not in terms of "a person" or "the subject" but rather of "I" and "me." That is to say, they purport to articulate certain features of the concrete cognitional process in which you and I experience ourselves as being engaged. For each of the steps that I will now explicate, checking their accuracy will at root be a matter of comparing them not to what we have read in books by other authors, but rather to what we discover when we carefully read the book of ourselves.

Now let me comment in more detail, first on Owens' argument and then on Lonergan's.

On Owens' analysis, (1) the *culminating act* I experience myself performing whenever I APPARENTLY come to know a particular thing first-hand is *judgmentally intuiting* a particular intelligible content. But (2) the expression *"judgmentally intuiting"* means *intellectually apprehending* a particular intelligible content's *concrete actual synthesizing* as *immediately given in the context of sense-experience.* That is to say, I "intellectually see" and thus cognitionally grasp a concrete dynamic factor that both integrates the various facets of an intelligible content and actualizes them. Hence, (A) the *culminating act* I experience myself performing whenever I APPARENTLY come to know a particular thing first-hand is *intellectually apprehending* and thus *cognitionally manifesting* a particular intelligible content's *concrete actual synthesizing* as *immediately given in the context of sense-experience.*

Next, Owens (3) identifies the particular intelligible content's *concrete actual synthesizing* with the *culminating component* of the thing's *genuine reality.* In other words, the thing's "genuine reality" consists of the diverse facets of an intelligible content precisely as integrated and actualized by the concrete dynamic factor that I intellectually apprehend as immediately given. And from this it follows that (B) the *culminating act* I experience myself performing whenever I APPARENTLY come to know a particular thing first-hand is *intellectually apprehending* and thus *cognitionally manifesting the culminating component* of a particular thing's *genuine reality* as *immediately given in the context of sense-experience.*

Finally, Owens (4) identifies *cognitionally manifesting the culminating component* of a particular thing's *genuine reality* as *immediately given in the context of sense-experience* with the basic meaning of *"an act of genuine knowing."* For it seems obvious enough that an act of genuine knowing is nothing other than an act that discloses something of genuine reality. And this leads to Owens' final conclusion, namely, that (C) the *culminating act* I experience myself performing whenever I APPARENTLY come to know a particular thing first-hand is *an act of genuine knowing.*

Now let me turn to Lonergan's account. On his analysis, (1) the *culminating act* I experience myself performing whenever I APPARENTLY come to know a particular thing first-hand is *reasonably affirming* a particular intelligible content. Now (2) the expression "reasonably affirming" denotes an activity that proceeds within a primordial horizon. That primordial horizon is grounded in the very structure of my concrete subjectivity; and it is dynamically projected as encompassing the anticipated goal of my natural, radically unrestricted yearning to know whatever is intrinsically knowable – and to know and possess whatever is intrinsically lovable. Proceeding within that horizon, and moved by sufficient evidence, I posit a particular intelligible content as part of the total goal for which I yearn, I assert and thus know the particular content as partially satisfying my unrestricted cognitional and affective intending. Hence, (A) the *culminating act* I experience myself performing whenever I APPARENTLY come to know a particular thing first-hand is positing and thus cognitionally manifesting a particular intelligible content as *part of the total goal* that by nature I cognitionally (and affectively) intend.

Next, Lonergan (3) identifies the *total goal that by nature I cognitionally (and affectively) intend* with *the totality of genuine reality*. That is to say, "genuine reality" is pinned down operationally as what I primordially yearn to know and possess; and "the totality of genuine reality" is pinned down operationally as the totality of what I primordially yearn to known and possess. From this it follows that (B) the *culminating act* I experience myself performing whenever I APPARENTLY come to know a particular thing first-hand is *positing* and thus *cognitionally manifesting* a particular intelligible content as *part of the totality of genuine reality*.

Finally, Lonergan (4) identifies *cognitionally manifesting* a particular intelligible content as *part of the totality of genuine reality* with the basic meaning of *"an act of genuine knowing."* For it seems clear enough that an act of genuine knowing is nothing other than an act that discloses something of genuine reality. And this leads to Lonergan's final conclusion, namely, that (C) the *culminating act* I experience myself performing whenever I APPARENTLY come to know a particular thing first-hand is *an act of genuine knowing*.

What is the key point of comparison between these opposed accounts of my process of genuine knowing, accounts that both Owens and Lonergan – when wearing their caps as historians of philosophy – contend were maintained at least implicitly by Thomas Aquinas? I would say that the key difference is that between the respective first premises (with their meanings amplified by the respective second premises). In Owens' view, careful self-study discloses my judgmental intuition of a concrete, dynamic, synthesizing and actualizing component of this or that particular thing, a factor that Owens subsequently identifies with the culminating component of the thing's genuine reality. In Lonergan's view, by contrast, careful self-study discloses no such judgmental intuition. What it does disclose, however, is the primordial cognitional and affective yearning that is a constitutive feature of my concrete subjectivity. The total goal of this yearning stands to posited particular contents as anticipated total satisfaction stands to achieved partial satisfactions – and, in Lonergan's subsequent identification, as the intended totality of genuine reality stands to the particular realities that I actually know and love.

Is Owens' account the more accurate, or is Lonergan's the more accurate, or are both of them importantly mistaken? That of course is the sixty-four-dollar question. And while the findings of my own extended self-study decisively move me to answer that question with a nod to Lonergan's account, it remains that I cannot answer it for you. If I might reiterate an earlier point, what is fundamentally at issue here are not competing *abstract theories* of *"the human subject"* but competing *concrete descriptions* of *certain conscious processes of you and me*; and each of us can decide between those concrete descriptions only through personal research in the laboratory of ourselves.

Still, if I cannot resolve the issue for you, perhaps I can conclude by clarifying it just a little more. Specifically, let me relate the issue explicitly to "limina," the topic of our symposium. A moment ago I suggested that the key difference between Owens' account and Lonergan's account is whether the most fundamental element of my cognitional process is a *judgmental intuiting* of what makes a particular thing genuinely real, or a *primordial intending* of the totality of genuine reality. Now, I have entitled my presentation, "Affirming a Limit and Transcending It"; and I intended that title to highlight the way in which persons who favor a Lonergan-type view purport to meet the most common objection levelled against them by persons who favor an Owens-type view.

The objection has a variety of forms, but all of them boil down to something like this: It is plainly wrong-headed to argue that the most fundamental way to characterize reality is in terms of the total goal of my desire to know and love, for on such an approach one is specifying reality in terms of the mind. But I cannot presume to assert ahead of time that what is in my mind corresponds to what is outside my mind, namely, reality! It is illegitimate to suppose that the total goal of my yearning encompasses, even if just in anticipatory fashion, everything that is. Might there not be at least some range of reality that lies beyond the horizon of my primordial yearning?

The response to this objection has two steps. The first step is to note that the objection has a presupposition, namely, that my *primordial yearning* is something like seeing, the *total goal* of my primordial yearning is like everything that stands within a visual field, and the *horizon* of my primordial yearning is like a high wall around that field. On the basis of that presupposition, it makes perfect sense to be suspicious of the claim that all of reality falls within my horizon; for the fact that my vision is limited by a wall does not exclude the possibility that there might be all sorts of things beyond the wall.

The second step of the response is to reject the objection's "visual" presupposition. My *primordial yearning* is not analogous to seeing – or, indeed, to any other kind of sensing. Rather, it is the radical dynamism of my spirit – the spiritual hunger to which Aristotle alludes when (in the first line of his *Metaphysics*) he asserts that all humans by nature desire to know, to which Augustine alludes when (in the first paragraph his *Confessions*) he observes that our hearts are restless until they rest in God, to which Aquinas alludes when (throughout Book One of his *Summa contra gentiles*) he speaks of our natural desire to know God's essence, to which Kant alludes when (in his *Kritik der praktischen Vernunft*) he describes our fundamental orientation to know and choose what is morally good, to which Joseph Maréchal alludes when (in *Le Point de départ de la métaphysique*) he discusses the natural finality of the human intellect.[2] And the *total goal* of my primordial yearning is not analogous to everything standing within a visual field, with the field's *horizon* like a wall around it. Rather, the total goal of my primordial yearning is unrestricted, infinite, unbounded, not limited by any horizon beyond which there might be more. Whenever I attempt to *affirm* some limit as ultimate, I inevitably *transcend* that limit; for the ultimate limit I would affirm is always surpassed by the unrestricted yearning that my every act of affirmation operationally presupposes. In other words, when all I see is what lies within a visual field, I cannot say with confidence that nothing lies beyond the limit of that field. But when all I yearn for is what lies within an unrestricted field, then by anticipation (if not yet by actual achievement) I transcend every limit. I can say with utter confidence that nothing lies beyond what I yearn for, since I yearn for everything. It is wholly legitimate, indeed obligatory, to identify the totality of reality with the total goal of my yearning, for beyond what I yearn for there is absolutely nothing at all.

WORKS CITED

Lonergan, Bernard, "The Concept of *Verbum* in the Writings of St. Thomas Aquinas," *Theological Studies* 7(1946) 349-92; 8(1947) 35-79, 404-44; 10(1949) 3-40, 359-93 [*Verbum: Word and Idea in Aquinas*, Notre Dame: University of Notre Dame Press, 1967; second edition, *Collected Works of Bernard Lonergan*, vol. 2, Toronto: University of Toronto Press, 1997].

---

[2] The point of these examples is to illustrate widespread recognition of a primordial dynamism of the human spirit, not to suggest that all the thinkers mentioned envision that dynamism's goal in exactly the same way.

Lonergan, Bernard, *Insight: A Study of Human Understanding*, London: Longmans, Green, 1957 [fifth edition, *Collected Works of Bernard Lonergan*, vol. 3, Toronto: University of Toronto Press, 1992].

Lonergan, Bernard, *Method in Theology*, London: Darton, Longman & Todd; New York: Herder and Herder, 1972.

Owens, Joseph, *An Elementary Christian Metaphysics*, Milwaukee: Bruce, 1963.

Owens, Joseph, *An Interpretation of Existence*, Milwaukee: Bruce, 1968.

CAROLINE TOLTON

BOUNDING ORTHODOXY:
MNEMONIC IMAGES IN THE SERMONS
OF PETER CHRYSOLOGUS

ABSTRACT. Peter Chrysologus, Bishop of Ravenna 430-450 C.E., braced his congregation against invading Arian beliefs by planting in his hearers' minds a memory of orthodox Christian subject matter. This paper will focus on Peter's portrayal of Mary's womb, a liminal space that he describes in vivid detail to safeguard the doctrine of Mary's perpetual virginity.

In the post-Ephesian and pre-Chalcedonian period of Peter Chrysologus' episcopate (c. 430-450 C.E.), Christology was at the forefront of religious debate throughout the Roman empire. But in the empire's western capital, the Ravennese confronted their own set of questions surrounding Christ's identity. The Gothic invasions of the fifth century had introduced into Ravenna an Arian Christology that Peter perceived as negating both the doctrines of Christ's divine nature and Mary's perpetual virginity (Benericetti 1995: 47).[1] The booming commercial capital had also attracted a large Jewish population who also rejected these doctrines (Sottocornola 1973: 52). One also imagines that even some non-Arian Christians refuted Mary's perpetual virginity – a notion opposed in late fourth-century Rome by Helvidius who affirmed that after Mary gave birth to Christ (*post partum*) she led a normal married life and was a model of motherhood (Jouassard, 1944: 145). Simi-

---

[1] Though 'Latin Arianism' has traditionally been viewed as not denying the Virgin birth (Simonetti 1967: 725), Peter folded the Nestorian debate over Mary as Theotokos into Arianism, so that he perceived one heresy, Arianism, which denied that Mary bore the Son of God.

Limina: Thresholds and Borders - A St. Michael's College Symposium
Joseph Goering, Francesco Guardiani, Giulio Silano eds. Ottawa: Legas, 2005

larly, the monk Jovinian had stridently argued against Mary's virginity both during birth (*in partu*) and thereafter (*post partum*). [2]

Peter Chrysologus preached a calculated defense against these denials of Christ's divine nature and Mary's perpetual virginity. Whereas the Arians appealed to those biblical passages that describe Christ's human experiences – his hunger, thirst, sleep, fear, and suffering – Peter's sermons pay scant attention to these. Rather, they expound upon the mysteries of Christ's life that point to his divinity, namely, his birth and resurrection. In particular, Peter develops the Marian theme at the service of the Christological one to demonstrate Christ's divinity from the moment of his conception in Mary's womb. By Peter's logic, "since a virgin conceives, the seed is not terrestrial, but celestial. A virgin gives birth, but God receives a son."[3] That which enters and leaves the virginal womb without breaking its seal must be divine.[4] Thus, according to Peter's Christology, the Virgin birth is the bedrock of Christ's divinity.

But how was Peter to explain convincingly an event that defies all logical plausibility? Peter himself describes the Virgin birth as an "ineffable mystery" that one should merely believe rather than discuss.[5] It is the aim of this paper to explain the mnemonic rhetorical strategy that Peter uses for cognitive effect. Peter circumvents the difficulty of explaining the mechanism of a virginal conception and birth by capturing the implausible doctrine in verbal pictures from the Bible. This coupling of an idea with a mental image is a rhetorical technique prescribed in

---

[2] Helvidius and Jovinian would not also have denied Christ's divine nature, but they recognized the direct link between the doctrine of the Virgin birth and Christ's divinity. They pointed to the latent Docetism in a doctrine that asserts that Christ suddenly appeared from the womb of Mary – without a normal birth, Jesus could not be human. To their minds, the Virgin birth emphasized Christ's divine nature too much.

[3] 144,51-53: *Videtis quia quod concipit virgo non terrenum germen est, sed caeleste. Virgo peperit, sed deus suscepit filium,.* See too 148,4-7: Quando *concipit virgo, virgo partit, manet virgo, non est consuetudo, sed signum; non est ratio, sed virtus; auctor est, non natura; non est commune, sed solum; divinum est, non humanum.* All references to Peter are from *CCL*, 24B. Translations from the Latin are mine unless otherwise indicated. The Latin will appear in the footnote with sermon and verse number.

[4] 142,51-53: "He who enters and leaves and leaves no trace of his entering and leaving is a divine dweller, not human. And he who preserves her virgin in her conception, and leaves her virgin in her birth, is not a terrestrial man, but a celestial one." (*Qui ingreditur et egreditur, et introitus sui et exitus sui nulla vestigia relinquit, divinus habitator est, non humanus. Et qui conceptu suo virginem servat, et ortu suo relinquit virginem, non terrenus homo est, sed caelestis.*)

[5] 140ter,7-10: *Non enim, fratres, ineffabile divine generationis contendimus aperire mysterium, sed nostrae salutis magnum et mirabile gestimus gaudium nuntiare..*; for, 143,3-4: *Debetur quidem vobis natalitius sermo, sed ineffabile nativitatis dominicae sacramentum credere magis convenit quam referre.*

ancient sources on the art of memory.[6] Peter drew from these principles of the mnemotechnical craft in order to implant within his hearers the Christian images with which they would think. By associating the Virgin birth with key images of enclosure and fecundity, Peter made the doctrine conceivable and, therefore, plausible.

This paper will present two examples of Peter's use of mnemonic imagery: first, the closed garden and sealed fountain from Song of Songs 4:12; and second, biblical water imagery. Both sets of images relate to Mary's virginal maternity. These examples will be followed later in the paper by an analysis of a more extensive use of topographical imagery which takes the form of a virtual voyage into Mary's womb.

Peter argued his case for Mary's perpetual virginity exegetically, sealing the virginity of Mary in the image of the *hortus clausus, fons signatus* (closed garden, sealed fountain) of Song of Songs 4:12.[7] In Sermon 145, he couples Psalm 109:1 ("The Lord said to my Lord: sit at my right hand") with Psalm 131:11 ("from the fruit of your womb") to imply that the descendant of David already sits at the right hand of God.[8] Then, by a rhetorical sleight of hand that specifies that the "womb" (*ventris*) in *de fructu ventris tui* is truly Mary's "*utero*," Peter appropriates Psalm 131 in a Marian sense to show that the descendant of David sitting at the right of God is in fact her divine offspring. He proceeds to explain Mary's virginity *in partu* and *post partum* with the governing metaphor of Mary's womb as an edifice:

> the celestial host, the supernal inhabitant, so descended into the hospitality of the uterus as not to know the gates of the body, and he so departed from the little abode of the womb that the virginal door would not be harmed.[9]

Mary's virginity, he concludes, is in fulfillment of Song of Songs 4:12, "My spouse is a garden enclosed, a sealed fountain." The images of a closed garden and of a sealed fountain act as a thematic montage of the

---

[6] Memory was added as the fourth part of rhetoric in the 3rd c. B.C. E. by the Stoics: Invention, Disposition, Style, Memory, Delivery (Kennedy 1994: 6).

[7]145,53-58: *'Ioseph, fili David.' Tali voce ad David prolata fuerat promissio dei patris: 'Iuravit dominus David veritatem, et non frustrabitur eum : de fructu ventris tui ponam super sedem meam.'* [Ps. 131.11] *Quod factum quidem tale tali gloriatur in cantico : 'Dixit dominus domino meo : sede a dextris meis.'* [Ps. 109.1] *'De fructu ventris tui.'* [Ps. 131.11] *Bene 'de fructu ventris tui,' bene de utero, quia caelestis hospes, supernus habitator, sic in uteri descendit hospitium, ut corporis claustra nesciret ; sic de habitaculo ventris exiit, ut virginalis ianua non pateret, et impleretur illud, quod cantatur in Cantico Canticorum : 'Sponsa mea hortus clausus, fons signatus.'* [Cant. 4:12]

[8] 145,52-53: *'Dixit dominus domino meo : sede a dextris meis.' 'De fructu ventris tui.'*

[9] 145,53-58: *quia caelestis hospes, supernus habitator, sic in uteri descendit hospitium, ut corporis claustra nesciret; sic de habitaculo ventris exiit, ut virginalis ianua non pateret.*

miraculous conception and birth. Like flashcards, the images function mnemonically so that the picture calls to mind the doctrine, and vice versa. The correlation between the image and the idea creates a lasting resonance in both. The doctrine of the Virgin birth absorbs the suggestion of closed fecundity while Marian overtones now reverberate back in the biblical verse.

In *De Oratore*, Cicero discusses the means by which one renders the inconceivable conceivable. This topic arises in his section on memory (2.86.350-2.88.360) because, as Mary Carruthers has aptly demonstrated, the art of memory belonged to the arts of thinking (Carruthers 1998: 9). To the ancients, memoria was the "store-house of invention" ("thesaurus inventorum," *Rhet. ad Her.* 3.16.28), "guardian of all the parts of rhetoric" ("*omnium partium custodem rhetoricae*," ibid.), and the "treasury of eloquence" ("*thesaurus eloquentiae*," Quintilian, Inst. orat., 11.2.1). It housed an inventory of images from which all thinking, all imagining, all creativity arose. Inconceivable notions were those which the thinker could not picture. Cicero refers to them as res caecas, things hidden from the mental view of the thinker (*De orat.* 2.87.357). For the thinker to "picture" them, they must be given some "figure, image or shape" (*De orat.* 2.87.357). Figuration brings an obscure notion into the visual field of the thinker so that, in Cicero's words, "we keep hold of as it were by an act of sight things that we can scarcely embrace by an act of thought" (2.87.358).[10] Embodying the inconceivable in an image makes it perceivable and conceivable.

Peter Chrysologus, well trained in classical rhetoric, would have incorporated into his oratorical practice Cicero's teaching (or at least the rhetorical tradition dependent on Cicero) that the sense of sight forms the keenest pictures in the mind (*De Orat.*, 2.87.357). Peter's biblical typologies allowed his audience to "apprehend thoughts by means of images" (*De Orat.*, 2.88.359) and thus come to share their preacher's 'view' of orthodox doctrine. He brought the otherwise unimaginable Virgin birth into focus before his audience through the lens of biblical representation. The logically inexplicable doctrine could thus be apprehended metaphorically through the image of the "closed garden" and "sealed fountain" of Song of Songs 4:12.

Key to ancient mnemotechnique was the division of material to be memorized into discrete, manageable sections (*Inst. Orat.* 11.2.36). Each section of an oration would be encapsulated in one symbol; an anchor,

---

[10] ...*ut ea quae cogitando complecti vix possemus intuendo quasi teneremus.*

for example, might trigger the recall of a discourse on a naval battle. The student of rhetoric was taught to find a representation that would "give shape to a complete thought by an image consisting of a single word." Puns and synecdoche could also prompt memory (Cicero, *De orat.* 2.87.358). Quintilian supplements Cicero's advice, suggesting that "symbols acquire even more binding force when people transfer memory from some similar object to the item which has to be remembered" (*Inst. orat.* 11.2.30). In order to remember the name Cicero, for instance, the student might take recourse to the root meaning of the word, *cicer*, and picture a chickpea; or, to remember the name Aurelius, the student would think of an *auris*, ear (*Inst. orat.* 11.2.31). One thus begins with the familiar and moves to the unfamiliar object of memory.

Peter Chrysologus employs just this strategy. But rather than ask his hearers to devise their own associative images for Christian doctrine, Peter encapsulates doctrine in images for them. In Sermon 146 he etymologizes Mary's name in its homonym, *Maria*, "seas": he asks, *"Maria mater vocatur; et quando non Maria mater?"* ("Mary was the name of the mother; and when were the seas/Mary not a mother?"). [11] He finds biblical warrant for his etymology in the description of the seas of Genesis 1:10, which he promptly cites: "The gathering together of the waters, he called seas (*Maria*)." Peter tightly interweaves biblical water images with Mary's name to illustrate that her virginal maternity has always been a historical force. The seas of Genesis 1:10 metamorphose into the Red Sea of Exodus 14:15-31 that "conceives in its one womb (*concepit uno utero*) the people fleeing from Egypt that they might emerge as a heavenly offspring reborn into a new creation."[12] The pun acquires further resonance in *Maria*, sister of Aaron, who "emerges" from the conceiving seas as a "life-bearing wave" (*unda genetrix*) that sends her people into the light (Ex. 15:20-21).[13] Peter then portrays all of the water references thus

---

[11] 146,71. Where might the pun on Mary's name as '*mare*' have begun? This is the earliest attestation I have come across. Peter's Marian appropriation of Genesis 1:10 is new; the verse appears seventeen times in the writings of Origen and Ambrose but unrelated to Mary.

[12] 146,72-74: *Nonne haec exeuntem de Aegypto populum concepit uno utero, ut emergeret caelestis in novam creaturam renata progenies?* The verbs *exeo, emergo, concipio, renascor*, the synecdochic personification of the sea as *uno utero*, and the characterization of the Crossing of the Red Sea as the birth of a *progenies*, reborn into a *nova creatura*, are all products of Peter "reading backwards" into the biblical text in order to accentuate its typological relevance to the argument that Mary was always a mother.

[13] 146,75-7: *Et ut semper Maria humanae praevia sit salutis, populum, quem unda genetrix misit in lucem, ipsa divino praecessit in cantico.*

far as the baptismal sea of 1 Corinthians 10:1-2: "Our fathers were baptized in the sea (*in mari*)."[14] The pun culminates in *Maria*'s song: "Mary...sister of Aaron, lifting a tambourine in her hand said: 'Let us sing to the Lord, for he is gloriously magnified.'"[15]

The superimposed imagery illustrates the symbolic inner logic Peter wishes his hearers – turned spectators – to see between Genesis 1:10, Exodus 14:15-31, 1 Corinthians 10:1-2, and Exodus 15:20-21. This inner logic is summarized in one symbol (*signum*), *Maria*, that functions mnemonically to call to mind the entire subject-matter (*res*) of Mary's virginal maternity. Indeed, Peter's conclusion to this passage indicates that he feels he has succeeded in this task:

> This name is related to prophecy and salutary to those reborn. It is the mark (*insigne*) of virginity, the glory of purity, the indication (*indicium*) of chastity, the sacrificial gift of God, the height of hospitality, the sum total (*collegium*) of sanctity. Rightly, therefore, is the motherly name that of the mother of Christ.[16]

Peter treats the name Maria as a distinguishable "mark" (*insigne*), like the mnemonic images one chooses to represent long passages of speech (*Inst. orat.* 11.2.22). The name *Maria* is the "sum total" or "association" (*collegium*) of all the epithets Peter has employed to portray her virginal maternity. In the process of re-collection, Mary thus emerges as a closed garden, a sealed fountain, and a life-bearing wave swelling with virginal fecundity. Peter has superimposed passages of biblical text onto Mary, and at the same time projected her body into the very same verses of Scripture. Peter's auditors will hereafter read the Old and New Testaments synchronically: Song of Songs 4:12 evokes Mary's closed womb, and the creation waters of Genesis, the Red Sea, and baptism itself call to mind the Virgin birth. The images combine to create an image of Mary as *ecclesia*, parting her virginal gate as the new Christological crea-

---

[14] 146,74-75: *Iuxta illud apostoli: 'Patres in mari baptizati sunt.'* Whereas Paul argues in 1 Corinthians 10:1-2 from the Red Sea to baptism, Peter interposes Mary into the argument: Red Sea – Mary - baptism.

[15] 146,75-79: *'Maria,' inquit, 'soror Aaron, sumens tympanum in manu sua dixit : Cantemus domino, gloriose enim honorificatus est.'* Peter establishes the parallel between Mary, sister of Aaron, who gives birth to the freed Israelites, and the virgin Mary who gives birth to a Christian creation.

[16] 146,79-83: *Nomen hoc prophetiae germanum, hoc renascentibus salutare, hoc virginitatis insigne, hoc pudicitiae decus, hoc indicium castitatis, hoc dei sacrificium, hoc hospitalitatis virtus, hoc collegium sanctitatis. Merito ergo, merito Christi nomen est hoc maternum.*

tion pours forth.[17] The biblical backdrop upon which Mary is projected defines her image, just as she, in turn, illuminates it. Peter Chrysologus has thus encompassed in her name "the record of an entire matter by one notation, a single image," as advised in the anonymous *Rhetorica ad Herennium*.[18]

Peter relied on images like the polyvalent image of *Maria* (i.e., as "seas"), or the "closed garden, sealed fountain" of Song of Songs, to insinuate themselves into his hearers' consciousness. In Sermon 98, he describes his understanding of the rhetorical effect of the image on the hearer in the metaphor of the mustard seed (Carruthers 1998: 64):

> if we would only sow this grain of the mustard seed in our chest in such a way that it will grow into a great tree of knowledge, and to the full extent of our consciousness be raised toward the sky, that it will spread out into all the branches of the sciences, that it will burn our tingling mouths with the pungent taste of its seed! Thus it will burn for us with all the fire of its seed, and break into flame in our heart.[19]

"*Maria*," the "*hortus clausus*" and the "*fons signatus*," act as shorthand images for a more expansive idea of virginal maternity. This "brief but plentiful" (*brevis et copis*) property of Peter's imagery is the mainstay of the memory for subject-matter (*memoria rerum*) described in the art of memory (Carruthers 1998: 64); the image is the *signum* that points to the *res*, the complex idea encapsulated in a single, simple notation. Carruthers explains that the images one possessed were considered the "ethical templates, the predispositions and even the moods, for virtually all subsequent ethical, religious, cultural and intellectual activity" (Carruthers 1998:90). Sharing the same common store of memories (*res memorabiles*) constructed "above all else... the web of a community or commonality"(Carruthers 1998:44). Evidently, Peter relied on the power of the images one possesses to shape individual character. He planted images that, like the mustard seed, took root and branched out along the cognitive pathways of his hearers into one tree of Christian knowledge.

---

[17] Of course, this is the very opposite image to *virginitas in partu*, but often that which Peter negates is that to which he inevitably points. This is in keeping with Cameron's observation that the treatises and sermons on the Virgin that began to emerge in the late fourth century "worked by metaphor and paradox, and... boldly exploited the very imagery it was ostensibly denying" (Cameron 1991: 170).

[18] *Rhet. ad Her.*, 3.20.33: *Rei totius memoriam saepe una nota et imagine simplici conprehendimus.*

[19] 98, 28-33: *si modo hoc granum sinapis nos sic nostris seminemus in pectore, ut intelligentiae magnam nobis in arborem crescat, et sensus altitudine tota levetur ad caelum, ac totum scientiarum diffundatur in ramos, atque ita ora nostra ferventia vivido fructus sui sapore succendat, et ita igne seminis sui toto nobis ardeat, flammetur in pectore.*

My third and final example of Peter's use of topographical images represents a more elaborate development of his mnemonic art, a virtual voyage into Mary's womb. Peter used the rhetorical device of *ekphrasis*, a technique of vivid description whose rhetorical goal is "to recreate for the listener the effect of its subject on the viewer, who is the speaker" (James-Webb 1991: 9). As Margaret Mitchell observes in *The Heavenly Trumpet*, what was "most distinctive about the *ekphrasis* was its foremost persuasive purpose" (Mitchell 2000: 103). It was persuasive because it implanted in people's minds detailed pictures that matched the imagination of the audience to that of the speaker. This rhetorical mode was certainly in the interest of the didactic Christian preacher.

In the following *ekphrastic* picture of Mary's womb, Peter casts the relationship of the observer to Mary in the metaphor of a journey. He uses the regal itinerary of Song of Songs, in which the king leads his bride into the private nuptial chamber, to portray to his audience the inaccessibility of the Virgin birth:

> How secret are the sleeping quarters of a king! With what reverence, with what trembling should the space be treated where the very power of the ruler rests! This place shall open and permit access to no stranger, no impure person, and no unfaithful. How clean, how chaste, how faithful are the services to be awaited there! This is made clear by the marks of a royal palace. What cheap or unworthy person would approach these palace doors? Certainly no one is admitted to the nuptial bed of the spouse unless sufficiently close, intimate, of good conscience, of laudable reputation, and of acceptable life. In truth, he [the ruler] receives into the inner chamber only that one virgin herself; she alone, virginity intact, is accepted there.[20]

Peter's speech leaves room for his hearers to feel some small spark of curiosity, some hope that they are perhaps the exception to the statement that "no one is admitted." The speech invites the auditor to ask: am I *satis proximus, intimus, bonae conscientiae, laudabilis famae* and *probabilis vitae* to gain access *ad thalamum sponsi*? Or am I merely *extraneo, inmundo,* and *infideli*? With his imperative *cogita*, Peter guides his audience into a spiritual contemplation at the end of which his hearers should realize

---

[20] 141,3-12: *Quantum secretum cubiculi sit regalis, quali reverentia, quo tremore locus habeatur, ubi ipsa principis requiescit potestas; quam nulli extraneo, inmundo nemini, nulli infideli pateat illuc et permittatur accessus; quam munda, quam casta, quam fidelia ibidem praestolentur obsequia, imperialis aulae manifestis docetur insignibus. Quis ad ipsas palatii fores vilis, quis propinquat indignus? Certe ad thalamum sponsi nisi satis proximus, nisi satis intimus, nisi bonae conscientiae, nisi laudabilis famae, nisi probabilis vitae, nullus admittitur. Intra thalamum vero ipsum virginem capit solam, suscipitur sola virginitas inlibata.*

their complete unworthiness in approaching the womb. On this virtual voyage, the observer is invited to come through to (*pervenire*) the bedroom of Christ's breast, where the supernal king and the entirety of divine majesty rest. He is invited to give heed (*adtendere*) with human eyes and bodily senses to the virginal conception, to gaze (*intueri*) at the very hands of God constructing for himself Christ's body within her womb, and, thus gazing, to lay bare (*conspectibus...nudare mysterium*) the mystery hidden through the ages, in order to reveal for himself (*revelare tibi*) the sacrament invisible to the very angels, and, thereby, to preside over the celestial production in Mary's womb (*caelesti fabricae praesidere*).[21] As head of the celestial warehouse, the itinerant must assist God in figuring out...

> ...how God will enter the inner part of her closed flesh; how he will paint the outlines of a holy body in that venerable uterus without the virgin's awareness; how, without her sensation of the conception, he will have solidified the bones that will abide for ages, just as he will have produced the true form of man outside the order of human generation; how without the care of flesh he will assume the whole truth of flesh, by reason of which, beyond nature, he will have taken up the whole quality of our nature.[22]

At the inception of the contemplation, Peter asked his hearers to "estimate who you are, how great you are, what kind of person you are." [23] By the end of the contemplation, after the itinerant has found himself in charge of God's celestial warehouse, Peter no doubt expects his point to be well made: do not ask how it is done, just admire!

Ultimately, the meditation serves as a visual metric against which the individual gauges his worthiness to discuss the virgin birth. Though Peter expresses the relationship of the observer to Mary in the journey

[21] 141,13-30: *Unde, homo, his admonitus exemplis aestima quis sis, quantus sis, et tunc demum cogita utrum possis dominicae nativitatis penetrare secretum; utrum merearis ad illius pectoris cubiculum pervenire, ubi tota superni regis, tota divinitatis requiescit maiestas; utrum debeas humanis oculis, corporeis sensibus, conceptum virginis temerarius discussor adtendere; utrum possis ipsas dei manus operantes sanctum sibi corporis templum intra alveum genetricis audax et curiosus arbiter intueri, conspectibus tuis absconditum saeculis nudare mysterium, revelare tibi ipsis angelis invisibile sacramentum, et ita caelesti fabricae praesidere...*

[22] 141,13-30....*.et ita caelesti fabricae praesidere, ut deprehendas liquido tu quomodo deus penetrale clausae carnis intraverit, quemadmodum sacri corporis in illo venerabili utero praeter virginis conscientiam liniamenta pinxerit, quomodo praeter concipientis sensum mansura saeculis ossa solidaverit, qualiter praeter hominis ordinem hominis veram produxerit formam, quemadmodum praeter carnis sollicitudinem totam carnis adsumpserit veritatem, qua ratione praeter naturam naturae nostrae integram susceperit qualitatem.*

[23] 141,13-14: *aestima quis sis, quantus sis, qualis sis.*

metaphor, it is a journey that the itinerant should not make, because no one is worthy to break through to Christ's innermost quarters. In Peter's sermons on the Nativity, there is no prayer for the itinerant to become worthy of the Spouse, Word, Wisdom, Jesus Christ, as there is, for instance, at the end of Origen's *Homeliae in Canticum Canticorum* (2.13).[24] No matter how detailed the mystical map into Mary that Peter proffers, it is an *invitation au "non"-voyage*:[25] map in hand, the Christian should not presume to use it. The scene of Mary's womb serves, rather, as the visual equivalent of a stop sign. Peter's *ekphrastic* description is designed to silence discussion on the subject.

Peter defines the orthodox Christian as one who couples the correct meaning with the obscure notion to make the latter spark with its true meaning:[26]

> Fire remains cold in flint and lies dormant in steel. However, fire is brought to flame through the collision of stone and flint. Similarly, an obscure word glows through the collision of the word with its meaning. Surely, if there were no mystical meanings, there would remain no distinction between the infidel and the faithful and between the pious and the impious.[27]

Peter struck steel to flint in his sermons as he clarified obscure doctrines in biblical images. Like all good rhetoricians, Peter was, above all, practical; in order to help his audience believe correct doctrine, he let them see it. Peter's exegetical genius lay in his persuasive rhetorical strategy to make opaque doctrine perceivable and therefore conceivable. He strove to make the soteriological landmarks of the Bible the topographical coordinates of his hearers' imagination. These doctrinally orthodox coordinates formed the Christian matrix within which all cogitation was bounded. He thus projected the topological axes of orthodoxy upon the Ravennese and braced them for contact with invading Arian beliefs.

---

[24] *Quapropter consurgentes deprecemur Deum, ut digni efficiamur sponso, sermone, sapientia, Christo Iesu, 'cui est gloris et imperium in saecula saeculorum. Amen !'*

[25] Baudelaire's famous poem "L'Invitation au voyage" can be found in *Les Fleurs du mal* (1857).

[26] The 'stumbling block' of the notion of a 'virgin mother' causes the heretic to fall, but coupled with correct meaning it propels the believer deeper into the mystery and the paradox. See Origen's hermeneutical implementation of *skandalon* in *On First Principles*.

[27] 96:6-10: *In lapide friget ignis, latet ignis in ferro, ipse tamen ignis ferri ac lapidis conlisione flammatur; sic obscurum verbum verbi ac sensus conlatione resplendet. Certe si mystica non essent, inter infidelem fidelemque. inter inpium atque pium discretio non maneret."* See Carruthers p. 45 for a short discussion of the passage.

WORKS CITED

Benericetti, Ruggero. *Il Cristo nei sermoni di s. Pier Crisologo*. Cesena: Centro Studi e Ricerche sulla Antica Provincia Ecclesiastica Ravennate,1995.

Cameron, Averil. *Christianity and the Rhetoric of Empire: The Development of Christian Discourse*. Berkeley/London: University of California Press, 1991.

Carruthers, Mary. *The Craft of Thought: Meditation, Rhetoric and the Making of Images 400-1200*. New York: University Press, 1998.

Cicero. *De Oratore*. Trans. E. W. Sutton. LCL 348. Cambridge: Harvard University Press, 1942.

[Cicero]. *Rhetorica ad Herennium*. Trans. H. Caplan. LCL 403. Cambridge: Harvard University Press, 1954.

James, Liz and Ruth Webb. "'To Understand Ultimate Things and Enter Secret Places': Ekphrasis and Art in Byzantium." *Art History* 14 (1991), 1-17.

Jouassard, G. "La Personnalité d'Helvidius." In *Mélanges J. Saunier*. Lyons: Faculté catholique, 1944.

Kennedy, George. *A New History of Classical Rhetoric*. Princeton: Princeton University Press, 1994.

Kochaniewicz, Boguslaw, OP. *La Vergine Maria nei sermoni di san Pietro Crisologo*. Dissertationes ad Lauream in Pontificia Facultate Theologica "Marianum" 77. Rome, 1998.

Mitchell, Margaret M. *The Heavenly Trumpet: John Chrysostom and the Art of Pauline Interpretation*. Tübingen: Mohr Siebeck, 2000.

Origène. *Homélies sur le Cantique des Cantiques*. Intro. and trans. Dom O. Rousseau. SC 37. Paris: Cerf, 1953.

Saint Peter Chrysologus: Selected Sermons; and Saint Valerian, Homilies. Trans. George E. Ganss. FC. New York: Father of the Church, 1953.

Petrus Chrysologus. *Sancti Petri Chrysologi Collectio sermonum a Felice Episcopo parata, sermonibus extravagantibus adiectis*. Ed. Alexandro Olivar. CCSL 24B. Tournhout: Brepols, 1982.

Quintilian. The Orator's Education. Trans. Donald A. Russell. LCL 494. Cambridge: Harvard University Press, 2001.

Simonetti, M. "Arianesimo latino." *Studi medievali* 8 (1967): 663-744.

Sottocornola, Franco. *L'Anno liturgico nei sermoni di Pietro Crisologo: Ricerca storico-critica sulla liturgia di Ravenna antica*. Cesena: Centro studi e ricerche sulla antica provincia ecclesiastica ravennate, 1973.

Elmar J. Kremer

Was Descartes the Father of Modern Philosophy?

ABSTRACT. Descartes's philosophical work did not determine the nature of the philosophy to which it gave rise. This is verified in the debate between Antoine Arnauld and Nicolas Malebranche, the two leading Cartesians of the seventeenth century. I will concentrate on two topics in the debate: scepticism and the relation between faith and reason.

Was Descartes "The Father of Modern Philosophy"?[1] To be sure, he marked the beginning of a new era of philosophy, and his work had a profound influence on philosophy for at least a century after his death in 1650. Between father and offspring, however, there is a likeness of kind, and it is not clear that such a likeness obtains between Descartes's philosophy and the philosophy that is typical of the modern period. In this brief paper, I want to consider whether two philosophical themes of the Enlightenment were already present in Descartes: the tendency toward skepticism regarding the external world, and the dominance of reason over revelation as the basis of human belief.[2]

I shall look at Descartes from the point of view of the two leading Cartesians in the second half of the seventeenth-century, Antoine Ar-

---

[1] It is not easy to determine the origin of this title, so often bestowed upon Descartes. Hans-Peter Schütt cites Victor Cousin's use of the title in 1824, in the *Prospectus* for his new edition of Descartes's works. See Schütt's *Die Adoption des "Vaters der modernen Philosophie,"* Frankfurt am Main: Vittorio Klostermann, 1998, p. 87-8. My thanks to Dan Garber for referring me to this book.

[2] According to Peter Schouls, political considerations led Descartes sometimes to downplay what were in fact the seeds of the Enlightenment present in his work. Schouls says that the Enlightenment was the natural outcome of a "Cartesianism of the radical revolutionary kind--that promulgated by Descartes when he did not feel constrained to say less than he would through fear for the loss of personal safety and respect." Peter A. Schouls, "Arnauld and the Modern Mind," in Elmar J. Kremer, ed., *Interpreting Arnauld*, Toronto: University of Toronto Press, 1996, p. 45. See also Peter A. Schouls, *Descartes and the Enlightenment*, Kingston, Ont.: The McGill-Queen's University Press, 1989.

Limina: Thresholds and Borders - A St. Michael's College Symposium
Joseph Goering, Francesco Guardiani, Giulio Silano eds. Ottawa: Legas, 2005

nauld and Nicolas Malebranche. Malebranche and Arnauld engaged in a long written controversy, which lasted from 1680 to 1704 and was one of the most widely followed intellectual events of the *siècle des lumières*. They disagreed about a wide range of philosophical and theological questions, including the nature of ideas, the nature and extent of human knowledge, the relation between philosophy and theology, the problem of evil, and the compatibility of human freedom and divine providence.

They also disagreed about the meaning of Cartesian philosophy. Although they were both deeply influenced by Descartes, they offer sharply different interpretations of Descartes's philosophy. Arnauld saw in Malebranche a version of Cartesianism that would lead to the positions characteristic of the Enlightenment, in other words, to much of what we have come to think of as "modern philosophy." Arnauld himself offered a different interpretation, designed to make of Descartes's philosophy a support rather than an enemy of the Christian faith, and a useful tool for Christian theologians. This situation suggests that, at least with respect to the themes I am discussing, it may be misleading to say that Descartes was the Father of the Enlightenment. It may be that Descartes's philosophy was open to interpretations that pointed toward, and interpretations that pointed away from, the Enlightenment.

I: Arnauld's Interpretation of Methodic Doubt as a Pretend-Doubt

Arnauld is often taken to be an unadventurous follower of Descartes. For example, Nicholas Jolley, discussing Arnauld's Objections to Descartes's Meditations, says, "Unlike Hobbes or Gassendi, Arnauld was a sympathetic critic of Descartes' philosophy; his aim was to make the system more watertight. Arnauld in fact was a fairly orthodox Cartesian, and he became a champion of Descartes' philosophy, not merely against its outright enemies, but also against unorthodox interpreters such as Malebranche."[3] A more important witness is Leibniz, who said, in 1691, that Arnauld had been "in all ways for Descartes for a long time."[4]

But Jolley and Leibniz overlook two facts. First, in the *Fourth Objections*, Arnauld not only presents sharp objections to several of Descartes's arguments, but also expresses a certain wariness about the acceptability of Descartes's philosophy for Christian theologians. Second,

---

[3] Nicholas Jolley, "The reception of Descartes' philosophy," in John Cottingham, ed., *The Cambridge Companion to Descartes*, Cambridge: Cambridge University Press, 1992, p. 400-401.

[4] Quoted in R. C. Sleigh, Jr., *Leibniz and Arnauld, A Commentary on their Correspondence*, New Haven: Yale University Press, 1990. P. 31.

although Arnauld was an enthusiastic supporter of Descartes's physics and some of his metaphysics, he did not think highly of Descartes as a theologian. Thus, in a letter of uncertain date, Arnauld says, "I find it quite strange that this good religious man takes Descartes to be exceedingly enlightened in matters of religion, whereas his letters are full of Pelagianism and, outside of the points of which he was convinced by his philosophy—like the existence of God and the immortality of the soul—all that can be said of him to his greatest advantage is that he always seemed to submit to the Church."[5]

One of points which Arnauld, in the *Fourth Objections*, says "may cause difficulty to theologians" is described as follows: "First, I am afraid that the author's somewhat free style of philosophizing, which calls everything into doubt, may cause offence to some people."[6] Arnauld goes on to recommend two changes in the *Meditations*: "The First Meditation should be furnished with a brief preface which explains that there is no serious doubt cast on these matters but that the purpose is to isolate temporarily those matters which leave room for even the 'slightest' and most 'exaggerated' doubt. . . Following on from this point, where we find the clause 'since I did not know the author of my being', I would suggest a substitution of the clause 'since I was pretending that I did not know.'"

In reply, Descartes begins by saying that he "completely agrees with" all of Arnauld's arguments in the theological part of the *Fourth Objections*, excepting Arnauld's objection that the Cartesian account of the nature of matter is inconsistent with the doctrine of transubstantiation.[7] But Descartes did not adopt the first of Arnauld's two suggested revisions. Perhaps he thought that the point was already covered in the "Synopsis" of the *Meditations*.[8] Descartes did adopt Arnauld's second suggestion, however, by adding some words in parenthesis to his rehearsal of the reasons for doubt in the "Sixth Meditation," thus: "The second reason for doubt was that since I did not know the author of my being (or at least was pretending not to), I saw nothing to rule out the possibility

---

[5] Quoted from *Oeuvres de Messire Antoine Arnauld*, Volume I, p 671, by R.C. Sleigh, Jr., *op.cit.*, p. 31-32.

[6] *Fourth Set of Objections*, in *The Philosophical Writings of Descartes*, translated by John Cottingham, *et al*, Cambridge: Cambridge University Press, Vol. II, 1984, p.151. Hereafter this volume is referred to as "Cottingham."

[7] Cottingham, p. 172.

[8] In a text to which Arnauld himself had referred, when he said. "I agree that the risk of offence is somewhat reduced in the Synopsis" (*Fourth Objections*, Cottingham, p. 151).

that my natural constitution made me prone to error even in matters which seemed to me most true."[9]

It is not entirely clear, however, whether Descartes meant to accept Arnauld's interpretation of the methodic doubt as a pretend doubt. For Descartes opens the later *Principles of Philosophy* with the remark, "It seems that the only way of freeing ourselves from these [prejudices of childhood] is to make the effort, once in the course of our life, to doubt everything which we find to contain even the smallest suspicion of error."[10] This remark suggests that Descartes meant the qualification "at least pretending not to know" to apply only to the existence of God, and not to the existence of an external, material world. Or again, Descartes may mean the qualification as just another way of saying that the doubts raised in the "First Meditation" are "exaggerated" and "metaphysical."

It is clear, however, that Arnauld wants Descartes to say that he was only "pretending" to withhold assent from the proposition that God exists. It is not hard to see why a Christian theologian would disapprove of a method that involved even temporarily suspending belief in the existence of God. But Arnauld disapproved of the use of real methodic doubt even about the existence of bodies. He could no more accept a method that involved temporarily suspending belief in the existence of the Bible, or, indeed, of the Savior, Jesus Christ, than he could one that involved doubting whether there is a God.

Furthermore, in the famous Port-Royal logic, *The Art of Thinking*, Arnauld and his co-author, Pierre Nicole, seem to assume that for Descartes, the methodic doubt is in general only a pretend doubt. Arnauld and Nicole categorically reject the idea that it might be useful to doubt whether "Everything contained in the clear and distinct idea of a thing can be truthfully affirmed of that thing." "This principle," they say, "cannot be contested without destroying everything evident and establishing a ridiculous Pyrrhonism."[11] They also say that it is psychologically impossible to maintain that "sleeping could not be distinguished from waking, or madness from sanity." A little earlier in the same work they say what would be true if one could deny those things:

---

[9] Cottingham, p. 53.

[10] Cottingham, *et al*, Vol. I, p. 193.

[11] Antoine Arnauld and Pierre Nicole, *Logic or the Art of Thinking*, translated by Jill Vance Buroker, Cambridge: Cambridge University Press, 1996, p. 247.

If there were people able to doubt that they were not sleeping or were not mad, or who could even believe that the existence of everything external is uncertain, and that it is doubtful whether there is a sun, a moon, or matter, at least no one could doubt, as St. Augustine says, that one exists, that one is thinking, or that they are alive. . . . Likewise is impossible to doubt one's perceptions, separating them from their objects. Whether there is or is not a sun or an earth, I am certain that I imagine seeing one. I am certain that I am doubting when I doubt . . . So . . . we find countless clear instances of knowledge that is impossible to doubt." They go on to say that "this consideration can help us" to settle the question of "whether the things we know only by the mind or more or less certain than those known by the senses."[12]

Notice that in this text, there is no suggestion that one can in fact doubt, let alone that one ought to doubt, even temporarily, that there is a sun, a moon, an earth, or more generally an external, material world. The line of argument is attributed to St. Augustine rather than Descartes. However, *The Art of Thinking* as a whole is clearly based on Descartes's views, and Arnauld had asserted from the very beginning of the *Fourth Objections* that the line of thought leading up to Descartes's "cogito" had been anticipated by St. Augustine. (Arnauld had insisted upon this point, I should add, to the annoyance of Descartes.) The version of Descartes presented in *The Art of Thinking*, then, is one in which the methodic doubt is a pretend doubt, or, if you prefer, a theoretical doubt, not a real doubt. The same is true of the rest of Arnauld's philosophical work.

II: Malebranche on the Problem of the Existence of an External, Material World

It is instructive to contrast this interpretation of Cartesian doubt with that offered by Malebranche. In *The Search after Truth*, Malebranche praises Descartes for following the rule that "we should never give complete consent except to propositions which seem so evidently true that we cannot refuse it of them without feeling an inward pain and the secret reproaches of reason."[13] Applying this rule to beliefs about bodies, Malebranche says that we ought to believe that it is "entirely probable" that there are bodies, but not to give complete consent to the

---

[12] Op.cit., p. 228.

[13] Nicolas Malebranche, *The Search after Truth*, translated and edited by Thomas M. Lennon, Cambridge: Cambridge University Press, 1997, p. 10, 13.

proposition that there are bodies.[14] In *Dialogues on Metaphysics and Religion*, the best overall presentation of his mature thought, he goes further. He begins that work by emphasizing that we do not perceive external material objects directly, but rather ideas; and that we live in a world of "intelligible" objects, or ideas, rather than actual material things. For this reason the existence of an external, material world is problematic. To be sure, early in the work, Malebranche denies that anyone doubts the existence of an external world. Thus, Theodore, the teacher in the dialogues, says to Aristes, the student, "Many more principles than you think are required to demonstrate what no one doubts. For where are those who doubt that they have a body, that they are walking on solid ground, that they live in a material world?"[15] But before long, Theodore is commending Aristes for beginning to doubt the existence of an external, material world. "What you say evokes a very strange thought in my mind," says Aristes, "I am beginning to doubt that bodies exist." Theodore responds, "I am not lacking in proofs which are certain and capable of dispelling your doubt, and I am pleased such a doubt has occurred to you. For, after all, doubting that bodies exist for reasons that make it impossible to doubt God's existence and the incorporeality of the soul is a certain sign that we have risen above our prejudices . . ."[16] So it seems that Malebranche finds it possible, and even commendable, to actually doubt the existence of bodies. He does not explicitly attribute this view to Descartes, but the view is expressed in thoroughly Cartesian terms.

The Arnauld-Malebranche controversy was occasioned by Malebranche's publication, in 1680, of his *Treatise of Nature and Grace*, an attempt to solve the problem of why not all men are saved, given God's goodness and indeed universal salvific will. But the first blow in the controversy was struck by Arnauld in 1683, and was aimed at Malebranche's theory of the nature of ideas. In *Of True and False Ideas*, Arnauld argues that Malebranche's theory of ideas, among its various failures, led to Pyrrhonism. Arnauld is referring specifically to scepticism with regard to the existence of an external, material world. According to Arnauld, Malebranche's theory not only made the existence of bodies problematic, it made the problem unsolvable.

When Arnauld says that Malebranche's theory of ideas leads to "Pyrrhonism," he is suggesting that Malebranche might give aid and comfort

---

[14] *op.cit.*, p. 574.

[15] Nicolas Malebranche, *Dialogues on Metaphysics and Religion*, edited by Nicholas Jolley and translated by David Scott, Cambridge: Cambridge University Press, 1997, p. 9.

[16] *op. cit.*, p. 94-95.

to a group of Descartes's contemporaries whom Arnauld, Malebranche, and Descartes, alike repudiated. Arnauld makes a subtle reference to this group in the *Fourth Objections* when he says that theologians might take offense at Descartes's "somewhat free (liberior)" way of philosophising. The suggestion is that Descartes's way of philosophizing might be thought to resemble that of "les libertins" or "les libertins érudits." This was a group of bright, well-placed young Frenchmen in the early 1600s who practiced scepticism combined with a blind fideistic Catholicism.[17] As Graeme Hunter points out, "another name frequently used for the libertines . . . [was] 'esprits forts.'"—bold spirits or bold minds.[18] And bold they were; for their scepticism expressed an attitude of self-assertiveness, an unwillingness to subject oneself to an independent reality. As to their advocacy of blind religious faith, Hunter suggests that faith may have meant no more to them than "religious behavior, without any claim to truth." Malebranche repudiated *les libertins* every bit as strongly as Arnauld did. But Arnauld thought that Malebranche's work was even more dangerous than that of the rather superficial libertines, because Malebranche had a well deserved reputation as a serious thinker, and also because he claimed to be a follower of Descartes.

III: Descartes, Arnauld, and Malebranche on the Relation of Faith and Reason

I turn now to a second way in which Arnauld thought Malebranche was dangerous: he thought that Malebranche was willing to concoct confused philosophical theories in the effort to solve a theological problem, the problem of why not all men are saved, and in the process to distort the relation between theology and philosophy, between faith and reason.

As I pointed out above, the written controversy between Malebranche and Arnauld was occasioned by Malebranche's publication of his *Treatise of Nature and Grace* in 1680, although Arnauld did not open the hostilities

---

[17] Richard Popkin lists the chief members of the group: "Gabriel Naudé, librarian to Richelieu and Mazarin and secretary to Cardinal Bagni; Guy Patin, a learned medical doctor who became Rector of the medical school of the Sorbonne; Leonard Marandé, a secretary of Richelieu's; François de La Mothe Le Vayer, the teacher of the King's brother; Petrus Gassendi, the great philosopher and priest, who became Professor of Mathematics at the Collège Royal; and Samuel Sorbière, the editor of Gassendi's works." Richard H. Popkin, *The History of Scepticism from Erasmus to Descartes*, Assen, Netherlands: Van Corcum & Comp., 1960, p. 89.

[18] Hunter describes Pascal's criticism of "les libertins" in "Motion and Rest in the *Pensées*," *International Journal for the Philosophy of Religion*, 47(2000), p. 87-99. I quote from p. 90.

until 1683. In Malebranche's treatise, Arnauld saw a second kind of boldness, the boldness of those prepared to call God's actions in creating the world to the bar of human justice, and to concoct philosophical and theological "novelties (nouvautés)" to acquit Him. Malebranche provides a general account of God's reasons for creating a world with the evils that the world in fact contains. But he is mainly interested in one particular evil, namely the fact that not all men are saved, and he is concerned to reconcile this particular evil with God's omnipotence and a particular aspect of God's benevolence, namely, God's "sincere will" that everyone be saved.[19] Malebranche took it as a given of Christian revelation that many human beings are not saved. He held that this state of affairs is consistent with God's sincere will to save all men and God's omnipotence, because God has a reason, indeed a determining reason, for choosing to create a world in which not everyone is saved. Furthermore, he tries to specify what that reason is, and how it leads God to save certain human beings rather than others.

This is not the place to discuss Malebranche's complicated theodicy of nature and grace in detail. However, his solution to the central problem of the work is the culmination of two lines of thought. First: (a) God's reason for creating the world is that it should honor him; (b) the only way in which a created world could honor God is that it should be united to the divine nature itself; and (c) this occurs through the union of men with Jesus Christ in the Church. Second: (a) God's wisdom dictates that he carry out his creation in such a way that it best combines the perfection of the world created (thus the perfection of the Church) with the simplicity of the volitions by which he creates; and (b) therefore, God's wisdom dictates that God build up the Church in answer to the prayers of Jesus Christ, acting in His human nature as an "occasional cause" of grace; but (c) since the human nature of Jesus is finite, his prayers are not directed in a precise way to each human being, with the result that many people do not get the graces they need for their salvation, and others get graces that turn out to be wasted.

Now Arnauld thought that this "novel" theory involved a failure to distinguish clearly between philosophy and theology. A good example is the proposition, "God cannot act externally except in order to procure for himself an honor worthy of himself." Malebranche uses this premise in order to arrive at a theological conclusion, "That God could have no other purpose (dessin) in the creation of the world than the incarnation

---

[19] See *Traité de la Nature et de la Grace*, in *Oeuvres complètes de Malebranche*, hereinafter *OC* 5, p. xliv.

of his Son and the establishment of the Church." Arnauld points out that the premise in question is found neither in Scripture nor in tradition. But neither does Malebranche defend it by any clear philosophical argument.[20]

At the same time, Arnauld thought that Malebranche's fundamental mistakes were philosophical, and that his philosophical mistakes led him into theological error, and indeed into heresy.[21]As Arnauld saw it, Malebranche began with the question, why not everyone is saved, and then created a theory that left God no choice but to create a world in which not everyone is saved. As Robert Sleigh says, "What Arnauld took to be Descartes's main virtue with respect to theology—his reluctance to construct philosophical hypotheses in order to resolve theological problems—he found lacking in Malebranche and Leibniz. In them he saw the boldness of reason which would, in time, spark the Enlightenment."[22]

Now Malebranche does not attribute his own views about the relation of philosophy and theology to Descartes. But those views are derived from Malebranche's theory of the nature of ideas. According to that theory, our clear and distinct perceptions have God's ideas as their immediate objects; in Malebranche's famous phrase, "We see all things in God." Furthermore, in the *Treatise of Nature and Grace*, Malebranche, referring to his theory of ideas, says, "If I were not persuaded that all men are reasonable only because they are enlightened by eternal wisdom, I would, no doubt, be very bold to speak of God's plans and to try to discover certain of his ways in the production of his work"[23]

With Malebranche's theory of ideas we make contact one final time with Descartes. Unlike Arnauld, Malebranche does not claim that his theory is found in Descartes. Rather, he says that Descartes "never examined seriously the question of the nature of ideas."[24] Malebranche

---

[20] *Réflexions philosophiques et théologiques sur le Nouveau Systeme de la Nature et de la Grace*, OA 39, p. 423 ff. Arnauld thought that the premise in question was false: God created the world, he says, "out of an entirely gratuitous goodness, a free overflow of his being." "It would be to lower [God] to the condition of men . . . if one said that he could decide to create me, me and the other creatures, only for some advantage he wanted to procure for himself by creating us" (p. 429).

[21] In the "Conclusion" of the *Réflexions*, he accuses Malebranche of Nestorianism. See OA 39, p. 845.

[22] R. C. Sleigh, Jr., *op. cit,* p. 47.

[23] *Traité de la Nature et de la Grace,* OC 5, p. 25

[24] *Trois Lettres de l'Auteur de la Recherche de la Verité touchant la Défense de Mr. Arnauld contre la Réponse au Livre des vrayes & fausses Idées,* OC 6, 218.

claims, in effect, that his own theory of ideas is what Descartes ought to have said, and would have said if he had thought more seriously about the question. Once again, the direction that Cartesian philosophy was to take was not determined by the text of Descartes. It may be true that some of Descartes's followers, including Malebranche, spawned the Enlightenment, But what Descartes wrote might have become a useful tool for tradition-minded theologians like Arnauld. Descartes may have been in some sense the Father of Modern Philosophy. But he was not the Father of the Enlightenment.

MARY DZON

THE LIMINALITY OF CHILDHOOD
AND ADOLESCENCE IN LATE MEDIEVAL
LIVES OF CHRIST

ABSTRACT. Using Arnold van Gennep's model of the limen as an area of transition between two spaces, my paper will consider how apocryphal texts portray Christ's childhood
and adolescence as a period of liminality between his infancy and adulthood that prepares
him uniquely for a radical life of preaching and miracle-working..

It is easy to overlook the middle years of Christ's life, those extending
from his early childhood until his young manhood,[1] when he made his
public debut at the Jordan, for the Gospels are silent concerning this
period of his life. Moreover, the Christian liturgical year does not remind
the faithful of Christ's boyhood and adolescence, hinging as it does

---

[1] Classical and medieval writers had various schemes for the ages of man. Isidore of
Seville, for instance, divides the human life-cycle into six stages: "infantia, pueritia, ado-
lescentia, iuventus, gravitas atque senectus." The first, second and third stages in this
scheme last until ages seven, fourteen and twenty-eight, respectively. Thus, according to
Isidore's model, Christ was an *infans* when he was born, a *puer* when he was found sitting
among the doctors and a *iuvenis* when he died. Although Isidore makes a distinction
between infants and children, he says that one of the three ways in which one may be
called a *puer* is "pro nativitate, ut Esaias (9, 6): 'Puer natus est nobis,'" *Etymologiae*, ed. W.
M. Lindsay, vol. 2 (Oxford, 1911), 11.2.11. Although the Vulgate has *parvulus* rather than
puer for this verse, the late fifteenth-century Missale Romanum of Milan, which takes its
introit for the third Mass of Christmas Day from Isaiah 9:6, has "Puer natus est nobis,"
Missale Romanum Mediolani, 1474, ed. Robert Lippe, Henry Bradshaw Society, Vol. 17.1
(London, 1899), p. 19. The same holds true for the *The Sarum Missal*, ed. J. Wickham
Legg (Oxford, 1916). Luke uses *puer* in speaking of both the infant Jesus and the twelve-
year-old Jesus. Although I will refer to the infant Jesus as the Christ-Child, in this paper
I am mainly concerned with the life of Jesus from the time after the Epiphany until his
baptism in the Jordan.

Limina: Thresholds and Borders - A St. Michael's College Symposium
Joseph Goering, Francesco Guardiani, Giulio Silano eds. Ottawa: Legas, 2005

upon Christmas, Lent and Easter.[2] The hidden quality of Christ's childhood and adolescence becomes more noticeable when we consider that this period is bordered on both sides by wonders, such as the star that led the Magi to the child, on the one hand, and the miracles that Christ performed as an adult, on the other.[3] In what follows I will consider the liminality of Christ's early years, in the sense of their being a time of obscurity between the more dramatic stages of his life during which he manifested his divinity to those around him, and as a stage of waiting until he reached the perfect age,[4] when it became socially acceptable for him to begin his public ministry.

The finding of the twelve-year-old Jesus in the Temple is, of course, the exceptional high point in the lowly valley of Christ's youth. It presents the possibility that Jesus could have begun teaching at an early age because he already possessed divine wisdom.[5] Some patristic and medieval exegetes interpreted the Christ-Child in this scene as a *puer-senex* — that is, as a holy boy endowed with the wisdom and maturity of an old man, a topos common in hagiographical literature.[6] Jerome, for instance, says that when "the Savior had completed twelve years, and questioned the elders in the Temple about points of the law, he taught while he wisely questioned" (Hilberg 1996: 449). Jerome emphasizes the unobtrusive way in which the boy Jesus instructed the doctors; like Socrates, Christ taught by means of questioning. Most exegetes, however, say

---

[2] In other words, apart from the feasts of the Epiphany and the Presentation of the Lord in the Temple, the Church does not celebrate any major events in the early life of Christ. Luke's narration of the finding of the child Jesus in the Temple (Lk. 2:42-52) was the gospel reading for the Sunday within the octave of Epiphany in the *Missale Romanum* and the *Sarum Missal*, but this Sunday was not designated explicitly as a feast of the boy Jesus.

[3] Peter Comestor, for example, in his commentary on John 2:11, calls attention to the miracles that Christ worked in the beginning of his life: "'Hoc enim initio signorum manifestavit Jesus gloriam suam.' Nec dicitur hoc esse initium, quin et prius signa fecisset, nascendo de Virgine, magos stella praevia ducendo, quadraginta diebus et noctibus jejunando, et hujusmodi," *Historia scholastica*, PL 198, col. 1559d.

[4] Although medieval writers use the term *perfecta aetas* in different senses depending upon the context, they usually use it to refer to manhood.

[5] Luke 2:46-8: "et factum est post triduum invenerunt illum in templo sedentem in medio doctorum audientem illos et interrogantem eos. Stupebant autem omnes qui eum audiebant super prudentia et responsis eius et videntes admirati sunt." Luke's statements here as to what exactly Christ was doing are somewhat ambiguous. This ambiguity gave rise to a variety of interpretations.

[6] On this motif, see Ernst Robert Curtius, *European Literature and the Latin Middle Ages*, trans. Willard R. Trask (Princeton, 1973), pp. 98-101.

nothing about the teaching of the boy Jesus, but emphasize his docility.[7] Bede, for one, remarks that "the fact that he himself in his twelfth year sat in the Temple in the midst of the doctors hearing them and asking them questions is an example of human humility, to be sure, an extraordinary example of humility which we ought to learn" (Hurst 1955: 135-6). Here Bede suggests paradoxically that by not teaching Christ was in fact teaching an important lesson. Medieval clerics considered such an example of docility particularly useful for schoolboys.[8] Irenaeus of Lyons in his treatise *Against Heresies* expresses a similar idea, namely, that Christ passed through all the ages of man in order to sanctify and give an example of pious behavior to each age (Rousseau and Doutreleau 1982: 220-2). In the early Church it was necessary to safeguard the doctrine of the humanity of Christ and therefore to emphasize that he passed through the normal human life-cycle. In the later Middle Ages, however, when the doctrine of Christ's humanity was no longer a point of contention, it was still necessary that Christ be thought of as having been an ordinary child so that he might serve as an example for normal children.[9]

Medieval clerics were worried that youths would presume to teach before they possessed the knowledge and authority necessary to undertake

---

[7] In his commentary on the Gospel of Luke, Bonaventure interprets the phrase "audientem illos et interrogantem" as meaning that the child Jesus was first a disciple and then a teacher. He quotes the passage from Jerome that I have cited above in his interpretation of "interrogantem," *Commentarius in Evangelium S. Lucae*, in *Opera Omnia*, vol. 7 (Quaracchi, 1895), p. 67.

[8] Humbert of Romans, for instance, in his *ad status* sermon *ad pueros* (chapter 87) refers to the finding of the child Jesus in the midst of the doctors (Luke 2:46) in order to bolster the authority that teachers have over their pupils. "Notandum autem quod [pueri] instruendi sunt...a doctoribus, iuxta illud quod dicitur de puero Jesu (Luc. ii): Invenerunt eum sedentem in medio doctorum audientem illos," *Sermones ad diuersos status* (Hagenau, 1508). Cf. *The De instructione puerorum of William of Tournai, O.P.*, ed. James A. Corbett (Notre Dame, 1955), p. 45.

[9] Christian Gnilka summarizes the issue as follows: "In the background of such remarks [i.e. the insistence of the Fathers on the normality of Christ's childhood] are Christological problems: the childhood of the Redeemer was not allowed to be too intensified with the element of wonder since the natural childhood and generally the natural sequence of Christ's life guaranteed his true humanity. Perhaps this explains why the Church Fathers often hesitated to provide the Christ-Child with the features of an old man," *Aetas Spiritalis: Die Überwindung der natürlichen Altersstufen als Ideal frühchristlichen Lebens* (Bonn, 1972), p. 241, translation mine. John Burrow also refers to this passage in his discussion of how medieval writers handled the life of Christ. Some of the themes I develop in this paper pertaining to the life of Christ have been touched upon by Burrow, *The Ages of Man: A Study in Medieval Writing and Thought* (Oxford, 1986).

that office. They used the example of the docile Christ-Child to counteract the examples of precocious boys found in the Bible, such as Daniel and Jeremiah. Commenting on Ezekiel's confession that he received the spirit of prophesy at age thirty (Ez. 1:1), Gregory the Great says that this fact

> indicates to us something we ought to consider, namely, that the faculty of preaching – because it necessitates the exercise of reason – is not granted except in the perfect age. Whence even the Lord himself in his twelfth year sitting in the midst of the doctors wished to be found not teaching, but asking questions. In order that men should not dare to preach while their age is still weak, he deigned in his twelfth year to ask questions of men on earth, who in his divinity always teaches the angels in heaven. (Adriaen 1971: 18)

The reason that Gregory alleges for the inappropriateness of boys and adolescents teaching is that they have not yet fully developed their reasoning faculty, and presumably lack experience and the prudence which stems from it.

This view of the deficiencies of the early stages of life fits into the classical and medieval conception of the life-cycle as a sort of bell-curve, consisting of the increase of youth, the fleeting culmination of the perfect age, and the steady decline of old age.[10] Dante, a medieval proponent of this schema, says that the first stage (*adolescenzia*) lasts until twenty-five, and describes it using the image of a threshold: "the first of these stages is the gateway and path by which we enter into the life of excellence befitting to us as human beings." He calls the second stage (*gioventute*) "the city where the life of excellence is enjoyed" (Ryan 1989: 185). Like Gregory, Dante also points out youth's deficiency in the rational faculty: "Since until that time our soul directs its energies to bringing about physical growth...and our body, consequently, under-

---

[10] See Burrow on Aristotle's view of the three stages of life (as put forth in the *De anima*), and Dante's reference to it in *Il convivio* (bk. 4, ch. 23), where he uses the image of the arc to describe the course of human life, *Ages of Man*, pp. 6-7. For the passage in Aristotle, see *On the Soul* in *The Basic Works of Aristotle*, trans. Richard McKeon (New York, 1941), 434a 24-5. Dante places the climax of life at age thirty-five. He supports this view by the fact that Christ died a little before that time, at age thirty-four, "because on the one hand it was not fitting that his divinity should be present in something that was in decline, and on the other it really is unthinkable that he should not have wished to live his life here below to its climax after experiencing the lowly condition of childhood," *The Banquet*, trans. Christopher Ryan (Saratoga, California, 1989), bk. 4, ch. 23, sections 10-11, p. 182.

goes many significant changes, our rational part cannot perfectly exercise its power of discrimination" (Ryan 1989: 183).

This discussion of the disabilities of youth brings us to the issue of the creation and maintenance of a power-structure based on age. The English proverb "children should be seen and not heard" embodies the expectations of adults that children be unobtrusive and submissive to their authority.[11] In most societies, children are obliged to pass through a long stage of formation and relative powerlessness before they are formally incorporated into the adult community and allowed to assume positions of importance. Yet, adults may argue, the liminality assigned to children is not simply a consequence of the attempt of grown-ups to guard their own power. Gregory the Great, in his *Pastoral Care*, adopts this rhetoric when he says that it is for their own good that the office of preaching be withheld from those who are immature:

> Those are to be reproved, who are debarred from the office of preaching either by imperfection or age, and who yet are impelled to it by reckless haste, lest when they precipitously assume the burden of so great an office, they cut themselves off from the way of subsequent improvement....They should be admonished to consider that if fledglings desire to fly before the perfection of their wings, although they wish to fly on high, they are plunged into the depths. (Rommel 1992: 434)

An example of a child who preaches at an early age and dies shortly thereafter is that of St. Rumwold. This Anglo-Saxon saint purportedly demanded baptism as soon as he was born, after which he preached a pious sermon, and died two days later (Love 1996: 93-115).[12] This just goes to show, as Gregory warned, how dangerous it is to preach at too young an age!

Gregory tells young men to heed Christ's admonition to his disciples before his Ascension (Lk. 24:49): "but stay you in the city till you be endued with power from on high." The city, Gregory explains, is a

---

[11] *The Oxford Dictionary of English Proverbs*, ed. William George Smith, 2nd edition (Oxford, 1963), p. 92. Smith cites a version of this saying in Mirk's *Festial*: "For hyt ys an old Englysch sawe: 'A mayde schuld be seen, but not herd.'" Mirk applies this to the Virgin Mary, who "spak no oftyr but foure syþes," *Mirk's Festial: A Collection of Homilies*, ed. Theodor Erbe, EETS e.s. 96 (Millwood, New York, 1975), p. 230. Apparently, this proverb originally referred to maidens and was later applied to children.

[12] *Vita S. Rumwoldi*, in *Three Eleventh-Century Anglo-Latin Saints' Lives*, ed. Rosalind C. Love (Oxford, 1996), pp. 93-115. For a discussion of the cult of saintly children in the later medieval period, see Patricia Healy Wasyliw, "The Pious Infant: Developments in Popular Piety during the High Middle Ages," in *Lay Sanctity, Medieval and Modern: A Search for Models*, ed. Ann W. Astell (Notre Dame, 2000), pp. 105-15.

metaphor for the "cloister of our minds [*mentium nostrarum claustra*]," within which those who are not prepared to preach should stay by not speaking publicly (Rommel 1992: 436). Whereas Dante uses the image of youths not yet being able to enter the city, Gregory says that they should not go out of it. In either case, youths are assigned a status of liminality with respect to the exercise of the privileges of adulthood. Gregory then proceeds to give the example of the twelve-year-old Jesus, repeating what he said in his commentary on Ezekiel. In his treatise *On the Instruction of Preachers*, Humbert of Romans quotes these texts from Gregory to argue that one who wishes to be a preacher "ought to have attained the proper age" (Humbert 1677: 437). The notion of youths' inadequacy to assume major leadership positions in the Church is also evident from medieval canon law. Although boys in the Middle Ages were able to attain to the minor orders, males were not admitted to the priesthood or the episcopate until the age of thirty "since," as Peter Lombard states, "even the Lord himself was baptized at age thirty and thus began to teach" (Lombard 1981: 415-16).[13]

In the *Tertia pars* of the *Summa theologiae*, Thomas Aquinas reiterates the opinions of the Fathers concerning the hidden years of Christ's life. Jean-Pierre Torrell notes that the Christological questions 27-59 in the *Tertia pars* were popularized in France under the name *Vie de Jésus* (Torrell 1996: 261-2), and it is this Dominican life of Christ that I would now like to consider before turning to other medieval lives.[14]

Thomas raises the question of whether the nativity of Christ ought to have been manifested to all and responds by saying that Christ is a hid-

---

[13] René Metz notes that "primitivement l'âge de trente ans avait été exigé, lui aussi, pour la prêtrise. Cette mesure avait été justifiée par des raison symboliques: le Christ avait commencé son ministére public à trente ans. Dès le milieu du VIIIe siècle, l'âge a été rabaissé, pour le case de nécessité, à ving-cinq ans par le pape Zacharie dans une décrétale de 751. Clément V (1305-1314) a fait de l'âge de ving-cinq ans le règle," "L'accession des mineurs à la cléricature et aux bénéfices ecclésiastiques dans le droit canonique médiéval," in *Recueil de mémoires et travaux: Mélanges Roger Aubenas* (Montpellier, 1974), p. 554. Cf. *Decretum Magistri Gratiani*, ed. A. Friedberg (Graz, 1955), prima pars, dist. 78, ch. 2, ch. 5; *Clementis Papae V Constitutiones*, ed. A. Friedberg, liber 1, titulus 6, ch. 3.

[14] Thomas's discussion of the life of Christ is divided into four sections, the first and second of which are the entrance (*ingressus*) of the incarnate Son of God into this world and the progress (*progressus*) of his life in it. That Thomas ends the first section with the baptism of Christ (q. 39) seems to indicate that he considers the whole first part of Christ's life a sort of incubation period preparatory to his public life, Passion and death, *Summa Theologiae, Tertia Pars* (Madrid, 1958), prologue to q. 27.

den God (*ST*, III, q. 36, a. 1, sed contra).[15] On the basis of this principle, Thomas thinks that Christ's childhood must have been obscure. In another question, in response to the objection that the book called *The Infancy of the Savior* implies that the Christ-Child made himself known because it describes him working miracles, Thomas says that this book is apocryphal (*ST*, III, q. 36, a. 4, ad 3). He refers to an argument made by John Chrysostom in his twenty-first homily on the Gospel of John that if Christ had worked miracles in his youth then the Jews would not have stood in need of John the Baptist to point him out to them (Goggin 1957: 205).[16] Referring presumably to Christ's Jewish contemporaries, Thomas adds that if the Christ-Child had been a wonder-worker then "they would have thought his Incarnation an illusion and, overcome by jealousy, would have handed him over to be crucified before the opportune time."[17]

---

[15] Thomas here is referring to Isaiah 45:15: "vere tu es Deus absconditus Deus Israhel salvator."

[16] Chrysostom also argues for the falsity of the legends about Christ's childhood miracles in homily 17. Here too his argument rests on the necessity of John the Baptist's pointing out Christ to the crowds. Interestingly, Chrysostom offers two explanations for John the Baptist's statement about Christ in John 1:31: "And I knew him not." First, John may not have known him "for he had spent the whole time previously in the desert, and was away from his father's house," *Commentary on Saint John* (New York, 1957), p. 166. Second, John may not have known Christ because "the miracles which took place when He was a child, such as those regarding the magi, and others like them, happened long before, when John himself also was still a child. Moroever, since a long period had elapsed in the meantime, He probably was unknown to all," p. 167. Here Chrysostom calls attention to the long years of obscurity that Jesus had endured in his childhood and adolescence. He also makes reference to the view that John the Baptist undertook the eremetical life at an early age. On this point, compare the *Meditations* of Alexander of Ashby, who says of John the Baptist: "Ille namque antra deserti teneris sub annis civium turmas fugiens petivit," ed. Thomas H. Bestul, *Mediaeval Studies* 52 (1990): 52. See also the *Meditaciones Vite Christi*, which describes the Holy Family coming upon the boy John the Baptist in the desert on their return from Egypt, ed. M. Stallings-Taney (Turnout, 1997), ch. 13, p. 59. Whereas medieval people were willing to entertain the idea of a boy being a hermit, they were not comfortable with the idea of a boy being a preacher.

[17] Although the subject of Thomas' sentence is unexpressed in Latin, a couple of sentences before this one, Thomas speaks of the "Israelitae" being in need of John the Baptist to point Christ out to them. Cf. *ST*, III, q. 43, a. 3, respondeo. In this hypothetical situation in which he imagines the Jews dispatching the boy Jesus if he had publicized his divinity at an early age, Thomas expresses well what we see enacted in the legends of Christ's childhood circulating in the later Middle Ages. The Jews are portrayed as being filled with envy and malice, as well as eager to put the Christ-Child to death. For instance, in the apocryphal Gospel of Pseudo-Matthew, Jesus' teacher Levi, confounded by the boy's superior wisdom, exclaims: "Num debet iste super terra vivere? Imo in

The issue of timeliness comes up again in Thomas' consideration of the age when Christ was baptized (*ST*, III, q. 39, a. 3). Thomas raises an objection based upon the idea of Christ's baptism being a rite of passage, after undergoing which he was authorized to teach and work miracles. It would have been more useful, one might be tempted to think, if Christ had begun to teach and work miracles before he turned thirty, the age when he was baptized. Thomas answers this objection by referring again to the argument that Christ's contemporaries would have disbelieved in his humanity if he had been a wonder-child. Such a situation would also be detrimental to the humility of youths who would be encouraged to assume the office of governing or teaching before the perfect age. Another objection Thomas entertains is that "the sign of divinely infused wisdom ought especially to have been manifested in Christ" (objection 3). If it was manifested in a *puer-senex* such as Daniel, then much more should it have been manifested in the boy Jesus, Wisdom incarnate. Thomas counters it with an argument we have heard before, namely, that "it was necessary that what is appropriate to all according to the common law be shown in Christ: namely, that he should teach when he reached the perfect age."[18]

In another question (*ST*, III, q. 43, a. 3), Thomas considers whether Christ began to work miracles at the wedding feast of Cana, which occurred after his baptism. He points out that Christ worked miracles only after he began to teach as a way of confirming his doctrine, and that he did not begin to teach until he reached the perfect age. In all of these questions, Thomas makes the crucial distinction between Christ's ability to teach and work miracles at a premature age and the suitability of his doing so, giving priority to the latter consideration.

Whereas Aquinas seems to portray the youthful Jesus as a good Dominican novice, waiting until he reaches the proper age before he begins

---

magna cruce dignus est appendi," *Evangelia Apocrypha*, ed. C. Tischendorf (Hildesheim, 1966), ch. 31, p. 101. This portrayal of the Jews as being eager to kill the Christ-Child is reflective of medieval views of the Jews as killers of Christ. See the monograph by Jeremy Cohen, "The Jews as the Killers of Christ in the Latin Tradition, from Augustine to the Friars," *Traditio* 39 (1983): 1-27. With regard to Thomas' statement that childhood would have been an inopportune time for Christ to die, it is worthwhile to compare what he says elsewhere: Christ died at the most opportune time because by giving up his life at the perfect age, he demonstrated his great love for humanity, *ST*, III, q. 46, a. 9, ad 4.

[18] In other words, Christ had to serve as an example for ordinary children and adolescents. Thomas adds that it is by "a special dispensation" that some children, such as Jeremiah, assume the office of teaching at an early age.

preaching, the Franciscan John de Caulibus, author of the popular devotional text *Meditations on the Life of Christ*, emphasizes the Franciscan virtues exemplified in Christ's childhood and adolescence. In particular, he calls attention to the lowliness, poverty and hardship that Christ not only endured but embraced in his early life. In his chapters on the Holy Family's flight into Egypt and their return, John seeks to arouse compassion for the poverty they suffered and the manual labor they engaged in to support themselves. He pictures Jesus as Mary's little domestic helper and agent in her home-based sewing business, quoting one of the psalms (87:16): "I am poor, and in labours from my youth *(iuventus mea)*" (Stallings-Taney 1997: 58). In the chapter on what Christ did between the ages of twelve and thirty, John calls Christ *Deus absconditus* (Is. 45:15) in his meditation upon the lowly manner in which the child Jesus conducted his life among the Holy Family, praying late at night and sleeping upon a little cot (Stalling-Taney 1997: 71).[19] In the following chapter, John envisions Jesus persuading John the Baptist to baptize him without revealing his identity since his "time has not yet come" (Stalling-Taney 1997: 75). This serves as the author's cue to interject a long exposition on the virtue of humility as manifested so perfectly by Christ in his youth.[20] John refers implicitly to the idea of God as a *Deus absconditus* to express his amazement at how Christ humbly remained silent at his baptism despite the fact that the Father publicly recognized him as his Son and commanded that he be heard: "This is my beloved Son, in whom I am well pleased: hear ye him." (Stallings-Taney 1997: 83):[21]

> For a long time you have been quiet, for an exceedingly long time....How long...as someone weak and foolish *(quasi infirmus aliquis et insipiens)*, will you hide yourself among the people? How long...will you suffer yourself to be called and likewise thought of as the son of a carpenter? O humility,...how greatly you confound the pride of my vanity!...I am not able to be quiet, impudently and imprudently obtruding and showing off, "prompt to speak,

---

[19] John refers to the idea of Christ as a *Deus absconditus* in the beginning of the *Meditations*. Explaining why it was fitting for Mary to have a husband and for Jesus to cry as an infant and suffer tribulations like other human beings, John says that by living an ordinary life the Son of God was able to hide his divinity from the Devil: "ut diabolo partus Filii Dei occultaretur," *Meditaciones*, ch. 6, p. 28, ll. 9-10; "ad occultandum se, ne a demonio cognosceretur," ch. 8, p. 38, ll. 43-4; "ut se diabolo occultaret," ch. 12, p. 49, ll. 31-2 .

[20] In the course of this discussion, John refers to Mt. 18:3-4, which holds out a child as the exemplar of humility.

[21] John here conflates the Father's words spoken at the Baptism (Mt. 3:17) and the Transfiguration of Christ (Mt. 17:5). Only in the latter passage does the Father command that Jesus be heard.

quick to teach, slow to hear" (James 1:19). Did Christ fear vainglory, since he was silent for such a long time, since he hid himself (*seipsum absconde-bat*)?...He feared it on our account....He was silent in speech, but he instructed by his deeds, and that which afterwards he taught by word, now he proclaimed by example: "Learn from me, for I am meek and humble of heart" (Mt. 11:29). (Stallings-Taney 1997: 83)[22]

John tells his readers to imagine the boy Jesus "sitting among the doctors, with a serene, wise and reverent countenance; he listened as if ignorant, which he did out of humility" (Stallings-Taney 1997: 63). He offers an unusual interpretation of Luke's statement that "Jesus advanced in wisdom, and age, and grace with God and men"(Lk. 2:52), a problematic scriptural passage for medieval exegetes who found it difficult to reconcile Christ's growth in knowledge with his possession of divine wisdom.[23] John, however, is not troubled with this Christological mystery, but rather with reconciling two other notions. On the one hand, Luke says that Christ grew in wisdom and implies that he increased in respect in the eyes of the people who knew him. On the other hand, the Gospel indicates that Jesus was the object of people's reproach when he began his public ministry: "Is not this the carpenter's son?" (Mt. 13:55). To explain this apparent contradiction, John suggests that Luke 2:52 only referred to Christ's development up to his twelfth year. He devotes a whole chapter (chapter fifteen) to filling in the gap between Christ's twelfth and thirtieth year, in which he portrays Jesus as a teenager (*iuvenis*) devoid of accomplishments.[24] John reasons that Christ must not have done anything all those years, because if he did, surely someone would have written it down. He takes pains to say that Christ was not lazy (*ociosus*), although he was lowly and obscure, arguing

---

[22] In this passage we hear echoes of the views expressed by the Church Fathers concerning the Christ-Child's humility manifested by not teaching the doctors in the Temple and the argument put forth by Gregory and others that Christ did not preach at any early age lest he encourage youths to imitate him.

[23] See Kevin Madigan, "Did Jesus 'Progress in Wisdom'? Thomas Aquinas on Luke 2:52 in Ancient and High-Medieval Context," *Traditio* 52 (1997): 181-200.

[24] Jaime R. Vidal summarizes well John de Caulibus' treatment of the childhood of Christ: "The hidden life at Nazareth has hidden from his people the wonders which the Infancy Narrative has shown to us, and thus made plausible the Messianic secret and the possibility of rejection," *The Infancy Narrative in Pseudo-Bonaventure's Meditationes Vitae Christi: A Study in Medieval Franciscan Christ-Piety (c. 1300)*, Ph.D. thesis, Fordham University, 1984, p. 328.

paradoxically that Christ was actually doing marvelous things by not doing anything worth mentioning (Stallings-Taney 1997: 64 & 100).[25]

> Therefore the highest teacher who later was going to teach virtues and the way of life, began to do virtuous deeds from his youth (*iuventus*); but in a wonderful manner....Namely, by rendering himself useless (*inutilis*), abject (*abiectus*) and foolish (*insipiens*) in the sight of men....He went to the Synagogue....He stood there long in prayer, taking quite a lowly place. He went home, he stayed with his mother and sometimes helped his foster-father. All wondered, seeing so comely a youth do nothing which seemed worthy of praise, for they expected that he would do great things. (Stallings-Taney 1997: 65)

John says that Christ emptied himself (Phil. 2:7) and made himself into a worm (Ps. 21:7) so that he might teach us worms humility. (Stallings-Taney 1997: 61-2, 66 & 68). John's choice of words to describe how people perceived the adolescent Christ suggests that Christ assumed the role of a fool: *idiota, insipiens, stultus, uilis, abiectus, inutilis* (Stallings-Taney 1997: 65 & 66).[26] This, of course, is not surprising considering John's admiration of St. Francis.[27]

John's ideal of manliness is clearly a far cry from the heroic. To commend the adolescent Christ's humility and lowliness he quotes Proverbs 16:32: "The patient man is better than the valiant: and he that ruleth his spirit, than he that taketh cities" (Stallings-Taney 1997: 66). John also contrasts Christ with powerful men of the world by the way he portrays him going forth from his mother at age thirty:

> The Lord of the world walks alone, for he did not yet have disciples...barefoot for such a long journey....Where are your barons and counts, your generals and soldiers, your horses and camels, your elephants and chariots?...How is it that you proceed so unpretentiously? (Stallings-Taney 1997: 73)

In this passage, John seems to have in mind an exotic ruler like Alexander the Great who sought to display and increase his power. It is use-

---

[25] Nicholas Love, a Carthusian who translated the *Meditations* into English in the fifteenth century, renders *ociosus* as *ydul.* See *Nicholas Love's Mirror of the Blessed Life of Jesus Christ*, ed. Michael G. Sargent (New York, 1992), ch. 13, p. 61, l. 6; cf. ch. 17, p. 84, l. 4.

[26] Nicholas Love uses the following words to describe Christ from age twelve to age thirty: *ydul, vnkonnyng, abiecte, vnworþi, foule, an ydiote, a fole.* See *Nicholas Love's Mirror*, p. 61, ll. 20, 41-2; p. 62, ll. 4, 12.

[27] On the importance of the fool in the Christian tradition, see John Saward's monograph *Perfect Fools: Folly for Christ's Sake in Catholic and Orthodox Spirituality* (Oxford, 1980), especially chapter six, which discusses Franciscan folly.

ful to consider how Walter of Chatillon in his twelfth-century epic poem The Alexandreis depicts Alexander behaving as a boy, for this boy's impetuosity stands in stark contrast to the meekness embraced by Christ in his early years.

> Although still a boy, [Alexander] longed eagerly for arms.... "Alas, how long must I suffer the inactivity of childhood (*quies pueris*)?...Will I never be allowed to shatter the Persians' yoke?...Is it really true that Hercules once upon a time, when a boy in his cradle, crushed two snakes by seizing their throats?" (Pritchard 1986: 36-7)[28]

The boy Alexander presents the type of a boy-hero who is eager (and ready) to perform valiant deeds.[29] Most medieval people did not think of the Christ-Child behaving in such a way, although he too was destined for greatness.

Another type of hero is the one who seems unpromising in his youth.[30] Such a hero is Beowulf, who surprisingly *is* like the young Christ in the sense that both were considered to lack potential in their youths.[31] Upon returning to his people, Beowulf tells his king about his victory over the monsters and the rewards he has been given. The poet then tells us that this news had the greater effect on the Geats because they did not think that Beowulf, judging from his youthful unassertiveness, had such heroic mettle in him:

> Hean wæs lange,
> swa hyne Geata bearn godne ne tealdon,
> ne hyne on medobence micles wyrðne
> drihten Wereda gedon wolde;

---

[28] For the Latin, see *Galteri de Castellione Alexandreis*, ed. Marvin L. Colker (Passau, 1978), bk. 1, ll. 29-30, 32-5, ll. 39-41, ll. 56-8, pp. 8-10.

[29] In his section on marvels, Stith Thompson lists the motif "hero's precocious strength" F611.3.2, which he cross-references with motif F628.1.3.2: "child tears to pieces a live snake with his own bare hands," the prime example of which is Hercules, *Motif-Index of Folk-Literature*, vol. 3 (Bloomington, Indiana, 1975).

[30] Stith Thompson lists "the unpromising hero" as a category of the motifs L100-L199, many of which involve children, *Motif-Index of Folk-Literature*, vol. 5 (Bloomington, Indiana, 1975). The young Beowulf and the young Christ differ from the type of hero who lives a completely obscure youth, such as the young swineherd who later becomes a prince (L113.1.3). Beowulf, for one, was the son of great warrior. The Christ-Child, for his part, attracted people's attention on account of his great beauty, according to John de Caulibus, *Meditaciones*, ch. 15, p. 65, ll. 27-9. Cf. *Nicholas Love's Mirror*, p. 61, ch. 13, ll. 32-5.

[31] The *Beowulf*-poet does not seem to be consistent in his characterization of his hero because in the beginning of the poem Beowulf recounts some of the daring deeds he performed in his youth; see ll. 406-25, 506-80.

swyðe wendon, þæt he sleac wære,
æðeling unfrom. Edwenden cwom
tireadigum menn torna gehwylces. (Klaeber 1950: 82)

[Long was he despised so that the sons of the Geats did not consider him worthy, nor would the lord of hosts do him much honor on the mead-bench. They had very much thought that he was indolent, an idle prince.]

The key Old English adjectives in this passage are *sleac* and *unfrom*. Our modern word "slack" and our denomination of a lazy person as a "slacker" derive from *sleac*, which means "slow and slothful." *Unfrom* means "inactive and feeble."[32] These Old English adjectives are similar to the term of reproach that the people leveled against the young Jesus, according to John de Caulibus: to them he seemed *ociosus* (or idle). In other words, both the young Beowulf and the young Jesus are accused of being slackers.

Another text that I would like to consider briefly is Langland's *Piers Plowman*, which covers the life of Christ impressionistically in a dream-mode. As a result of Langland's depiction of Christ as a knight whose goal is to fight the devil,[33] his Christ-Child is different from the meek child we have seen so far, because – like the boy Alexander – he is anxious to take up arms. The dreamer says that Jesus must wait in the chamber of Mary's womb and then in his childhood until the fullness of time comes when he may joust with the fiend over human souls.

And in þe wombe of þat wenche was he fourty wokes
And bycame man of þat maide, mankynde to saue,
Byg and abydyng, and bold in his barnhed
To haue yfouthte with þe fende ar fol tyme come. (Pearsall 1994: 299)

The adverb "ar" ("before") indicates that the Christ-Child wished to perform knightly deeds before he became an adult. The phrase "fol tyme" refers to Christ's early thirties (the *perfecta aetas*) when he was finally able to preach, work miracles and suffer on the cross. The description of Jesus as a bulging baby-boy is significant because it makes him

---

[32] See the glossary to Klaeber's edition. Klaeber notes that "the introduction of the commonplace story of the sluggish youth is not very convincing," p. 207, note to 2183 ff.

[33] Langland's Christ is different from the one we usually meet in late medieval devotional literature, which tends to emphasize the bodily suffering of a human Christ. Cf. Malcolm Godden, *The Making of Piers Plowman* (London, 1990), pp. 127-8; David Aers, "Christ's Humanity and *Piers Plowman*: Contexts and Political Implications," *The Yearbook of Langland Studies* 8 (1994): 107-25.

seem like a child hero who already possesses the muscularity needed to fight his enemy.[34] Although Langland's Christ-Child is eager to get on the road to Calvary, he must first be trained in leechcraft, an art considered necessary for young apprentice-knights to learn: "Ac *Liberum Arbitrium* lechecraeft hym tauhte / Til *plenitudo temporis* hy tyme aprochede" (Pearsall 1994: 299). David Aers argues that Langland's portrayal of the young Christ being "guided from fighting the devil prematurely (from a premature exertion of his full Godhead)" demonstrates the poet's notion "that the Creator in his Incarnation is obliged to learn creaturely limitation" (Aers 1975: 108-9). This interpretation seems to be consistent with that of medieval theologians that Christ was able to increase in knowledge of an experiential kind,[35] such as knowledge of what it feels like to suffer physical pain and perhaps even what it feels like to await patiently the fullness of time.

The apocryphal infancy gospels may also be classified as lives of Christ. Written in the early Church to satisfy pious curiosity about the hidden years of Christ's childhood and transmitted to the later Middle Ages, these stories dramatize the tension latent in the unique situation of an incarnate God having to pass through the liminal stage of boyhood in an ordinary manner. Christ's parents and their Jewish neighbors try to restrain him, but the child's omniscient wisdom and almighty power are too great to be held in check. This Christ-Child is portrayed as existing on the margins of the Jewish community, spending all of his time playing outside rather than helping at home, learning at school or praying at the synagogue. Wishing to exert his freedom from control and his superiority over others, and also simply to amuse himself, the boy Jesus assumes the role of a trickster who exasperates the Jewish elders and his parents to whom they complain.[36] For example, Christ induces his playmates to imitate his sitting on a sunbeam, but they end up breaking their

---

[34] Mary Dove makes a similar observation in the chapter "*Hy tyme* in *Piers Plowman*," in her book *The Perfect Age of Man's Life* (Cambridge, 1986), p. 119.

[35] See Madigan, op. cit.

[36] A few scholars have characterized the Christ-Child in these legends as a trickster: Claude Gaignebet, *Le carnaval: essais de mythologie populaire* (Paris, 1974), p. 50-1; Kathleen M. Ashley, "The Guiler Beguiled: Christ and Satan as Theological Tricksters in Medieval Religious Literature," *Criticism* 24 (1982): 132-3; Thomas N. Hall, "The Miracles of the Lengthened Beam in Apocryphal and Hagiographic Tradition," in *Marvels, Monsters, and Miracles: Studies in the Medieval and Early Modern Imaginations*, ed. Timothy S. Jones and David A. Sprunger (Kalamazoo, Michigan, 2002), p.115.

necks.[37] When the Jewish parents hide their children from this dangerous boy by putting them in an oven, Jesus asks the man who is guarding
it what is in there. When the man lies to him by telling him that the oven
contains pigs, Jesus transforms the children into these creatures.[38] An
example of Jesus the trickster breaking a taboo is the story of his making
live birds from clay on the Sabbath. When the Jews hear about this, they

---

[37] This incident is described in some of the Middle English poems on the childhood
of Jesus. See MS Harley 2399, *Sammlung Altenglischer Legenden*, ed. C. Horstmann
(Heilbronn, 1878), p. 118, ll. 453-64; MS Additional 31042, "Nachträge zu den
Legenden," ed. Carl Horstmann, *Archiv für das Studium der neueren Sprachen und Literaturen*
74 (1885): 333, ll. 472-83; MS Laud 108, *Altenglische Legenden*, ed. C. Horstmann
(Paderborn, 1875), pp. 36-7, ll. 1051-82; MS University of Minnesota Z822 N81, *The
Middle English Stanzaic Versions of the Life of Saint Anne*, ed. Roscoe E. Parker (Oxford,
1971), p. 61, ll. 2341-67; pp. 62-3, ll. 2401-12. Medieval French poems on the childhood
of Jesus also relate this incident. See *The Old French Évangile de l'Enfance*, ed. Maureen
Boulton (Toronto, 1984), pp. 68-71; 1491-1580; *Les Enfaunces de Jesu Crist*, ed. Maureen
Boulton, Anglo-Norman Text Society no. 43 (London, 1985), pp. 65-7; ll.1157-1232.
The manuscript which served as the base text for the latter edition (Oxford, Bodleian
Library, MS Selden Supra 38) includes a miniature depicting this event, *Les Enfaunces*, p.
5. This scene is also illustrated in the *Holkham Bible Picture Book*, W. O. Hassall (London,
1954), folio 15v. As Hassall points out, this story is found in one of the manuscripts that
Constantine Tischendorf used for his edition of Pseudo-Matthew, p. 97. Tischendorf
prints this story (found in Florence, Biblioteca Medicea Laurenziana, MS *Gaddi* 208) in
the footnote to chapter 37 of his edition of Pseudo-Matthew: "Et cum Iesus cum aliis
infantulis super radios solis ubique plures ascenderet et sederet, multique simili modo
facere coeperunt, praecipitabantur, et eorum crura frangebantur et brachia. Sed dominus
Iesus sanabat omnes," *Evangelia Apocrypha*, p. 106.

[38] Cf. MS Harley 3954, *Sammlung*, pp. 107-8, ll. 487-530; MS Harley 2399, *Sammlung*,
pp. 116-17, ll. 361-96; MS Addit. 31042, "Nachträge," p. 332, ll. 364-99; MS Laud 108,
Altenglische Legenden, pp. 34-6, ll. 997-1050; *Les Enfaunces*, pp. 64-5; ll. 1101-56; *The Old
French Évangile*, p. 67-8, ll. 1437-90. In this anecdote the Christ-Child is portrayed as a
trickster because his transformation of the children into animals Jews regarded as
unclean alludes to the breaking of a taboo. A similar story in the Arabic Gospel of the
Infancy, in which the animals are goats, is believed to be the source, or at least an
analogue, of the pig episode found in later medieval poems. See *Evangelium infantiae
Arabicum*, in *Evangelia apocrypha*, p. 202. The pig scene is also illustrated in the Holkham
Bible Picture Book on folio 16r. Commenting on this picture, M.R. James notes that "in
the written stories of this miracle the metamorphosed children are changed back to their
proper forms; here the change is regarded as permanent, for it is said that the miracle is
the reason why Jews do not eat pork," "An English Bible-Picture Book of the
Fourteenth Century (Holkham MS. 666)," in *The Eleventh Volume of the Walpole Society
1922-23* (Oxford, 1969), p. 16. The scribe who wrote MS Laud 108 also gives this
explanation for the Jewish dietary custom: "And euereft sethþe for þis / þe Gyv for
broþur heold i wis / Euerech swyn in heore manere / ... / Ne neuere eft fram þat to þis
/ Gywes ne eten of swynes flechs," *Altenglische Legenden*, p. 36, ll. 1043-8. The pigs are
not described as being transformed back into children in this poem, nor are they
changed back in the two French poems cited above.

tell Joseph that his son is sacrilegious.[39] In these apocryphal legends, Jesus does not suffer a liminal period of youthful obscurity. Yet he *is* a liminal character in the sense that he is anti-social and never peacefully incorporated into the Jewish community.

Most medieval writers, however, who reflected upon the early life of Christ were impressed by the ordinariness of Christ's childhood and adolescence, and the humility that this implied in a God not used to being subject to the slow passage of time. In the young Christ, they saw an example of one who also serves who only stands and waits.

WORKS CITED

Aers, David. "Christ's Humanity and *Piers Plowman*: Contexts and Political Implications." *The Yearbook of Langland Studies* 8 (1994): 107-25.

_____. *Piers Plowman and Christian Allegory*. London: Edward Arnold, 1975.

Alexander Ashby. "The Meditations of Alexander of Ashby: An Edition." Ed. Thomas H. Bestul. *Mediaeval Studies* 52 (1990): 24-81.

Aquinas, Thomas. *Summa Theologiae, Tertia Pars*. Madrid: Biblioteca de Autores Cristianos, 1958.

Aristotle. *On the Soul*. In *The Basic Works of Aristotle*. Trans. Richard McKeon. New York: Random House, 1941.

Ashley, Kathleen M. "The Guiler Beguiled: Christ and Satan as Theological Tricksters in Medieval Religious Literature." *Criticism* 24 (1982): 126-37.

Bede. *Homeliarum Evangelii Libri II: Opera Homiletica: Pars III*. Ed. D. Hurst. CCSL 122. Turnhout: Brepols, 1955.

Biblia sacra iuxta vulgatam versionem. Ed. Robert Weber. 2 vols. Stuttgart: Deutsche Bibelgesellschaft, 1983.

Bonaventure. *Commentarius in Evangelium S. Lucae*. In *Opera Omnia*. Vol. 7. Quaracchi, 1895.

Boulton, Maureen. *Les Enfaunces de Jesu Crist*. Anglo-Norman Text Society no. 43. London: Anglo-Norman Text Society, 1985.

_____. *The Old French Evangile de l'Enfance*. Toronto: Pontifical Institute of Mediaeval Studies, 1984.

Burrow, J. A. *The Ages of Man: A Study in Medieval Writing and Thought*. Oxford: Clarendon Press, 1986.

---

[39] See, for example, *Evangelia apocrypha*, ch. 27, pp. 95.

Chrysostom, John. *Commentary on Saint John the Apostle and Evangelist: Homilies 1-47*. Trans. Sister Thomas Aquinas Goggin. New York:---, 1957.

Cohen, Jeremy. "The Jews as the Killers of Christ in the Latin Tradition, from Augustine to the Friars." *Traditio* 39 (1983): 1-27.

Comestor, Peter. *Historia Scholastica. Patrologia Latina* 198.

Curtius, Ernst Robert. *European Literature and the Latin Middle Ages*. Trans. Willard R. Trask. Princeton: Princeton University Press, 1973.

Dante. *The Banquet*. Trans. Christopher Ryan. Saratoga, California: Anma Libri, 1989.

Dove, Mary. *The Perfect Age of Man's Life*. Cambridge: Cambridge University Press, 1986.

Friedberg, A., ed. *Clementis Papae V Constitutiones*. In *Corpus Iuris Canonici*. Vol. 2. Graz: Akademische Druck-U. Verlagsanstalt, 1955.

Gaignebet, Claude. *Le carnaval: essais de mythologie populaire*. Paris: Payot, 1974.

Gnilka, Christian. *Aetas Spiritalis: Die Überwindung der natürlichen Altersstufen als Ideal frühchristlichen Lebens*. Bonn: Peter Hanstein Verlag, 1972.

Godden, Malcolm. *The Making of Piers Plowman*. London: Longman, 1990.

Gratian. *Decretum Magistri Gratiani*. Ed. A. Friedberg. Vol. 1. Graz: Akademische Druck-U. Verlagsanstalt, 1955.

Gregory the Great. *Homiliae in Hiezechihelem Prophetam*. Ed. Marcus Adriaen. CCSL 142. Turnhout: Brepols, 1971.

_____. *Règle Pastorale*. Ed. Floribert Rommel. Vol. 2. Paris: Les Éditions du Cerf, 1992.

Hall, Thomas N. "The Miracles of the Lengthened Beam in Apocryphal and Hagiographic Tradition." In *Marvels, Monsters, and Miracles: Studies in the Medieval and Early Modern Imaginations*. Ed. Timothy S. Jones and David A. Sprunger. Kalamazoo, Michigan: Medieval Institute Publications, 2002.

Hassall, W.O., ed. *Holkham Bible Picture Book*. 2nd edition. London: ---, 1954.

The Holy Bible Translated from the Latin Vulgate. Rockford, Illinois: Tan Books, 1971.

Horstmann, Carl, ed. *Altenglische Legenden: Kindheit Jesu, Geburt Jesu, Barlaam und Josaphat, St. Patrik's Fegefeuer*. Paderborn: Ferdinand Schöningh, 1875. [MS Laud 108]

_____. ed. "Nachträge zu den Legenden." *Archiv für das Studium der neueren Sprachen und Literaturen* 74 (1885): 327-39. [MS Additional 31042]

_____. ed. *Sammlung Altenglischer Legenden*. Heilbronn: Verlag Von Gebr. Henniger, 1878. [MS Harley 2399 & 3954]

Humbert of Romans. *De eruditione praedicatorum*. In *Maxima Bibliotheca Veterum Patrum*. Vol. 25. Lyons, 1677.

_____. *Sermones ad diuersos status*. Hagenau, 1508.

Irenaeus of Lyons. *Irénée de Lyons: Contre les hérésies: Livre II*. Ed. Adeline Rousseau and Louis Doutreleau. Vol. 2. Sources Chrétiennes. Paris: Les Éditions du Cerf, 1982.

Isidore of Seville. *Etymologiae*. Ed. W. M. Lindsay. Vol. 2. Oxford: Clarendon Press, 1911.

James, M.R. "An English Bible-Picture Book of the Fourteenth Century (Holkham MS. 666)." In *The Eleventh Volume of the Walpole Society 1922-23*. Oxford, 1969; reprint of 1923 edition.

Jerome. *Sancti Eusebii Hieronymi Epistolae: Pars I: Epistolae I-LXX*. Ed. Isidore Hilberg. CCEL 54. Turnhout: Brepols, 1996.

John de Caulibus. *Meditaciones Vite Christi*. Ed. M. Stallings-Taney. Turnhout: Brepols, 1997.

Klaeber, F., ed. *Beowulf and the Fight at Finnsburg*. 3rd edition. Lexington, Massachusetts, D.C. Heath and Co., 1950.

Langland, William. *Piers Plowman: The C-Text*. Ed. Derek Pearsall. Exeter: University of Exeter Press, 1994.

Legg, J. Wickham, ed. *The Sarum Missal Edited from Three Early English Manuscripts*. Oxford: Clarendon Press, 1916.

Lippe, Robert, ed. *Missale Romanum Mediolani, 1474*. Henry Bradshaw Society. Vol. 17.2. London: Harrison and Sons, 1899.

Lombard, Peter. *Sententiae in IV libris distinctae*. Vol. 2. Grottaferrata, 1981.

Love, Nicholas. *Nicholas Love's Mirror of the Blessed Life of Jesus Christ*. Ed. Michael Sargent. New York: Garland, 1992.

Love, Rosalind C., ed. *Vita S. Rumwoldi*. In *Three Eleventh-Century Anglo-Latin Saints' Lives*. Oxford: Clarendon Press, 1996.

Madigan, Kevin. "Did Jesus 'Progress in Wisdom'? Thomas Aquinas on Luke 2:52 in Ancient and High-Medieval Context." *Traditio* 52 (1997): 181-200.

Metz, René. "L'accession des mineurs à la cléricature et aux bénéfices ecclésiastiques dans le droit canonique médiéval." In *Recueil de mémoires et travaux: Mélanges Roger Aubenas*. Montpellier: Faculté de droit et des sciences économiques de Montpellier, 1974. Reprinted in *Le femme et l'enfant dans le droit canonique médiéval*. London: Variorum Reprints, 1985.

Mirk, John. *Mirk's Festial: A Collection of Homilies*. Ed. Theodor Erbe. EETS e.s. 96. Millwood, New York: Kraus, 1975; reprint of 1905 ed.

Parker, Roscoe E. *The Middle English Stanzaic Versions of the Life of Saint Anne*. EETS o.s. 174. New York: Kraus, 1971; reprint of 1928 ed.

Saward, John. *Perfect Fools: Folly for Christ's Sake in Catholic and Orthodox Spirituality*. Oxford: Oxford University Press, 1980.

Smith, William George. *The Oxford Dictionary of English Proverbs*. 2nd edition. Oxford: Clarendon Press, 1963.

Torrell, Jean-Pierre. *Saint Thomas Aquinas: Volume I: The Person and His Work*. Trans. Robert Royal. Washington, D.C.: The Catholic University of America Press, 1996.

Thompson, Stith. *Motif-Index of Folk Literature*. Vol. 3 and Vol. 5. Indiana University Press, Bloomington, Indiana, 1975.

Tischendorf, Constantine, ed. *Evangelia Apocrypha*. Hildesheim: Georg Olms, Verlagsbuchhandlung, 1966; reprint of 1876 ed.

Walter of Chatillon. *The Alexandreis*. Trans. R. Telfryn Pritchard. Toronto: Pontifical Institute of Mediaeval Studies, 1986.

_____. *Galteri de Castellione Alexandreis*. Ed. Marvin L. Colker. Passau: In Aedibus Antenoreis, 1978.

William of Tournai. *The De instructione puerorum of William of Tournai, O. P.* Ed. James A. Corbett. Notre Dame, Indiana: The Mediaeval Institute, 1955.

Wasyliw, Patricia Healy. "The Pious Infant: Developments in Popular Piety during the High Middle Ages." In *Lay Sanctity, Medieval and Modern: A Search for Models*. Ed. Ann W. Astell. Notre Dame, Indiana: University of Notre Dame Press, 2000.

William of Tournai. *The De instructione puerorum of William of Tournai, O.P.* Ed. James A. Corbett. Notre Dame: The Mediaeval Institute of Notre Dame, 1955.

Missale Romanum Mediolani, 1474 [
In epiphania domini
Dominica infra octauam epyphanie (Luc. 2:42-52)
In octaua epiphanie (Ioan. 1.29-34)
Dominica secunda post epiphaniam (Ioan. 2.1-11)

The Sarum Missal Done into English, A. Harford Pearson [
The Epiphany (Matt.2:1-12)
The Octave of Epiphany (Matt. 3-13-17)
First Sunday after Epiphany (Luke 2:42-52)
i.e. First Sunday after the Octave of Epiphany
Second Sunday after Epiphany (John 2:1-11)

The Sarum Missal in English, Part 1, vol. 8
Trans. Frederick E. Warren, London: Alexander Moring, 1911
The Epiphany (Matt. 2:1-12)
Octave of Epiphany (Matt. 3:13-17)
Sunday after Octave of Epiphany (Luke 2:42-52)
Second Sunday after the Octave of Epiphany (John 2:1-11)

JANE RUPERT

FRANCIS BACON AND JOHN HENRY NEWMAN ON THE THRESHOLDS OF THOUGHT

ABSTRACT. An exploration of the reflections of John Henry Newman in *The Idea of a University* and of Francis Bacon in *The Advancement of Learning* on methods and the way modes of thought structure education.

The various modes of reasoning, such as induction or speculative thought, are portals which shape how we see the world. They stand at the threshold of thought and, as instruments, are determined by the end they serve. Through the observations of Francis Bacon in *The Advancement of Learning* (1605) and of John Henry Newman in *The Idea of a University (1852)*, I shall consider two different ends in education and, consequently, the methods which they cultivated.

In their writing on education both Bacon and Newman took a sanguine look at the state of learning in their periods. Bacon's purpose in *The Advancement of Learning* was to assess the strengths and deficiencies of the learning in his time. His mission in life was nothing less than to redirect radically the end of learning towards the area where it appeared most deficient: that is, towards useful knowledge, the study of the laws of the physical world with a view to their application in new ways for the material betterment of mankind. Bacon perceived that the thrust he gave towards the study of material nature heralded a new age for learning, away from the areas of truth concerning human affairs considered previously such as politics, ethics, or poetry. He believed that Greece and Rome occupied "the *middle part* of time," as "two exemplar states of the world for arms, learning, moral virtue, policy, and laws" (Bacon 1962: 74-5). In *the De Augmentis Scientiarum*, he writes of his own period as a time "in which learning seems to have now made her third visitation to men" which might "far surpass the Greek and Roman in learning" (Farrington 1951: 41-2). The new orientation of learning towards the

Limina: Thresholds and Borders - A St. Michael's College Symposium
Joseph Goering, Francesco Guardiani, Giulio Silano eds. Ottawa: Legas, 2005

material world was intended to effect a restoration or renewal of the first estate of Eden before man "lost the dominion over the creatures which was its highest privilege" and to provide relief for his suffering since from "want, sickness, and death" (Ellis, *Works of Francis Bacon*: 58).

Bacon believed passionately that the time had come to rectify the neglect of the study of the physical world. The reorientation of the end of learning towards useful knowledge was to be made possible through a refinement of the inductive method traditionally associated with the investigation of the physical sciences. Bacon noted in *The Advancement of Learning* that previous philosophy had erred in a too great mistrust of the senses and in paying too little attention to particulars essential to the inductive method. He believed that his *novum organon*, or new logic for the study of cause and effect in the physical world, would "suffice to obviate the deficiencies of sensory perception" (Farrington 1951: 137). The certainty obtained through reforming the "remiss proofs" in the method of induction had enormous potential for human control of the material domain. Knowledge of uniform laws would

> Enfranchise the power of man unto the greatest liberty and possibility of works and effects…For physical causes give light to new invention in *simili materia*, but whosoever knoweth any Form, knoweth the utmost possibility of super-inducing that nature upon any variety of matter. (Bacon 1962: 96)

What Bacon proposed was a great shift in learning from liberal knowledge towards applied knowledge. His zealous redirection of education towards a largely undeveloped kind of truth meant in effect a battle with the kind of learning which had predominated for two thousand years in order to dislodge this learning from its dominant position. To promote applied or useful knowledge, what had to be thrown off in particular was the speculative tradition in learning originating in Greek thought with its emphasis on first principles or ideas. Because this learning, exemplified in Plato and Aristotle, had no immediate practical application it was deemed unfruitful or useless. William Rawley, Bacon's secretary, remarks that Bacon "first fell into the dislike of the philosophy of Aristotle" when still a student at Cambridge. This dislike was based not on "the worthlessness of the author, to whom he would ever ascribe high attributes, but for the unfruitfulness of the way; being…only strong for disputations and contentions, but barren of the production of works for the benefit of the life of man."[1] In *The Advance-*

---

[1] "Dr. Rawley's Life of Bacon," *Works of Francis Bacon*, 4.

ment of Learning, Bacon criticizes Plato for making ideas the end of knowledge rather than the application of abstract laws to matter:

> Plato, in his opinion of Ideas,…did descry, *that Forms were the true object of knowledge;* but lost the real fruit of his opinion, by considering of Forms as absolutely abstracted from matter, and not confined and determined by matter; and so turning his opinion upon theology, wherewith all his natural philosophy is infected. But if any man shall keep a continual watchful and severe eye upon action, operation, and the use of knowledge, he may advise and take notice what are the Forms, the disclosures whereof are fruitful and important to the state of man. (94)[2]

So successful were Bacon's successors in generating a new departure for learning oriented towards the physical sciences along with the method appropriate to them that scarcely two hundred and fifty years later Newman sought to defend what risked being eclipsed. Already there was a need to defend the dignity of the liberal education that Bacon sought to displace in order to make room for the study of physical science. *In The Idea of a University,* Newman represents the uneasy relation between applied and liberal studies through reference to a public quarrel conducted in a review earlier in the century. In an exchange of articles, the devaluation of the classics by advocates of a socially useful education had prompted a retort by Oxford defenders of the classics. These defenders protested against the whole man being "shaped, pressed, and stiffened, in the exact mould of his technical character." For the person allowed *only* a professional education, "any interloping accomplishments, or a faculty which cannot be taken into public pay, if they are to be indulged in him at all, must creep along under the cloak of his more serviceable privileged merits."[3] The lines of demarcation had been clearly drawn: from the vantage point of the advocates of both the applied sciences and of professional education, humanist learning was useless; the humanists, for their part, perceived the training in judgment offered through a knowledge of first principles and a study of literature to be of comprehensive personal worth and, as such, valuable in the useful sci

---

[2] In his Preface to "Bacon's Philosophical Works," Robert Leslie Ellis suggests that Bacon uses the word "form" in the sense of law. "For instance, the Form of heat is a kind of local motion of the particles of which bodies are composed, and that of whiteness a mode of arrangement among those particles. This peculiar motion or arrangement corresponds to and engenders heat or whiteness, and this in every case in which those qualities exist." *Works of Francis Bacon,* 29.

[3] John Davison, cited by Newman, *Idea,* 129.

ences, in a merchant career, in the civil service, to a clergyman, in the home or amongst friends in the pleasures of good conversation.

What Newman champions in *The Idea of a University* includes the speculative knowledge that Bacon had rejected in the interests of promoting modern empirical science. Yet, in his arguments for liberal education Newman refers to the same principles as Bacon concerning the distinctions between the physical domain, the human, and the divine, and the different methods appropriate to different areas of truth. Indeed, Newman was familiar with Bacon's works and esteemed his thought. In *The Idea of a University*, there are more than twenty-four references to Bacon or the Baconian method where Newman draws several quotations from Bacon's *Advancement of Learning* and from its later Latin adaptation into the longer work, *De Augmentis Scientiarum* (1623).

The Idea of a University is in part a defense of the study of speculative knowledge and of literature which are at the heart of the university against the aggressions of the Baconian school, the successors of Bacon who declared liberal learning to be useless, that applied knowledge alone was of account. Newman praises the fruits of modern science and the school for which Bacon was the impetus, but he also indicates the need to recognize that only material benefits can be provided by the "Baconian school." In the Discourse in *The Idea of a University* entitled "Knowledge its Own End," Newman refers to the indebtedness of almost everyone in the period to the Baconian method for "his daily food, his health, and general well-being." He describes Bacon's mission as "the increase of physical enjoyment and social comfort," a design which he remarks had been "most wonderfully, most awfully... fulfilled." But he observes that while Bacon as the Prophet of Utility "was the divinely provided minister of temporal benefits to all of us," he nonetheless typified "the intellectual narrowness of his school." The Philosophy of Utility was "simply a Method whereby bodily discomforts and temporal wants are to be most effectually removed from the greatest number" (89-90).

The speculative thought defended by Newman involves the apprehension of fundamental ideas that are the starting-points of any issue or any branch of learning. Training of the mind in speculative thought is an education in perennial ideas, each grasped as the source of myriad facts. Like training in the habit of mind of literature, its purpose is personal: to refine the individual's judgment on contemporary issues in shifting historical circumstances through a personal grasp of fundamental underlying ideas. Newman exemplifies this judgment of contemporary issues through an understanding of underlying principles in *The Idea of a University* as he evaluates what is important to the nineteenth-century university through a clear definition of liberal knowledge as distinguished from applied knowledge. *The Idea of a University* is itself a demonstration of the value of speculative thought and the training provided by a liberal education.

Like Bacon, Newman was also profoundly aware of the influence of method. Bacon's *Novum Organum*, or new method, was a promotion of the rational instrument essential to the development of the modern physical sciences where Aristotle's *organon*, the verbal method of logic, could hold no sway. From Newman's vantage point in the nineteenth century, he recognized that the method promoted by Bacon had come to dominate the processes of thought, to be accepted increasingly as the sole rational instrument valid even in those subject-matters such as religion and theology where it could be no more effectual than Aristotle's logic applied to the physical sciences. While he admired Bacon and his clear distinction between methods and areas of truth, he deplored the Baconian successors who recognized only a single method and would apply it to all subject-matters. Indeed, Newman's final work, the *Grammar of Assent* (1870), was a response to unbelief in the scientific community when all areas of truth were subjected to the same criterion for evidence exacted by the physical sciences. In this final work, Newman argued for the validity of another *organon* associated with indemonstrable matters and commonly used in our daily decisions, in religious assents and in the reasoning of literature.

Bacon's battle against speculative thought was a new variation on the ancient quarrel over the relative merits of the active life and the contemplative life of *theoria*. A comparison of Aristotle's and Bacon's positions in the debate illustrates the shift advocated by Bacon towards a new direction in education. For Aristotle, both the practical and the theoretical were desirable in themselves because both are parts of our rational humanity, or, as Aristotle states in Book vi of *the Nicomachean Ethics*, because "each one of them is the virtue of a different part of the soul" (1144a). Aristotle values theoretical wisdom because it is simply the fulfilment of the intellectual part of our humanity and "what is by nature proper to each thing will be at once the best and the most pleasant for it" (1178a). As one classical scholar points out, Aristotle "rates experience very high indeed for practical purposes," as in the practice of medicine. "Nevertheless experience does not reach the level of Art of Science...till the universal implicit in experience is made explicit." It is when we "reach the stage of intellect" that the fully human level is attained (Burnet 1904: 67). For Aristotle, the debate on the active and contemplative lives is not an either-or question. Both practical and theoretical knowledge are important, but theoretical knowledge of any sort is of a higher order because it is more elemental.

In the final book of the *Ethics*, Aristotle describes theoretical or speculative wisdom as a divine element within us, "small in bulk" but surpassing "everything else in power and value." He observes: "One might even regard it as each man's true self, since it is the controlling and better part." He suggests that through speculative activity we "become immortal as far as that is possible;" this is for our own happiness in fulfilling our nature and because the gods "rejoice in what is best and most akin to them" (1177b, 1179a). Aristotle also observes that the nature of theoretical wisdom or speculative truth makes it susceptible to accusation of uselessness. Unlike practical wisdom, theoretical wisdom risks being called useless because, while practical wisdom deals with matters helpful to us, theoretical wisdom concerns not only pure science but "things which by their nature are valued most highly" and seeks a good which is not human but divine (1141b).

In his part in the debate over the relative merits of the active and contemplative lives, Bacon rejects Aristotle's view of the contemplative life as higher than the active life on the grounds that the contemplative life is private, making no contribution to the good of the greater body. In *The Advancement of Learning*, he points out that all the reasons Aristotle "bringeth for the contemplative are private, and respecting the pleasure and dignity of a man's self, (in which respects, no question, the contemplative life hath the pre-eminence)" (156). Bacon also cites Biblical examples of physical wants supplied, thus effectively rejecting Aristotle's claim that speculative thought more nearly approached the divine. He declares conclusively that the highest end for knowledge is "for the glory of the Creator and the relief of man's estate" (35). For this there is no need of what is merely personal or "useful only to the mind of the speculator." In his argument, Bacon effectively shifted the foundation of education by insisting on the greater importance of the common good as its end over individual good as its end and by claiming for material betterment as a goal in learning the same dignity traditionally accorded to personal intellectual cultivation.

The lines of battle were drawn. On the one hand, there was a Greek ideal in education transmitted through a continuous humanist tradition that was oriented towards a personal intellectual good; on the other

hand, there was the reorientation of learning towards the materially useful and the common good coupled with the rejection of the humanist
tradition. A mere two hundred and fifty years after the publication of
Bacon's *The Advancement of Learning*, the success of physical science had
been such that Newman spends the second half of his Discourses
defending humanist learning too easily dismissed as useless. He is
typically inclusive, resisting the mutilation of the circle of learning
through the exclusion of what Aristotle had considered its most
precious part. Although the most successful faculty at the Catholic
University of Ireland was the School of Medicine, Newman placed at
the centre of the University a training for all students in the habits of
mind of Letters and speculative thought. In his Inaugural Lecture to the
School of Philosophy and Letters, he states at the outset that "in spite of
the special historical connexion of University Institution with the
sciences of Theology, Law, and Medicine, a University, after all, should
be formally based (as it really is), and should emphatically live in, the
Faculty of Arts." He observes that "the studies which that Faculty
embraces are almost the direct subject-matter and the staple of the
mental exercises proper to a University" (*Idea*, 187).[4]

In the *Idea*, Newman draws particularly on Aristotle's arguments in the
Nicomachean Ethics to defend the continuous tradition of liberal education. Like Aristotle, he rests his defense on the claim that personal
thought and the personal understanding of principles are simply part of
our human nature and essential to our development as human beings.
He contends that Aristotle's definition of liberal knowledge, in contrast
to useful knowledge is an "archetypal idea"; it is "founded in our very
nature" and attested by its longevity in a "continuous historical tradition" (83). Just as Aristotle validates the exercise of the intellect in
speculative truth as the exercise of a part of our soul and so the fulfillment of part of our humanity, so in the *Idea* Newman states that the
word "liberal as applied to Knowledge and Education, expresses a specific idea, which ever has been, and ever will be, while the nature of man
is the same." Although the subjects that are considered liberal vary with
the age, the idea "varies not itself" as would be the case if it were "a mere
generalization" from the subject matters (83).

---

[4] Ironically, this Faculty was the least successful at the Catholic University of Ireland.
Newman wrote in a letter to John Hungerford Pollen (Nov. 26, 1857) that the Faculty of
Philosophy and Letters was the most lame, prospering less than Medicine and Science
because it had not attracted Irish youths. *The Letters and Diaries of John Henry Newman*,
187.

Like Aristotle, Newman also claims that what is natural to us is a source of pleasure. In defending liberal education, Newman refers directly to Aristotle's observation that we derive enjoyment from fulfilling the speculative part of our nature. He cites Aristotle's distinction between the useful and the liberal: "Of possessions, those rather are useful, which bear fruit; those *liberal which tend to enjoyment*" (82). Newman also elicits the testimony of Cicero in *The Offices* as familiar to his nineteenth-century audience. Cicero argued that the pursuit of truth is a delight, a "condition of our happiness," to be enjoyed in the leisure when the physical wants of our animal nature have been supplied and our duties fulfilled (79). Newman points again to the personal good of this pursuit, adding that "strange as such a procedure is to those who live after the rise of the Baconian philosophy,....The idea of benefiting society by means of "the pursuit of science and knowledge" did not enter at all into the motives which he [Cicero] would assign for their cultivation" (79-80).

In his contribution to the debate on the relative merits of contemplative and practical education, Newman, like Aristotle, recognizes both modes, clearly distinguishes between their goals, and defends the importance of the theoretical knowledge of underlying principles. He speaks in the *Idea* of "two ways of using Knowledge," and "two methods of Education;...the one rises towards general ideas, the other is exhausted upon what is particular and external." *Theoria* or philosophic knowledge is an end in itself because there is no further end beyond this highest activity which deals in first principles and leading ideas containing the germ of all that develops from them. For this reason, liberal or philosophical knowledge is the "principle of real dignity in Knowledge, its worth, its desirableness" (85).

Newman makes clear that what he is defending in his day against its disparagement by Baconian promoters of useful knowledge is a Greek educational ideal of habituating the individual to think independently especially through an understanding of *theoria*, of elemental ideas or principles. At the beginning of Discourse vi entitled "Knowledge Viewed in Relation to Learning," he regrets the lack of any English word that corresponds satisfactorily to the Greek word for a particular intellectual disposition achieved through the exercise and training of the mind or intellectual culture. Newman states:

> It were well if the English, like the Greek language, possessed some definite word to express, simply and generally, intellectual proficiency or perfection, such as "health," as used with reference to the animal frame, and "virtue,"

with reference to our moral nature... Every one knows practically what are the constituents of health or of virtue; and every one recognizes health and vir-tue as ends to be pursued; it is otherwise with intellectual excellence. (93-4)

He draws on the same analogy of the healthy state of the body which Aristotle uses in the Ethics to explain the usefulness of *theoria*. In the *Ethics*, Aristotle states that theoretical wisdom produces happiness "not as medicine produces health, but as health itself makes a person healthy" (1144a). Newman asks:

If a healthy body is a good in itself, why is not a healthy intellect? And if a College of Physicians is a useful institution, because it contemplates bodily health, why is not an Academical Body, though it were simply and solely engaged in imparting vigour and beauty and grasp to the intellectual portion of our nature? (*Idea*, 122)

Newman's view of liberal education stands clearly in the tradition of the Greek *paideia*. For Newman, a liberal education was not concerned with the physical betterment of mankind nor directly with the common good; it was concerned with the development of our human nature which requires an understanding of the principles behind things, a perspective essential to independent judgment. The Greek word *paideia*, which Cicero translated as *humanitas*, describes a humanism that had for its goal the most complete blossoming or development of the individual's personality. In Greek civilization, *paideia* assumed a resonance that evolved from referring simply to the technique for a child's education to suggesting the most complete realization of the person as person, the human ideal described in the word culture which for the Greek had a personalist rather than a collective sense. *Paideia* referred to a most precious good, i.e., the full development of an individual's human potential realized through the cultivation of the mind throughout one's life.

For Newman the training of the speculative intellect, as in the Greek *paideia*, is a personal task in which we learn to use our own minds as we use our own eyes. In the Idea, Newman describes this cultivation of the intellect, the aim of a liberal education, as the training of «intellectual eyes.» Through «research and systematizing» (95),through analysis, comparisons, and discriminations, the mind reduces matters to «order and meaning» (101), seizing on the strong point in a subject, reaching out to truth and grasping it. Newman describes this philosophic knowledge as «an acquired illumination,...a habit, a personal possession, and an inward endowment» (85). Such interior personal knowledge is a «state or condition of mind» and «something individual and permanent» (86).

The tradition of the Greek *paideia* as a personal development is reflected by Newman in the *Preface* to the *Idea* where he suggested that the University is for the sake of the students rather than for the «sake of the Sciences, which are to be the matter.» It is for the formation of the students, for «their exercise and growth in certain habits, moral or intellectual» (xxxviii-ix). Like Aristotle, Newman states that in seeking liberal knowledge as an end in itself, «we are satisfying a direct need of our nature in its very acquisition.» He says that this is how we realize or actualize ourselves:

> Our nature, unlike that of the inferior creation, does not at once reach its perfection, but depends, in order to it, on a number of external aids and appliances. Knowledge, as one of the principal of these, is valuable for what its very presence in us does for us after the manner of a habit, even though it be turned to no further account, nor subserve any direct end. (*Idea*, 78)

Newman's impassioned defense of humanist learning makes him, like Bacon, a champion engaged in the battle of warring ideas. Where Bacon sought to release learning from the tyranny of speculative thought, Newman sought to protect speculative thought from its exclusion by useful knowledge. Their differences proceed from the moments in history to which they belong; both were concerned about the state of learning in their time and sought to strengthen it where it was deficient. For Bacon, this meant a zealous reorientation of learning away from a long classical tradition towards physical science and the method associated with it; for Newman it meant advocating the central importance of humanist learning and the habits of mind of both Philosophy and Letters which risked dismissal by modern science.

Both Bacon and Newman caution against the exclusion of areas of truth or methods. Methods as liminal, or portals, determine what we see. Habituation to one way of looking at things, whether through methods suited to speculative knowledge or to physical science, leads to a neglect of those areas of truth which are not apprehended through the favoured method. At the Catholic University of Ireland, Newman sought to include all learning, from applied sciences like Engineering to contemplative thought or *theoria*. Because he considered *theoria* important to all students as the fulfilment of their intellectual nature, he wanted all of them to pursue liberal studies, adapted to their particular interests, for two years before specializing in their chosen professions. The inclusive ideal represented in this University is a model for our own times when the humanities must justify their role before the tribunal of useful knowledge.

WORKS CITED

Aristotle. *Nicomachean Ethics.* Indianapolis: Bobbs-Merrill, 1962.

Bacon, Francis. *The Advancement of Learning.* New York: Dutton, 1962.

Bacon, Francis. *Works of Francis Bacon*, vol. 1, Ed. James Spedding, Robert Leslie Ellis and Douglas Denon. London: Longmans, 1858.

Farrington, Benjamin. *Francis Bacon: Philosopher of Industrial Science.* London: Lawrence and Wishart, 1951.

Newman, John Henry. *The Idea of a University*, Ed. Martin J. Svaglic. Notre Dame: U. of Notre Dame P., 1986.

Newman, John Henry. *The Letters and Diaries of John Henry Newman.* Oxford: Clarendon, 1964-8.

NEIL HOBBS

GOING INTO HOSPITAL:
A BOUNDARY FOR THE ILL BETWEEN
THE INSTITUTION AND THE COMMUNITY

Dedicated to Maggie Cuvelier.
Without her kind of kindness and persistence
physicians might never learn their craft.

ABSTRACT. Admission into a Canadian hospital constitutes a significant event - the crossing of a threshold. This paper describes my reflections on palliative care, a regenerating
branch of medicine that delivers compassionate care to the dying patient and also has the
potential to heal the much deeper rift that has divided humanistic and scientific thought in
medicine..

As a family physician it is a rare opportunity to venture outside the
everyday world of medicine, a world that sometimes seems sealed off
from other fields of academic endeavour. Within the broad ambit of
medicine, the practice of clinical medicine may sometime be remote
from other medical sciences, and family medicine as a generalist discipline often lives apart from the world of specialists. Many of these divi-
sions relate to my topic today.

The split between the two worlds of science and the humanities is a
long and deep one. Do we place the origin of the split to the time of
Descartes and the 1700s? Or to Enlightenment thinking of the eighteenth century, and the resultant wave of discoveries in science. Whatever the cause of the rift, there is much to be done to heal the breach.

In this paper I would like to discuss the boundary that exists between
world inside the hospital and that outside in our homes and communities. When I have talked to patients about this boundary, there is instant
recognition and no shortage of information based on personal experience. Many patients have found the boundary a difficult one to cross in

Limina: Thresholds and Borders - A St. Michael's College Symposium
Joseph Goering, Francesco Guardiani, Giulio Silano eds. Ottawa: Legas, 2005

either direction, and two of my patients[1] will be discussed in this paper. The difficulties can be such that a patient of mine, an 87-year Scottish woman who I cared for recently at home as she died of esophageal cancer over a period of about six months, made me promise not to have her readmitted after her experiences in hospital when her illness was originally diagnosed[2].

I think that the process of going into hospital [even the words 'admission' and 'discharge' seem to denote some special process going on] is more than a physical one, and involves emotional, social and cultural factors that make for multiple *limina*. My interest in this process derives from my involvement in the *patient-centred care model of care* promoted in Canadian family medicine teaching programs for a number of years, and due in great part to the efforts of Joseph Levenstein and his fruitful collaboration with physicians based at the Department of Family Medicine of the University of Western Ontario in the 1980s.[3]

The patient-centred clinical method is complementary to the notion of *disease-centred models of care where the attentions of carers* are focussed around the nature of the illness. Such a dichotomy of view harks back to the early work of Carl Rogers[4] in sociological research of the 1950s and the

---

[1] I have had a half-time academic practice in the Department of Family Medicine at Queen's University for the last seventeen years. At last estimate there were about 750 patients in the practice. I have an interest in chronic pain and palliative care.

[2] Carcinoma of the esophagus is associated with pain, difficulty with eating and drinking, and the secondary effects of weight loss, weakness and fatigue. Diagnosis is made by examining the tumour through a fibre-optic device inserted down the esophagus. Punch biopsies are obtained to make a histological diagnosis. This patient, though, was chiefly concerned much more about the poor communication that existed at her time of diagnosis. She was in hospital on what is known within the hospital culture as '*Black Monday*', the first working day in July in Canadian Hospitals when all residencies and internships start. It is also traditional for consulting staff to rotate on a monthly basis, so that [as in this lady's case] all the consulting staff are usually encountering patients for the first time during that month's rotation.

[3] See particularly *Patient Centred Medicine: Transforming the Clinical Method*, 2nd edition, Moira Brown, Judith Belle Brown, Wayne Weston, Carol McWilliam and Thomas Freeman, 2003, Radcliffe Publications, Oxford, for further information on this topic.

[4] Rogers C [1951]. *Client-centred therapy; Its current practice implications and theory.* Cambridge MA: Riverside.

research of Michael Balint[5], a British psychiatrist as they tried to tease the notion of 'person [or patient]-centredness' away from the more classical models of disease-centred behaviour.

Patient-centred models of care teach that the patient's ideas and feelings about what it is to be ill, as well as their understanding of the doctor's role and their expectations of that physician have as important a part to play in holistic care as a competent understanding of the processes of illness. Not only should diseases be competently defined and managed but the physician should make an active attempt to understand the illness and the *personal experience of that illness* through the variety of contexts – social, geographical, political, educational, cultural, racial, lifecycle etc. that in Eric Cassell's words make up the 'topology of the person'[6]. For a number of years since the promulgation of ideas about illness experience Canadian family medicine programs have sought to emphasize in their teaching programs the interconnected roles of disease pathology and illness experience, including the modifying effect of the latter upon the former[7].

Patients' stories of their illness play a highly significant part in their life. As family physicians we have an important hermeneutic roles to interpret the significance of these 'illness narratives'. It is significant that Hermes' wings are included on the versions of the caduceus with the snake of Aeculapius. Hermes was the god of interpretation besides his other rôles as messenger of the Gods, and the god of commerce, the winds and air, gymnastics and exercise, thieves and traitors...and luck at

---

[5] Balint M [1957]. *The doctor, his [sic] patient and the illness.* New York: International Universities Press.

[6] See Cassell E *The Meaning of suffering and the goals of medicine* New England Journal of Medicine *306*, 11; 639-645 March 1982. For a further description of the topology of the person. Eric Cassell has appropriated the notion of topology from mathematics where it is intimately concerned with the properties and behaviours of surfaces and the boundaries that delineate those surfaces.

[7] For a fuller description of the educational role in undergraduate medicine curricula see the College of Family Physicians of Canada's discussion paper '*The Present and Promise of Family Medicine in Undergraduate Education*' published in September 2000. Wayne Weston MD [also a co-author of *Patient-Centre Medicine (op. cit.)* writes specifically of the social and community context of illness in ch. 5 '*What we Bring*' pp.33-43]

games. Sadly, medical students have often never heard of the meanings of both these icons of their profession.[8]

The importance of narrative[9] explains why I have chosen a quasi-narrative presentation to model the experience of my two patients, Maggie C. and Peter V. On occasion I have digressed slightly to explain some of the significant medical details of their illness.

Maggie C.

It was a bright and frosty night last December as I pulled up in my car outside a condominium in a ten-year-old development just outside the centre of Kingston. I have practised here in this city as a family physician with a special interest in palliative care for over fifteen years.

I was on my way to see Mrs. Maggie C., a fifty-five-year old woman who had been referred to me through our palliative care service earlier in the month. It was Maggie who really provided me with the initial impetus to crystallize my ideas about the boundaries that exist between institutions and the home. She [and others] have helped me reflect on other related boundaries: between the insouciance of being healthy and the pains and uncertainties of being ill, and about the ultimate boundary between life and death.

---

[8] Forms and symbolism of various forms of the caduceus are hotly disputed by medical historians. Although the word derives from καδηκειος□□ the staff of Hermes, the various representations may go back to Babylonian times. The presence of Mercurial winged sandals may in fact derive from the use of the element mercury in the treatment of eye diseases, and some caducei do not possess wings. For a fuller discussion of the forms and use of the caduceus see Hart, Gerald D *The Earliest Use of the Caduceus* Canadian Medical Association Journal 9[Dec 1972], 1107-9; and Geelhoed, Glenn W *The Caduceus as a Medical Emblem: Heritage or Heresy?* Southern Medical Journal 81 [Sept 1988], 1155-58.

[9] See *Narrative Based Medicine: Dialogue and discourse in clinical practice* eds. Trisha Greenhalgh and Brian Hurwitz 1998, British Medical Journal Books, London for a fuller description of the role of narrative in the daily interchanges of physicians and patients. *Following the Story: continuity of care in general practice* by Iona Heath and *Stories we hear and stories we tell...analysing talk in general practice* by Glyn Elwyn and Richard Gwyn particularly illustrate the importance of comprehending the role of narrative in family medicine. If we are to construct meaningful *pathographies* in the manner of Mary Catherine Bodden's hagiographies described in *Limiting Women's Speech, Limiting Women's Sanctity*, we will need to include far more than mere clinical information to provide a coherent whole.

A digression on some aspects of palliative care

Palliative care has been defined as a "concept of compassionate, competent care where cure is no longer an achievable objective" and brings care, not only to the seriously ill, but to their circle of loved ones. Palliative care [from *pallium,* a cloak, or the shelter associated with such an item of clothing] is what caregivers perhaps have *always* done with the sick.

The modern era of palliative care within the English-speaking world may be dated from the work of early hospices that included the foundation of St. Christopher's Hospice[10] in London, England, by Dame Cicely Saunders in 1967; and in Canada from the opening of the first palliative care unit in Winnipeg at Grey Nuns' Hospital in 1972.

It is hard to look back and see where my first involvement with palliative care began. It certainly predates my appointment to an academic unit of family medicine at Queen's in 1987. I think it dates from about 1980 when I was working as a government physician in the quite remote community of North-West River in Northern Labrador, about 20 miles north of Goose Bay[11].

I was asked to look after a 40-year-old woman with widespread cervical cancer, who I was told " had come from Hamilton...to die at home". And die is with difficulty what she later did, though it was not easy to look after her with the very little knowledge that I had about care of the dying. At that time I would have found it hard to articulate even the basic principles of palliative care came with later learning and experience. Certainly my hospital medical training in the late sixties came only a few years after St. Chrsitopher's had started operation, and the concepts of palliative care were barely formulated at that time.

---

[10] Although St. Christopher's Hospice was opened in 1967, as Saunders points out in *A Personal Therapeutic Journey [British medical Journal 313(December 1996), 1599-1601]* there were other pioneering hospices and other charitable institutions that built on time-honoured institutions of charitable care that had existed from the middle ages. St. Luke's Hospital and St Joseph's Hospice were two institutions that were doing early palliative work prior to the opening of St. Christopher's Hospice. Saunders worked at both of these intstitutions.

[11] The hospital in North-West River was one built by the Grenfell Association that was founded by the medical missionary, Wilfred Grenfell in 1914 to serve communities in Northern Newfoundland and Labrador. North West River hospital closed in the 1980s, but much of the infrastructure that was founded then has been absorbed in to the Health Labrador Corporation. See http://www.hlc.nf.ca and www.iga.nf.net/ for further information.

Now, taking the elevator to Maggie's apartment [and the only place we ever met in the months I have cared for her][12], I can appreciate the developments that have taken place in my community of 125,000 inhabitants since 1987. Now we have a team of seven physicians, mostly family physicians, working in two hospitals in the city as well as in the community. We work with numerous other health-care workers, especially nurses and community support workers. Maggie is one of over 500 patients to be similarly visited at home in 2002. Besides home visits there are consultations and visits in our two hospitals, one with a six-bedded palliative care unit, and in clinics in the Kingston regional cancer centre. Total physician visits last year were over one thousand. Our job would be next to impossible without the technical support of faxes, cell phones, e-mail and pagers especially as so much work is being done in the domiciliary context. Apart from pagers all such technology has come into common use since 1987, and do much to keep us connected.

Maggie's husband, Frank, lets me in to the apartment and I meet Maggie in a wheelchair in the comfortable living room[13]. Her referring physician had said, "...she really is in [a] very fragile condition and her husband Frank, recently retired, is very attentive..[she] has end-stage respiratory failure.."

The story as she told it was a remarkable one. I have often bridled at Osler's dictum to medical students that 'your patients are your best teachers'; as I age, I become ever more convinced that this dictum is true, and Maggie is an excellent examplar.

Her medical symptoms started over thirty years ago when she experienced multiple admissions to hospital with gastric, respiratory and neurological complaints. All of the symptoms had been exhaustively investigated to no avail. She had come to dread hospital as a place where she would have to tell her story anew each time, receive lengthy and often painful investigations...and be no nearer a diagnosis. Eventually she came to fear the oft-implied appraisal of her symptoms that they were 'all in her head'. As the years progressed, so did her symptoms of persistent weakness, problems with her vision and breathing, and unexplained nervous, muscular and digestive problems.

Five years ago, she came under the care of a new neurologist at Kingston General Hospital with an interest in neuro-muscular disorders. In

---

[12] Perhaps in retrospect her apartment was the *locus sanctissimus* referred to by Jennifer Harris in *Cluny as a Threshold between Heaven and Earth*.

[13] Sadly by the time this was written, Maggie's condition had deteriorated and she had become confined to bed.

1999 he decided to do a biopsy of some muscle and sent specimens to colleagues in California.

Thus was she finally diagnosed with a condition known as *mitochondrial neurogastrointestinal encephalomyopathy* [often shortened to *MNGIE*] inherited as a rare genetic disorder but with no other affected family members. As the name implies it is a disease occurring in the nervous system, the gastro-intestinal tract, and especially her muscles. Her biopsy showed highly abnormal muscle fibres and abnormal concentrations of organelles known as mitochondria[14] within her muscles.

Mitochondria, using 90% of the oxygen we breathe, provide most of the energy we require for our metabolic processes, particularly to muscles governing physical movements of the body, and to the contraction of visceral organs such as the intestinal tract.[15]

Besides the ever-present profound muscular weakness, some of Maggie's clinical symptoms are due to the accumulation of by-products of this defective metabolism, similar to the lactic acid accumulation that make muscles ache after exercise. Her increasing muscular pain had resulted in a request to be started on morphine, and the doses have gradually increased in the intervening months.

The most significant clinical effect for Maggie's overall disease has been on her respiratory muscles and she by the time I visit her she has already started home oxygen via an oxygen concentrator in her bedroom.

Maggie long ago found that she could not swallow food properly as the valve between her stomach and the esophagus would no longer op-

---

[14] Mitochondria are ubiquitous energy-providing components of animal cells. They are related to chloroplasts, organelles that today provide photosynthetic energy to plants, but it is postulated that far back in evolutionary time mitochondria were free-dwelling organelles that came to inhabit animal cells symbiotically. Interestingly, unlike many other components of cells, the DNA that governs inheritable characteristics is matrilineal, though this was not discovered until the 1980's.

[15] Mitochondria do this firstly through a process of glycolysis. Glucose molecules are broken down into smaller components; these breakdown products then pass through a process called the Kreb's cycle, first described by Hans Krebs in the 1930's, and then release an energy product called adenosine triphosphate. ATP is the one of the most significant energy providers of the body and powers most metabolic processes. There are alternative energy cycles within the body but they are often less efficient or provide by-products that are disadvantageous to the body.

erate effectively, being of smooth muscle. She thus also has a gastric tube that provides the bulk of her food and without it would either starve, or aspirate food into her lungs.

One of Maggie's chief concerns at our first meeting was that she might pick up an chest infection from someone. However, as I realized later, her fear was not so much that she might get a serious infection that she might die from...but that she might have to go back to hospital, an event which had always caused her various difficulties. As she eloquently put it, so many of the hospital admissions over the years meant yet another admission, to tell her medical story yet one more time and yet still be without a diagnosis.

Hospitalization had become associated with discomfort and separation from a strong caring family. Besides her very caring husband, she has three fine daughters, two of whom live locally; one is a nurse who lives in Texas.

Until 1988, when the first reports of mitochondrial diseases were published in the scientific journal *Nature*, the cause of her illness was unknown. MNGIE is one of a wide spectrum of disorders, though many of the disorders are extremely rare. For much of her life, then, Maggie suffered from a condition that was essentially undiagnosable, because the cause was unknown. Perhaps that is why her story speaks eloquently to the boundary issue we are discussing. Hospitals are the institutions we enter for the important purpose of diagnosis. As Wood[16], writing of the process of diagnosis, said in 1991, naming an illness can have great symbolic significance. The act of naming may say: 'you are not alone. Your illness is not some hidden menace, but a familiar thing'. If naming the illness cannot be done, then hospital admission may augur a series of futile encounters. Even though the cause of MNGIE is now known, effective therapies still elude us, hence Maggie's referral for palliation where cure was not the main intent. This is not to say that curative therapies need prevent comfort measures being offered, or stop tender loving care from being directed towards the person rather than the disease. Throughout Maggie's illness she and her family have demonstrated the bonds of caring love that can sustain through thick and thin.

Several important factors overlooked or ignored in hospital may have contributed to Maggie's concerns. The list of problems with hospital

---

[16] Wood ML *Naming the Illness: the Power of Words*. Family Medicine *23*[7], 543-538.

care that follow are culled from conversations over the years with patients and their families, and include more than the ones that Maggie mentioned. All are really due a basic misunderstanding about the fact that a hospital has a *cultural milieu* that is different from the milieu of the community.[17]

Among structural and environmental differences causing loss of personal freedoms, patients may refer to:

- Loss of privacy
- The surrendering of personal clothing, jewellery and money
- Physical connection to various pieces of equipment restricting freedom of movement
- The sharing of facilities with strangers: beds, toilets and the like
- The loss of the passage of time [many rooms in hospital are still without clocks]
- a daily routine not of their choosing
- permission that is required to leave the confines of the hospital.

Many of these differences are in partly 'understood' by patients and accepted as the 'price' for entering the confines of a hospital. More troubling to them are some of the differences of interaction that may take place between themselves and hospital staff[18]. These are mostly entirely unintentional and arise out of a lack of appreciation for the effect of a hospital milieu on patients, or often because the need to complete tasks in a timely fashion.

They include:

- Confusion about who does what in a physician hierarchy, especially a teaching hospital. Many patients do not understand the role of students, clerks, residents and consulting staff
- Confusion about who is mainly responsible for their care in hospital. This is particularly confusing when responsibility

---

[17] This was parodied to great effect by the anthropologist, Horace Miner. Writing in the *American Anthropologist* of 1956, he described the role of the '*latipsoh*' in *Body Ritual among the Nacirema*. Those adept at mentally reversing word order will have already deduced his drift!

[18] The recent quarantine regulations during the present SARS crisis has only accentuated the isolation of patients within hospital. It was clearly desirable for Maggie, as a patient with a major respiratory problem, to stay away from environments that might present her with a fatal infection.

rotates among consulting staff on a calendar basis, or when other specialities – sometimes a lot of them during a long or complex admission - are called on for an opinion.

- Confusion about the roles of support staff. As one patient said to me: 'I don't know how to tell the difference between the cleaning staff and the medical staff these days..they all have different coloured uniforms and I don't know which one is which!' This situation is worse for demented or confused patients.

- The important task of interpreting what is happening to patients is sometimes left out of the plan of management. Many patients coming to see me after being in hospital talk about their bewilderment at not understanding the overall plan for diagnosis or treatment. Often, the after-discharge plan is omitted in subsequent communication between the family physician and the hospital staff

- Hospital physicians often underestimate the complexity of information that is being communicated, or misunderstand patients' reactions to what is being told them. Often apprehension or fear about a medical process may worsen the miscommunication

- Patients and physicians may develop misunderstandings over decision-making, particularly when painful or difficult decisions need to be made.

Perhaps Peter V's case may help illustrate some of these issues.

Peter V.[19]

Peter V. is in his fifties, diabetic, and has been my patient for over ten years. He lives with his wife, Viola, in a village about ten miles outside Kingston. He came to my practice because he 'didn't get on with his previous physician'. It could have been the other way round, as very early on Peter and I agreed on, quite amicably, that non-compliance was one of his medical problems[20]!

---

[19] Names changed for patient confidentiality in this case.

[20] A fairly extensive bibliography exists on the compliance problems in diabetes. Greenhalgh and Hurwitz [Ch. 1 'Why study narrative?': op.cit.] describe an excellent narrative of a diabetic patient's example of being misunderstood. Other references include from the medical literature Funnell MM and Anderson RM The problem of compliance in diabetes. Journal of the American Medical As-

Those who have diabetes or know someone with the disease will agree that much is required of the individual who suffers from it. The diabetic has to pay attention to diet, blood testing, drug treatment and perhaps insulin. In addition they may have to come to terms with possible diabetic complications involving the heart, eyes, kidneys and skin, and that they have a higher than normal frequency of heart attacks and strokes.

Peter long ago abrogated much of his care to his wife, Viola. He would probably have died long ago without her. Although he is a larger than life character who enjoys regaling me with details of his old Hell's Angels connections, he is functionally illiterate and relies on Viola for a great deal of his well-being.

Recently, Peter came into my clinic feeling less well than usual, with weakness and shortness of breath. On doing a cardiogram it was clear that he had an abnormal heart rhythm. I referred him urgently to hospital. I was only half-surprised to receive a call a few days later from Viola to come and adjudicate in a disagreement Peter was having with hospital staff. I had been asked to 'interpret' Peter to staff during previous admissions. His somewhat cavalier attitude to doing what he liked and his colourful language did not facilitate his care within the hospital environment.

On this latest occasion a cardiology resident had wanted to inject dye into the coronary arteries through a catheter inserted into an artery in the thigh. As with all medical procedures the resident had been required to explain the risks and benefits of such procedures before obtaining the patient's consent. The intended procedure would have provided helpful information about treatment. Inexplicably Peter had declared his complete non-interest in such a procedure – I decline to use the exact words he chose – and demanded to leave the hospital.

Despite the somewhat tense environment on the coronary care unit it was not difficult to understand what had happened. 'Potential damage' to the kidneys had been listed as one of the possible risks of the procedure. Peter knew that diabetes already put his kidneys at risk and decided that there was no way that 'those doctors' were going to increase the risk. In his typically abrupt way, he had informed the resident of this, and said that he was going home if kidney damage was a possibility.

sociation 283 [13] Oct 2000, 1709. Funnell and Anderson have also written elsewhere of this in the journal *Diabetes Education*. For an example from the nursing literature see Callaghan D and Williams D *Living with Diabetes: issues for nursing practice*. Journal of Advanced Nursing 20[1]June 1994, 132-9.

Somehow the resident had interpreted this to mean that Peter was intending have to go home 'against medical advice'. Both Peter and his wife felt was this was not the case; he wasn't going home against advice, he was going home because he didn't intend to have a procedure that could cause him harm.

In the end Peter did go home, and care has continued pretty much as it did before. In this case, what decided treatment was an explanation including Peter's right to refuse treatment even if it was not the best one; and to make sure that patient knew this. To my mind it was one of a number of examples of how the management styles of people from essentially two different cultures clashed, and required some interpretation to bridge the gap. For family physicians using patient-centred models of care this is familiar territory. Just as physicians and patients earlier in the process have attempted to reach an understanding of the illness and the associated experience of being ill, so too they attempt to "reach common ground" over what is the most appropriate management or treatment. For family physicians, 'most appropriate' may not always be what is recommended by medical science

Perhaps the challenge of these stories is to understand better the significance of this boundary as seen by patients. McWhinney[21], writing in Patient-Centred Medicine about why we perhaps need a 'new clinical method', has described a new way of thinking about illness that is a reversed version of what we are often familiar with in disease-centred care. First, he says, should come a recognition of the sufferings of the patient and an understanding of the personal meaning of illness. Then follows the diagnostic search which may, or may not, reveal the cause of illness and finally comes the naming of the illness and the explanation, which hopefully would turn the patient's thinking about cause to thinking about healing, which may not always be synonymous with cure. Palliative care is a good base to come from when attempting an implementation of this new paradigm, focussing as it does on care rather than cure. In Maggie's case there are a goodly number of care measures coming from family and health-care professionals working together measures that may make her remaining life comfortable and dignified.

Perhaps Maggie should have the final word. Realising that she may not have the likelihood of recovering from her illness, or living very much longer, she said to me at the end of our first interview: 'you know, I have come to think that the role of my illness is to help people under-

---

[21] Ian McWhinney *Why we need a new clinical method* op. cit.pp 1-20.

stand what it is to be ill. It may be that I can teach them in ways that I never really appreciated when I first was ill'. Perhaps this talk is the one of the results of her wise thoughts.

INGRID LEMAN STEFANOVIC

CHALLENGING TRADITIONAL ACADEMIC
BORDERS THROUGH INTERDISCIPLINARITY

ABSTRACT. The history of universities is also a history of academic disciplines and the borders that have come to be established among them. This presentation will discuss both the problems and the opportunities of such re-definitions of academic borders that emerge through interdisciplinary teaching and research.

> In the beginning, God created the heavens and the earth. Now the earth was a formless void, there was darkness over the deep, and God's spirit hovered over the water. God said, 'Let there be light' and there was light. God saw that light was good, and God divided light from darkness...
>
> *Genesis*, I

Out of primal chaos, a world is created. Within that act of creation, limits arise to distinguish darkness from light. Essential to the process of establishing order out of chaos is the creation of borders to distinguish discrete moments, events, persons, societies and worldly objects. In this sense, limits and borders are manifestations of the sacred and are the condition of life itself.

French philosopher, Michel Serres, recognizes this point. "Deciding on markers and borders," he writes, "appears to be a moment of origin; without such decisions, there is no oasis separate from the desert, no clearing in the forests where peasants set themselves to farming, no sacred or profane space, isolated from each other by priestly gesture, no definition enclosing a domain and, therefore, no precise language on which to agree, nor any logic."[1] Meaning requires borders, as words themselves delimit and distinguish discrete concepts. To decipher order

---

[1] Michel Serres, *The Natural Contract*, trans. Elizabeth MacArthur and William Paulson, (Ann Arbor: University of Michigan Press, 1995) pp. 51-52.

Limina: Thresholds and Borders - A St. Michael's College Symposium
Joseph Goering, Francesco Guardiani, Giulio Silano eds. Ottawa: Legas, 2005

from chaos, limits are essential moments in the process of interpretation.

It is no surprise, then, that our highest educational institutions seek to order knowledge within the limits of discrete disciplines. As order is sought within a chaotic world, we compartmentalize areas of specialization in order to better understand that world. There is good reason for this move: demarcating fields of knowledge allows for increased concentration on specialized details. Experts dedicate themselves to a circumscribed domain and, thereby, come to know their areas of bounded rationality well.

Still, there are dangers. Limits can lead to closure: consider the prejudices that define nationalist hatreds or protectionist isolationism within political settings. In the academic world, closed-minded adherence to the limits of one's own field can inspire bias against other research methodologies and other disciplinary endeavours.

We need to distinguish between borders that inspire understanding and those that close off dialogue. To advance this discussion in some small way, I will consider some lessons to be learned from the example of interdisciplinary research. Sometimes, the epistemological borders that we draw around our disciplines may encourage abstraction and reifying limits that oversimplify and, therefore, denigrate the mystery and complexity of life. For this and other reasons, there is growing support within universities of interdisciplinary programmes of teaching and research.

The paper will begin with a historical outline of the rise of interdisciplinarity within the academic setting. Following a brief discussion of different *kinds* of interdisciplinarity and ways of moving beyond traditional, disciplinary borders, I will move on to discuss the case of environmental philosophy and what it reveals about ways of transcending limits.

The paper has two main objectives. First, I aim to show how moving beyond the borders of disciplines is best accomplished, not as a transcendent, synthetic endeavour but rather, one aiming towards the uncovering of prior, existing relationships and taken for granted foundations. Second, I hope to demonstrate that interdisciplinarity is best accomplished when it maintains an essential awareness and respect of disciplinary boundaries. I would like to suggest that the relationship of disciplines to interdisciplinarity can tell us much about the genuine meaning and purpose of borders themselves.

The Rise of Interdisciplinarity

In her excellent historical overview, Julie Thompson Klein suggests that the modern connotation of disciplinarity is a direct outcome of the 19th century.[2] A number of factors influenced the development of academic disciplines within universities, including the evolution of the modern, natural sciences and the overall "scientification" of knowledge that aimed to better understand a phenomenon by reducing it to its component parts. This reductionist approach to understanding the world arose within a linear epistemology that sought causal relations between well demarcated entities or concepts. In many respects, a calculative paradigm of thought grounded the emerging particularization of knowledge that focussed attention upon empirically defined, piecemeal measures.[3]

On the pragmatic side, there were a number of factors that promoted the increasing specialization within universities. Industry required specialists, trained to function as experts within the requisite fields. Students, consequently, began to be recruited to universities for instruction within specific, clearly demarcated disciplines. Finally, as more expensive and sophisticated instrumentation was required in individual fields, economic factors continued to drive the division – and the competition for funding – of disciplines.[4] The "professionalization" of knowledge ensured that the formal pursuit of education proceeded within the parameters of clearly prescribed fields.[5]

Nevertheless, in the first part of the 20th century, Liberal Arts Colleges began to promote the notion that the "whole person" could benefit from a "general" education as a precursor, or even an alternative to specialization. A "civic model" of education began to emerge, that assumed that a university-educated citizen required a broader, cultural awareness of literary and nonliterary "classics."[6] Reviving the notions of the "Renaissance man" and Cicero's *doctus orator* (one who is able to merge scientific knowledge with pragmatic realities), universities began to reflect upon the need to educate both the "generalist," as well as the specialist.

---

[2] Julie Thompson Klein, *Interdisciplinarity: History, Theory and Practice*, (Detroit: Wayne State University Press, 1990) p. 21.

[3] See Ingrid Leman Stefanovic, *Safeguarding Our Common Future: Rethinking Sustainable Development*, (Albany, NY: State University of New York Press, 2000.)

[4] Julie Thompson Klein, *op.cit.*

[5] According to Klein, the academic discipline of History was formalized in 1884; Economics in 1885; Political Science in 1903; and Sociology in 1905. (*Ibid*, p. 22.)

[6] *Ibid*, p. 23.

By the 1920s, the first, few funding agencies (for example, the American Social Science Research Council) were established, specifically to promote integration across the disciplines. It was mid-century, however, before a major reform and challenge to knowledge specialization arose in the structure of the 1945 Harvard "redbook," entitled *General Education in a Free Society*. This strategic document argued for the establishment of core curricula across the universities, that would cover literary texts, basic scientific principles, English composition as well as an additional course within each of the humanities, social sciences and natural sciences.[7] At this time, "synthetic" theories such as Marxism and Structuralism were also beginning to exert a powerful force on ways of thinking that called for changes in multiple disciplines from economics to art history.

Despite these growing challenges to specialized, disciplinary limits, it is nevertheless true that the real "watershed era" for interdisciplinarity emerged in the 1960s and 1970s. In fact, the Organization for Economic Cooperation and Development has suggested (perhaps not entirely accurately but with some merit) that the very concept of interdisciplinarity was developed in the 1960s.[8] Certainly, major professional organizations – from the Association for Integrative Studies to the International Association for the Study of Interdisciplinary Research – were formed and there was growing awareness that the emerging problems of a complex, technological society required interdisciplinary solutions.

Programmes in environmental studies also began to emerge at this time within university settings.[9] The Institute for Environmental Studies at the University of Toronto was formally established by the Statute of the Board of Governors in 1971. The Faculty of Environmental Studies at nearby York University was similarly founded in 1968. In my field of Environmental Philosophy, the landmark journal, *Environmental Ethics*, emerged in 1979 to provide the first interdisciplinary forum for reflection on questions of values and attitudes towards the natural world.

A variety of agencies began to support interdisciplinary activities during this time as well, both in America (for instance, the National Science

---

[7] *Ibid*, p. 28.

[8] The OECD reference is found in a brochure, calling for an international conference on "Interdisciplinarity Revisited," in Linköping, Sweden, 3-5 October, 1984. Nevertheless, the case can be made that the concepts of integration and epistemological bridge-building are hardly exclusively modern ideas, but can be traced back to the Ancient Greek philosophers. See Stefanovic, *op.cit.*, pp. 53ff.

[9] Julie Thompson Klein, *op.cit.*, p. 112.

Foundation, the Carnegie Foundation and others) as well as in Europe – most notably, the Paris-based Organization for Economic Cooperation and Development (OECD.) Klein is right to suggest that the 1972 OECD document entitled *Interdisciplinarity: Problems of Teaching and Research in Universities* was a seminal work, incorporating the general systems and structuralist approaches of leading theorists like Jean Piaget and Erich Jantsch into a "working tool" that remains the most widely cited reference on interdisciplinarity to this day.[10]

Finally, the complexity of problems that needed to be addressed – planetary, environmental change issues constitute the obvious example – pushed the disciplines into situations of cooperation and collaboration with others. Whether a matter of tool-borrowing in the natural sciences or building bridges in interdisciplines such as social psychology, biochemistry, geopolitics or environmental engineering, the emerging complexity of a technological world has driven educational institutions to devise new ways of moving beyond traditional, disciplinary borders. How, specifically, this move beyond limits was conceptually envisioned is a topic to which we turn next.

Varieties of Interdisciplinarity

In an essay written to provide advice to incoming undergraduate students to the University of Toronto, Professor Edmund O'Sullivan cautions: "We have brought the legacy of specialization into this new century, and the modern university...must be seen critically in that light. You should take care that you do not lose the expansiveness of your intelligence on pre-mature specialization. This is not the education you should be seeking."[11] Critiques of disciplinary boundaries have become so commonplace that, to some extent, they have become "the standard repertory of criticism from outside and inside American higher education."[12]

Nevertheless, *how* one chooses to move beyond the borders of disciplines – not to mention *where* one defines those borders – is hardly unproblematic. Klein defines a discipline in terms of "the tools, methods,

---

[10] *Ibid*, p. 36.

[11] Edmund O'Sullivan, "What Kind of Education Should You Experience at a University," in *On Higher Education: Thoughts and Reflections on the University Experience*, Edited by David Nam, (Toronto: University of Toronto, 2000) p. 35.

[12] David Riesman, "The Scholar at the Border: Staying Put and Moving Around inside the American University," *Columbia Forum*, Spring 1974, p. 26. Cited in Klein, *op.cit.*, p. 95.

procedures, concepts and theories that account coherently for a set of objects or subjects...[A] discipline comes to organize and concentrate experience into a particular 'world view.'"[13] Consequently, disciplines "put limits" on the kinds of questions that are asked, the methods that they use, the answers that they provide and criteria for truth and validity. In short, there is a "certain particularity about the images of reality in a given discipline."[14]

The rhetoric of interdisciplinarity challenges this particularity in different ways. Perhaps the most basic distinctions are drawn between multidisciplinarity and interdisciplinarity. "Multidisciplinarity" signifies the additive, rather than integrative juxtaposition of disciplines.[15] Quoting a number of different sources, Klein describes situations of *multidisciplinary* projects in this way:

> Even in a common environment, educators, researchers and practitioners still behave as disciplinarians with different perspectives. Their relationship may be mutual and cumulative but not interactive, for there is 'no apparent connection,' no real cooperation or 'explicit' relationships and, even perhaps a 'questionable eclecticism.' The participating disciplines are neither changed nor enriched, and the lack of a 'well-defined matrix' of interactions means disciplinary relationships are likely to be limited and transitory.[16]

Courses that are organized to present multiple, specialized perspectives on an issue are examples of multidisciplinarity, since integration and synthesis – primary characteristics of *interdisciplinary* endeavours – are lacking. Over the years, a number of different terms evolved, often with different meanings associated with them. For example, the Canadian Tri-Council research funding agency established some years ago used "interdisciplinary" and "cross-disciplinary" interchangeably, whereas others, such as Erich Jantsch and the OECD defined the latter concept in terms of unidirectional cooperation among disciplines.[17]

As discussions of interdisciplinarity proceeded, especially within the 1960s and 1970s, there seemed to be general agreement that as one moved towards higher planes of interdisciplinary teaching and research, one also moved towards increasing integration and synthesis of the dis-

---

[13] Julie Thompson Klein, *op.cit.*, p. 104.

[14] *Ibid.*

[15] *Ibid*, p. 56.

[16] *Ibid.*

[17] Erich Jantsch, "Towards Interdisciplinarity and Transdisciplinarity in Education and Innovation," in *Interdisciplinarity: Problems of Teaching and Research in Universities,* (Paris: Organization for Economic Cooperation and Development, 1972) pp. 104ff.

ciplines. The *multidisciplinary* juxtaposition of unrelated disciplines was less integrative than the *"pluridisciplinary"* relations between disciplines that were seen to be similar in nature (for example, mathematics and physics.) In *interdisciplinary* projects, those trained in different disciplines collaborated to address a common problem with continuous opportunities for communication. Finally, *"transdisciplinary"* research indicated domains such as "the science of man," Marxism, or phenomenology – all seen to be examples of a common system of axioms transcending specific, identifiable disciplines. In such a schema, it was not only the case that the "higher" one went on the scales of collaboration and cooperation, the more one was seen to "transcend" the limits of individual disciplines. Implicitly, there was also a sense that the higher one went, the "better" the interdisciplinary teaching and research.

There are, however, at least two, very different sorts of problems with what I shall call this "transcendent" model of interdisciplinary hierarchies. First, the image of "consolidating" differences in an all-encompassing, universalizing perspective risks the abandonment of rigorous, disciplinary grounding: one is supposed to know everything about everything and, in the end, one may end up with a superficial understanding about many things but not a comprehensive knowledge about genuine relationships and complex nuances of grounded theory and practice.

Second, an over-arching "synthetic" viewpoint may inadvertently seek to capture truth within new broader, but nevertheless static limits of a Super-Discipline. In that sense, the "synthesis" of interdisciplinarity risks collapsing into a reifying exercise that may have abstract, theoretical coherence but, once again, misses out on the genuine complexities of the world. Just as reality often exceeds the limits of simulation models, precisely because they are ultimately abstract constructions, so too might the complex subject of interdisciplinary study exceed the tidy boundaries of any single Super-Discipline. To investigate these issues further, let us consider Environmental Philosophy as a case in point.

The Case of Environmental Philosophy: Pushing the Limits of Disciplinarity

As with the lexicon of interdisciplinarity, the field of "environmental studies" has emerged into prominence within the last several decades. With the growing awareness of such critical challenges as global climate change, the impact of pollutants on human and ecological health and resource depletion, philosophers have engaged themselves in the process of analyzing the roots of these and similar problems, in an effort to seek viable solutions.

To be sure, it is incumbent upon every citizen to engage these matters of environmental degradation in our collective effort to improve the state of the planet and to ensure a healthy world for present and future generations. Aside from this generalized need, however, what happens to the discipline of philosophy proper when it pushes its borders to include these new and pressing issues?

First, I would argue that *new possibilities for thinking emerge*. By enforcing strict limits on philosophical domains, it is a fact that important insights can be missed. Consider, for example, the tendency within philosophy departments to distinguish between "history" and "problems" courses. Drawing this distinction can sometimes be misleading and confusing to students. After all, what "history" course in philosophy does not address philosophical problems? And are not "problems" historically situated? By invoking uncompromising limits, we risk excluding certain truths and, thereby, denying complex realities.

In fact, as philosophy pushes its own disciplinary boundaries to include environmental concerns, new philosophical questions arise. The obvious example relates to the impact of increased ecological awareness on the borders of philosophy itself. For centuries, the discipline had, in many respects, taken the natural world for granted, focussing ethical, metaphysical and epistemological questions on exclusively *human*, anthropocentric concerns. The confined subjectivism of philosophy has increasingly come under attack by environmental philosophers who question whether these narrow limits do justice to the genuine breadth of human understanding of the world and the wider cosmos. Certainly, any insular, subjectivistic understanding of the meaning of being human denies the real possibilities that emerge in a more comprehensive philosophical contemplation of the fullness of human experience of otherness, of difference and of the significance of relations between entities. Expanding the borders of philosophy to include ecological realities has made such broad-based thinking possible.

Moreover, as phenomenologist Martin Heidegger has pointed out, a reductionist approach to understanding phenomena focuses attention upon clearly demarcated *things*, whether objects or entities.[18] In the process, *relations between* things are taken for granted. The phenomenological

---

[18] See Martin Heidegger, *Being and Time*, trans. John Macquarrie and Edward Robinson, (New York: Harper & Row, Publishers, 1962.)

method itself focuses attention neither upon the human subjectivity nor the so-called "objective" world but, instead, explores the complexities of human "Being-in-the-world." The hyphenation is meant to suggest that the temporal process of existence is neither purely subjective nor objective but, rather, precedes these dualistic limitations as the primary condition of the possibility of their emergence in the first place.

As the science of ecology pays heed to the non-linear relations between organisms, so too environmental philosophy is forced to come to terms with the fact that the human subjectivity is in-the-world and this relation provides philosophy with a new paradigm – one that pushes discussions of ethics to include questions about the intrinsic value of animals or forests; pushes epistemology into addressing knowledge parameters in cases of risk assessment or pragmatic justification of judgment calls in instances of scientific uncertainty; pushes metaphysics into discussions of the reality of a natural world that is, in some sense, also socially constructed. In all such cases, the borders of the discipline of philosophy itself are enlarged, but only to enrich and renew the philosophical endeavour.

Finally, there is a pragmatic demand of environmental philosophy that ensures that theoretical reflection cannot legitimately remain at the level of abstract speculation. A primary motivation for this emerging field is the need to actually help to advance solutions to environmental problems, rather than to engage simply in academic reflection. I recall how a colleague proudly confessed that he was able to chase away one third of his introductory philosophy class within the first few weeks of term. That third, he explained, simply "shouldn't have been there in the first place" because they lacked the intellectual rigour to become "true philosophers." What a contrast to the Ancient Greek incentive to promote broad, philosophical dialogue within the agora! It is not only trained philosophers who ask themselves philosophical questions about the meaning of life and death, or the right way to live. Similarly, when philosophy becomes a narrowly specialized discipline contemplated in isolation from the lived world, it defeats its purpose as an essential human endeavour.

Final Reflections: The Place of Disciplinary Borders in Interdisciplinary Studies

It is significant that, while pushing the borders of traditional, human-centred approaches to ethics and metaphysics, environmental philosophy does not aim to "synthesize" all knowledge, nor to "merge" with

ecology and build a Superdiscipline. If anything, environmental philosophy (particularly environmental phenomenology, which defines my own
interest) aims to uncover taken for granted attitudes and values, revealing a plurality of interpretations about the world and inviting reflection
upon the pre-theoretical conditions of being-in-the-world. The transcendent model of interdisciplinarity does not square with this goal of
uncovering contexts, instead of building speculative, theoretical constructs.
Neither does this model square with the messy business of moving back
and forth between disciplinary borders and broader, interdisciplinary
dialogue, nor with the pragmatic demands of environmental decision
making. How, then, does one more rightly conceive of the relationship
between the disciplinary boundaries of philosophy and interdisciplinary,
environmental concerns?

Physicist and philosopher, Henri Bortoft, provides an interesting clue
to an answer. In his discussion of the meaning of "holism," he reflects
upon the liminal relation of parts to whole, suggesting that a genuine
whole is not an additive phenomenon or construction of a "Super-Part."
One example that he finds compelling relates to the hologram photo-
graphic plate produced with the light of a laser.[19] When an ordinary film
plate shatters, the image disperses in piecemeal segments. With a hologram, a different phenomenon occurs: the same, three-dimensional re-
construction of the original object is produced in each fragment of the
plate, although the smaller the piece, the less well defined it is. "What
can be seen straightaway about wholeness in this example," Bortoft explains, "is the way in which the whole is present in the parts. The entire
picture is wholly present in each part of the plate" – though the smaller
the fragment, the less clear the resolution of the image.

Bortoft uses the hologram to suggest that the whole cannot be properly perceived by "'standing back to get an overview.'" Instead, "the
whole is in some way reflected in the parts, it is to be encountered by
going further into the parts instead of by standing back from them."[20]
He further substantiates this claim by reference to the microscopic
world, which we tend to conceive as a collection of separate, independent sub-atomic particles interacting with one another through force
fields. The view that emerges from contemporary physics is, according

---

[19] Henri Bortoft, "Counterfeit and authentic wholes: Finding a means for dwelling in
nature" in David Seamon and Robert Mugerauer, *Dwelling, Place and Environment: Towards
a Phenomenology of Person and World*, (The Netherlands: Martinus Nijhoff, 1985.) Pp. 282 ff.
This volume has now been reprinted in Malabar, Florida: Krieger Publishing, 2000.

[20] *Ibid*, p. 284.

to Bortoft, quite different. The properties of any individual particle are determined by all the other particles which means that, in some sense, "every particle is a reflection of all the others."[21] Einstein explained how a single particle of matter would have no mass, were it not for the remaining matter in the universe. Bortoft concludes then, that "instead of trying to understand the universe by extrapolating from the local environment here and now to the universe as a whole, it may be useful to reverse the relationship and understand the local environment as being the result of the rest of the universe."[22]

Just as parts are not isolated fragments or isolated containers of mass, so too are disciplinary borders, properly understood, not merely independent, closed systems. Neither is interdisciplinarity a matter of simply "standing back" to picture "the whole." Rather, a reciprocal relation begins to emerge, defining legitimate disciplinary borders as reflections of broader experiences and interdisciplinary exchanges. While interdisciplinary, environmental studies may move one beyond traditional, disciplinary borders, philosophy as a discipline is itself enriched through the interaction with other, plural perspectives.

In such a scenario, boundaries become, in the words of philosopher Irene Klaver, "not places where things stop, but where they begin."[23] Disciplines are enriched, but not necessarily abandoned or transcended, in legitimate interdisciplinary endeavours. No longer a transcendent, synthesizing model of interdisciplinary research, this perspective provides legitimacy to original disciplinary borders, without defining them as closed, introverted systems. Klaver has it right when she points out how

> boundaries are places where different entities, different modes of being, different ontological domains, meet, interact with each other, give and take from each other – places of heterogeneity and diversity that call for negotiation, or translation. Translation is facilitated by so-called boundary objects... As vehicles of translation, they are crucial for developing and maintaining coherence across and within worlds, maximizing both the autonomy of and the communication between heterogeneous worlds.[24]

---

[21] *Ibid*, p. 283.

[22] *Ibid.*

[23] Irene J. Klaver, "Phenomenology on (the) rocks," in *Eco-Phenomenology: Back to the Earth Itself*, edited by Charles S. Brown and Ted Toadvine, (Albany, New York: State University of New York Press, 2003) p. 163.

[24] *Ibid*, pp. 162-3.

In a pragmatic sense, for these reasons, I support interdisciplinary programs that do not seek to collapse disciplinary difference in a unifying "school" of synthetic thought but instead, foster dialogue, preserving difference and plural interpretations of broader realities. Through the interdisciplinary exchange, individual disciplines can "gather" together meaningful reflections of the broader complexity of a universe that will always exceed finite, disciplinary borders, even though those borders are needed in order to focus our attention upon legitimate "parts" of the holistic discussion. Borders help us to define and understand the world but let us keep in mind that these same borders provide an opening for redefining our knowledge base, and communicating between diverse worlds. After all, as Gaston Bachelard reminds us, "everything comes alive precisely when contradictions accumulate."[25]

Kenneth Burke once said that "a way of seeing is also a way of not seeing."[26] It is dangerous to become entrenched in our habitual ways of seeing, within familiar limits. We should not conclude, however, that those limits can or should be abandoned. Rather, they might be more properly conceived as new beginnings for broader, more informed discourse.

---

[25] Gaston Bachelard, *The Poetics of Space*, trans. Maria Jolas, (Boston: Beacon Press, 1964) p. 39.

[26] Cited in Klein, *op.cit.*, p. 182.

AGMV Marquis

MEMBER OF SCABRINI MEDIA

Quebec, Canada
2005